The Flem Cup

A Story of Friendship, Love & Redemption

A memoir by

Scott Dow

The Flem Cup

First Printing: 2015

Published by Indaruf Publishing
P.O. Box 185, Landenberg, PA 19350

International Standard Book Number: 978-0692376812

Contents

Dedication

First, this book is dedicated to all those who love the game of golf along with the lasting friendships and glorious competition it inspires. A uniquely social game of skill and nerve grounded in etiquette, tradition and honor, it is truly the greatest game on earth.

Second, this book is dedicated to all those seekers who, deep inside, know there *must* be something more to this life than a temporary existence in this broken world that is far too often filled with grief, pain and loneliness. If you have the commitment and courage to seek with an open mind and an open heart, I promise you that there is hope for much, much more.

Acknowledgements

There are all my great friends on the England side - Joe, Swampy, Miffer, Richard, Milo, Greg, Singe, Mark and Paul Nelson, Jarvo, Phil and many more. None of this would have happened without you lads.

There is Caroline, Ian's angel who was with him through it all. Without you, I don't know what any of us would have done, least of all Ian, and we will always love you for who you are and what you did.

There are all my great friends on the U.S. side - the Tanis family, Lou, AJ, Matt, Pat, Terry and all the rest.

There is Theresa, love of my life, who has taught me so much about love. Your patience and encouragement were indispensable pieces in the final product.

Finally, there is Ian Jennings, my great friend. *Our* great friend. We miss you and love you, pal. The time we spent together was . . . *magic*.

Preface

There are times and events in life that, the further they recede into the past, the more incredible they become. The five Flem Cups between 2001 and 2005 were just such events. They were special times, an extraordinary mix of a highly competitive international golf match, great friendships, hilarious escapades and a whimsical "news" website that reported on the facts while taking any bits of rumor, innuendo and imagination and turning them into the latest news stories.

I was privileged to be an integral part of this experience, something I will never forget and wouldn't trade for the world. In setting up and posting stories and articles to the website, I didn't really set out to document it, much less write a book. I just wanted to have some laughs at the expense of my friends, my opponents and myself. Only in hindsight did it become clear what a truly incredible story it was, one that I could not have made up because, well, it was just too unbelievable.

Only a small portion of the original 110 or so articles written for the website are used in this book since my goal was to not simply republish them but to write the story from my personal perspective and experience. Many stories that did not make the cut are quite funny, left out simply because they really did not add to the story and I did not want them to needlessly get in the way.

Golf is a truly extraordinary game, one that uniquely places its highest value not just on results but on etiquette, tradition and honor as well. It brings out the best in the human experience, from the creation of a magnificent golf hole - a pure work of art that combines the human spirit and imagination with the majesty of God's creation - to the challenge of playing this impossibly difficult and frustrating game, a challenge that requires great skill, precise execution and iron-willed strength of mind to succeed at a high level. Kept in the proper perspective, it is also a game that feeds the competitive spirit while inspiring friendships and camaraderie rarely found in other sports.

The story that follows is not of my own making. I am the teller of the tale but that is only because it was given to me to tell, and for that I am and will forever remain humbly grateful. God's hand is always at work in our lives, often in improbable and unseen ways, and my most fervent wish is that this story will bring some of His light into your world.

I hope you enjoy *The Flem Cup!*

1

The Angel

"Ha! This should be good!"

Startled by the outburst, I turned to find Singe grinning broadly, staring at me as he held a quiz card aloft for the crowd to see. Squinting at the card through my drunken haze, I saw it was littered with X's signifying wrong answers. It was mine.

"You've got the snowball."

"You're joking" I groaned. With my card pulled from a bin filled with the night's 40 or 50 quiz cards, I would now be accorded the week's one and only chance to correctly answer the coveted snowball question and claim its cash prize. Although I didn't know exactly how much was at stake, I did know that half of every quiz night entry – at 10 quid a pop – went into the snowball fund and when it wasn't answered correctly, the pot rolled over to the next week. Anyone else would have welcomed a chance at the money, however slim, but my dismal performance – one lonely correct answer out of twenty – afforded me no comfort or optimism. Scanning my card, Singe laughed again.

"Judging from your performance 'ere . . . and the amount of beer you've 'ad . . . I don't think the snowball fund is in any immediate danger."

I shook my head as the crowd laughed, confident only of being even further humiliated as a solo act. Ian laughed as he slapped me on the shoulder.

"C'mon, lad. This should be a lark for a quiz-master like you!"

Smokin' Joe lifted his pint towards me in a good luck gesture. "'Asn't been won in over a month, you know. Should be quite substantial."

Shaking my head again, I managed a weak, resigned smile.

"All right, all right, let's get on with it."

The Angel Hotel had become my home away from home during my jaunts to England. Located near Sheffield in the tiny hamlet of Spinkhill, the Angel was the quintessential English pub, the cozy epicenter of the village's social life. Behind the 12 foot long bar with the polished brass foot rail stood the single most important element that made the Angel such a special place – St. John Harris. Of course, no one who knew him would ever think to call him "Saint" anything so he was just Singe to his friends. I'd always imagined his nickname being coined late one night by some thoroughly inebriated patron or friend trying to put "Saint" and "John" together into something coherent.

If you were in the mood for some exotic frozen concoction with a little plastic umbrella, you were in the wrong pub. In fact, you were in the wrong country. The obligatory assortment of lagers, bitters and ales were supplied by modern pressurized kegs kept in the basement but the Guinness was still poured the proper way – via an old-fashioned pump tap. The shelves behind the bar were stocked with an ample selection of gin, scotch, bourbon and other hard liquors. You'd get one ice cube in your drink and a strange look if you asked for two. Of course, standing at the rail was preferred to sitting on a bar stool.

The vast majority of my time at the Angel, though, was not spent in the main bar area. It was spent in a small room the locals dubbed the Rave Cave – perhaps 12 or 14 foot square and situated at the far right end of the bar. There, three or four tables and half a dozen tattered chairs in need of some new fabric were scattered haphazardly around the room. Above the fireplace, which I'd never seen used, was a mantle crowned with a few old trophies and mementos. The Rave Cave was where the most gregarious and fun-loving locals would inevitably congregate, a group led unofficially by my business partner and friend Ian Jennings, the nightly master of ceremonies.

Having retreated to its safety after the debacle of my quiz night performance, I'd been happily drowning my extremely limited sorrows in my favorite lager – Stella Artois – when Singe's pronouncement shattered my quietude. Now, 30 or 40 patrons stood frozen in place, peering down their noses and across the bar as Singe prepared to deliver their precious snowball question to someone who was, at best, a stranger. Avoiding their glances, I knew their attention was riveted on me for two reasons: respect for tradition and an unabashed desire to see me crash and burn.

With a wave of his hand, Singe signaled the start of solemn weekly ritual, immediately quieting the room. Everyone knew the routine, having seen it played out time after time, save one – me. He addressed the crowd.

"There must be total silence. No 'elping or the answer will be disqualified and the offending party banned from future quiz nights."

I chuckled to myself, unable to imagine anyone present wanting to help me succeed. Turning back to me, he continued, deadly serious in his role.

"You'll have 10 seconds to answer."

I could hear a pin drop as the crowd anxiously anticipated one last question on some obscure aspect of English tradition or history that they could claim to have known afterward. Drawing a folded piece of paper from a jar marked "Snowball", Singe officially began the process by reading the front of the folded paper to determine the category for the question.

"It's an 'istory question." he started, scanning the room as if he had just announced some monumentally significant development. Unfolding the slip, his lips moved slightly as he silently read the question. Slowly, his expression turned to one of complete disgust as his hand fell to his side.

"I don't believe it!"

"What?" I asked with a mix of suspicion and cautious optimism.

Swallowing hard, Singe looked up, a pained look etched on his face.

"It's a bloody Yank question!"

I cocked my head, smiling to myself as I considered the possibility that I might actually have a chance. Composing himself, Singe shook his head before reluctantly continuing.

"You'll have 10 seconds from when I finish the question. Ian, watch the time. Ready? In what year did John Hinckley attempt to assassinate American . . ."

"1981"

" . . President Ronald Reagan."

"Late March of 1981. To be precise."

Throwing the slip of paper up into the air, Singe slapped at it as it fluttered to the floor. There was no need for him to confirm my answer as correct. I knew I'd nailed it.

"Why? Why tonight? Of all nights, why tonight?!? I don't believe it . . . I just don't believe it."

Singe wasn't the only one who couldn't believe it. Weeks of faithfully contributing to the snowball fund in hope of a big payday had just gone down the tubes for the locals, and to an outsider, no less; an interloper! It just wasn't *right*. As the crowd slowly shuffled out, muttering under their collective breath and shaking their heads in disgust, a few glanced my way, daggers in their eyes. I gave a big smile and thumbs up but they seemed unamused. Finally, I turned to Singe, smiling.

"So how much did I win?"

"650 quid" Singe offered glumly. With the current $1.65 exchange rate, I quickly calculated that I'd won about $1,000 and, after letting out a low whistle, quickly decided it best to buy a few rounds for the Rave Cave stalwarts.

"Drinks are on me, Singe" I announced with a smile.

As Singe handled the sudden onslaught of orders, Ian returned to doing what he did best: *holding court*, as Joe called it.

Ian Jennings was, quite simply, the most extraordinary man I'd ever known. He could effortlessly dominate any social gathering, offering up jokes, funny stories and one-liners as easily as sipping a beer. There was no need to be in Ian's clique because he had none. He happily swapped laughs with anyone so inclined, making everyone feel welcome and comfortable in the process, even newcomers. His laugh, whether the infectious giggle that signaled the end of one of his corny jokes (and he had plenty of those) or the hearty laugh that came straight from his gut, made you laugh as well. No matter where we were, I always enjoyed my time with him.

Before long, Singe's girlfriend and pub partner Jude Jenkinson arrived, finished with her work and eagerly looking forward to a glass of wine.

"Hullo", she offered in a cheerful but tired voice.

"Scott won the snowball" Singe responded glumly.

"Oooo. That's lovely" she cooed as he poured her a red. I knew Jude had a soft spot for me – probably because I loved her cooking – and she seemed genuinely pleased that I'd won. Ian burst out laughing.

"Lovely?" he said incredulously. "'e certainly didn't earn it. Singe gave him a Yank question. Something about some President I've never 'eard of getting shot. They're all a bunch of cowboys over there, you know."

Eliciting a chuckle from the remaining regulars, it was all I could do to stand upright after too many pints to count. I laughed in what I imagined was a sarcastic tone.

"Ha, ha. Singe, can you get Ian some cheese to go with that whine?"

"Oh, c'mon. You din't get a single quiz question right and then you get a *Yank* snowball question."

"First of all . . . I did get one right – ONE. And now . . . I have TWO. But what can I say? You finally had a question about an important country."

"Hmmm. Well, we stick mainly with questions on culture and 'istory – and you actually need a country with some culture and 'istory for that to work, you see?"

The crowd erupted in laughter, awarding the exchange to Ian by default. To the Brits, we Americans were viewed as amusing but culturally inferior cousins at best; ungrateful barbarians at worst. After waiting for the laughter to subside to just the right level, he continued.

"Isn't anything in America built before World War II and still standing declared to be of great 'istorical significance?"

Even Smokin' Joe, who'd been slumping in the corner, perked up at that one, slurring "quite right" as he waved his cigarette in some ill-defined geometric pattern. Searching my Stella-soaked brain for a pithy response, I had nothing. Undeterred, I responded – clumsily.

"Is that what you call this? Culture?"

Even in my highly inebriated state I sensed I was in dangerous territory, teetering on the brink of gratuitously insulting everyone at The Angel – and England, for that matter. Sensing my tenuous position, I turned back to my pint for another sip, hoping the exchange would die a quiet death. Several seconds passed as the crowd seemingly held its collective breath in anticipation of what might come next. Finally, as Ian brought his pint up to his lips, the quiet comment slipped out.

"Well, it WAS only the snowball. Not like the Flem Cup. You'd have never won *that*."

Ah, the Flem Cup. Our annual team golf match, now approaching its 4th year. The one I went to great lengths to organize every year. The one I was a team captain for every year. The one that every single participant had won at least once - except me, that is.

A collective "*oooh*" emanated from the crowd, all of whom were well aware of the history. Having been hit where it really hurts – in my winless Cup record – all eyes were now on me, awaiting the inevitable return smash following a carelessly executed lob. Enunciating slowly and deliberately to compensate for my beer-addled state, I did not disappoint.

"I *would* have won last year . . . IF a certain someone . . . hadn't CHOKED!"

Joe, once again is slumping in the corner, stirred on cue, slurring a "quite right" as he waved his cigarette in Ian's general direction. Now it was Ian's turn for a clumsy return.

"I could describe what it's like to win, if you'd like to know."

Singe jumped in, trying to settle things down.

"Boys, boys. 'Ow 'bout another beer. Scott? Ian?"

Ignoring him, I pressed my momentary advantage, glaring at Ian as memories of the previous November flooded back.

"You could *also* tell me is how it feels to personally cost your team a win. An *epic* comeback win! Now *that* would be an interesting feeling . . . here, let me try to imagine it. Hmmm . . . "

Closing my eyes, I waved my head around like Stevie Wonder playing the keyboards.

"Nope . . . nothing." I said, reopening my eyes. "You'll have to describe it. I've had to go through 3 years as captain, making all the strategic match decisions – you just show up to play."

"Well, with that record, perhaps you should be sacked"

"You think you could do better? You think you'd be a better captain?"

Ian laughed, shaking his head.

"I don't think that – I know it. But no thanks. You'll just fix the teams and the handicaps to your advantage."

Over my rising anger, Joe's quiet voice once again piped up from the corner.

"Bring your own team."

Slowly, the four words registered, slowly penetrating my consciousness. Ian's expression changed as well, the idea slowly sinking in. Out of pure frustration and anger, without even beginning to understand its implications, I embraced Joe's idea.

"Yeah . . . you pick . . . your own damn team . . . and we'll play."

Ian cocked his head. "My own team?"

"Quite right" offered Joe as we turned towards him. "It'll be easy."

"Yeah. . . . . your own team."

"My own players?"

"Your own players."

"How many players?"

"How many can you get?"

Putting his beer down on the bar, a familiar look came over Ian's face, one that indicated he was fully engaged with a promising new idea.

"Right, so let me get this straight. You're saying I can assemble my own team on this side and we'll take on your American side?"

"That's what I'm saying. But no plus handicaps."

That was a loophole that needed to be closed right up front, before Ian recruited Paul Nelson or John Oates, two local pros who routinely shot under par.

Ian nodded, understanding that advantage would fatally tip the competitive balance. Pondering the idea, Ian sat silent for a few seconds, eyes averted.

"*That*, Joe, is a *brilliant* idea." he finally gushed, employing his highest compliment.

"Quite right" Joe mumbled, raising his beer to toast. "Quite right."

As we toasted Joe's brilliant idea, our brief, beer-fueled skirmish was quickly forgotten. The crowd, down to a few late night regulars, eagerly nodded their approval. His brow furrowing, Ian began to dig into the details.

"What do you think, Joe? 'Ow many should we get?"

"Eight. Same format we've been using. 8 man sides."

Ian nodded as I jumped in.

"I'll get a trophy – a trophy that the winner keeps each year. We'll do a best out of 5 match."

"OK. What are the stakes?" he asked. "Other than the trophy . . . and pride, I mean."

"Stakes? You mean just between you and me?"

Money was never a problem for Ian so whenever we concocted a wager, he left it to me to start the bidding. Feeling my oats after winning the snowball, I considered it for a few moments before making my opening bid.

"I'll put up the money I've got left from the snowball - call it $800 - and you match that. We'll each add $300 a year until someone wins. If we get to a fifth year, we'll up it to $500 each."

Doing some belated math in my head, I calculated the winnings would be $1,700 if the match went 3 years, $2,500 if we went the full 5. Taking a long sip from my pint, I sat back to wait for Ian's counter. Subdued conversations permeated the room as Ian took a sip from his beer, contemplating the wager. Stroking his considerable chin, he considered all possible pitfalls.

"What if I can't get eight men?"

"Well, then the bet's off."

Putting his pint down on the bar, he glanced at Joe, who gave him a small nod. Turning back to me, he stuck out his hand.

"Done."

With that simple gesture, the deal was sealed and the new, trans-Atlantic era of the Flem Cup had officially begun. As I sipped on a new pint, half-listening to Ian, Joe and Singe discuss players I didn't know, the magnitude of what had just happened began to sink in. Although just amateurs, we were all serious golfers and serious competitors and this would be a deadly serious competition. I also had no doubt that it would be an absolute hoot since, knowing Ian, he would pick players who were good golfers *and* fun guys to hang out with. I knew I'd end up sharing more than a few beers and laughs with these as yet unmet friends at our favorite Myrtle Beach hangout, BummZ at the Beach. The more I considered it, the more I knew this was going to be *awesome*.

Now, it is rare in life to have an event that you are really, really looking forward to actually lives up to expectations. It is rarer still for such an event to actually *exceed* those expectations but against all odds, that is exactly what the Flem Cup would do. Not for one year or two but for five amazing years the Cup would be firmly positioned at the very epicenter of our golfing world and although each year was unique and some of the characters would change, the bottom line was that each one of those five years would fill our lives with incredibly competitive golf, enduring friendships, hilarious escapades and fun-filled evenings.

In the end, though, its effect would go far deeper than merely a collection of wonderful memories. The events, good and bad, that would transpire over the five years of the Flem Cup would change lives – mine and others – in ways far more profound and important than I could ever have imagined. Looking back, the story of the Flem Cup is truly amazing, a story I was blessed to be an integral part of. This is the story of those five remarkable years.

2

Ian Jennings

I first met Ian Jennings in October of 1993 while attending a business conference called Enteract in Cincinnati. We were each co-owners of small companies that offered condition based monitoring services and products – basically high tech industrial maintenance. My company's area of expertise was vibration analysis on machinery while Ian's company, being larger, also offered services like thermal imaging, oil sampling and motor testing. The conference was put on by a software company we represented named Entek and it was split between the international sales meeting, which ran Wednesday through Friday, and the international user group meeting, which started the following Sunday evening and ran through Wednesday. Not so coincidentally, the weekend between coincided with Cincinnati's massive Oktoberfest celebration and with representatives coming in from all over the world, there was no shortage of fun and laughs.

Our launching point each evening was a little bar named Scully's, conveniently located in the maze of walkways connecting Cincinnati's downtown hotels. Where we landed from there was anyone's guess – riding a mechanical bull in Kentucky, dancing at a nightclub, climbing into a limo full of strangers, crashing a film preview party on Main Street or just laughing ourselves silly over countless pitchers of beer back at Scully's – but nearly anything was possible and in several years of conference attendance, my head never once saw the pillow before 3 am.

Adding to the fun was the fact that 1993 was the conference's first year and, with a cast of international characters and budding new friendships, it was truly a magical, unforgettable week.

On Saturday, we were invited to play in a golf outing organized by our hosts at Black Bear, a Jack Nicklaus signature course just north of Cincinnati. Barely able to roust myself for our noon tee time, I found myself paired with an English gentleman I'd only met briefly over the previous few days - Ian Jennings. Discovering a shared passion for competitive golf, I was amazed to learn that Ian, an 8 handicap, had only taken up the game 3 years earlier. A gifted athlete who had previously excelled at pretty much any sport he'd tried, he confronted the challenge of golf with typical gusto and focus, beginning with lessons in order to develop a technically sound swing and following through with regular practice and playing time. Within a few short years, he'd earned a single digit handicap that would eventually reach as low as 5.

Like me, Ian had an entrepreneurial streak a mile wide. In the mid-80s, he co-founded a consulting company, Monition, and within a few years he was employing dozens of people. Throughout that time, he increasingly plugged himself into the world of European Union projects and, being a connoisseur of the finer things in life, he embraced the role of international playboy and businessman. Despite that, he was equally comfortable – perhaps even more so – seated in a fun little bar like Scully's, telling jokes, laughing and drinking pitcher after pitcher of beer with friends, new and old.

At 6 feet tall and fairly fit, Ian's face sloped down from a thinning hairline to his strong chin. With his reddish blond hair and the freckles that so often accompany that complexion, he was not quite "model" handsome but was a very good looking fellow. He was also quite the ladies' man. If money and power are the two greatest aphrodisiacs, a great sense of humor runs a close third and Ian had that in spades. More than just being funny, Ian was *stylishly* funny. Being entirely comfortable in his own skin, he never had to think up a line or crack some awkward joke. He would simply start a conversation by making some funny little observation or comment, flash that impish smile and let his boyish charm and wit take over from there.

In day to day life, Ian would draw people to him like moths to a flame. He possessed not only an amazing memory for jokes and funny stories but also the personality and technique to deliver them with flair and style. Perhaps most extraordinary was his innate ability to make everyone around him feel comfortable. He cast a wide net of friendship and camaraderie wherever he went, drawing in friends and strangers alike.

As I got to know him better and better over the years, I came to understand that Ian was an entirely social creature, one who used his financial success to fund hobbies and activities he loved that, in turn, provided him the opportunity to spend time laughing and enjoying life with his friends and loved ones. He loved the challenge and competition of an intense golf match but the 19th hole was his favorite. He embraced the adrenaline rush of a double black diamond ski slope but loved the subsequent gathering around a roaring fire even more. His boat, a 17 meter wooden dual engine cruiser, was merely a stylish and mobile entertainment center for his guests. So while he loved his boat and his sports, the end game was always about surrounding himself with his friends, laughing and enjoying themselves.

Although we got to know each other during the round of golf at Black Bear, it was our second round together that really cemented our friendship. The day after our Black Bear outing, the organizer of the event, a fellow named Scott whom we'd played with at Black Bear and who was an outstanding golfer, approached us about playing a round at a course named Shaker Run, assuring us it was well worth playing. We eagerly agreed, grabbing a customer of mine named Don to round out our foursome. Bright and early Tuesday morning, we set off for Shaker Run.

Golf's handicap system is unique among sports because it allows players of widely disparate skills to play competitively against one another. The reason this can work is simple: the ultimate opponent is not a person but the golf course itself. A player's handicap is based on the average of the 10 best out of a golfer's most recent 20 rounds, meaning that handicap represents a significantly *above* average round. The more inconsistent a golfer is, the harder it is to play to one's handicap. Golf being what it is – an incredibly hard game requiring consistent skill and precise execution – any single digit handicap represents a very high level of golfing skill.

When playing in a "medal" or "stroke play" tournament, you simply add up all your strokes (your "gross" score) and deduct your handicap to obtain your "net" score. What many non-golfers do not realize is that there is another completely different way to play golf called match play. The Ryder Cup, a bi-annual match between the top European and U.S. golfers, is the most well-known team match play event. In match play, every hole is an individual match played within the larger 18 hole match. No matter how many strokes you win an individual hole by, you only win that one hole.

For matches between amateurs using handicaps, every individual hole on a golf course is assigned a handicap rating between 1 and 18 with the #1 handicap hole being the hardest and the #18 handicap hole being the easiest, an explanation that is a bit simplistic but suffices. If a 10 handicap golfer plays an 18 handicap golfer, the higher handicap player will get one shot on the 8 hardest holes or, more commonly, a percentage of those holes. If 75% is used in the above example, the higher handicap golfer would get a stroke on the 6 hardest holes. Although there are various formats, the most common team match play format is called 4 ball because four players are each playing their own ball. In 4 ball play, player's handicaps are calculated as if the lowest handicap player's handicap is zero and to win the hole for your team, your net score must beat *both* of your opponents.

With our host, Scott, as low handicap (playing off 4), Ian, playing off of 8, would be getting 3 shots (75% of the difference) while Don (playing off 12) would get 6 and I (playing off 14) would get 8. Having already played as a group on Saturday, and thus familiar which each other's level of play, we decided on a $20 per man match with Ian and Scott taking on me and Don.

By the time we were driving up the hill to the 4th tee on the Woodland 9, Don and I were 2 holes down and I was playing miserably, having carded two triple bogies and a double. Don's bogie net par on the 2nd hole had been our lone bright spot, enough at least to tie, or "halve", the hole. Things were looking a bit bleak early on.

On the plus side, Scott's assessment of Shaker Run being a "great" course turned out to be a bit of an understatement. Two excellent starting holes were followed by the spectacular par-4 3rd hole, followed one hole later by the equally spectacular par-3 5th hole. With fantastic holes interspersed with merely excellent ones, it wasn't long before we were comparing it to the best courses any of us had ever played. The weather was picture perfect - mid 70s and a piercingly blue, cloudless sky - and the fall foliage of mid-October was at its peak. With the lush greens and whites of the golf course set against the brilliant reds, oranges and yellows of the bushes and trees set against a brilliant blue October sky, it was a remarkable setting for what would become a memorable day.

Determined to get my game on track, I managed to scramble my way to a par on 4, enough to halve the hole, and followed that with one of my best strikes of the day on the next hole, a treacherous par 3. Playing 190 yards down a steep hill to an angled green guarded tightly all along the front by a creek, my crisply struck 5 iron never left the pin, finishing only 10 feet short. Although I missed the birdie putt, we won the hole and were back in the match at only 1 down. Settling into solid, steady golf, we eventually drew even by winning 7 and made the turn all square in what had become a tight, hard fought match.

Three times on the back 9 Ian and Scott took the lead only to see us counter by winning the very next hole. Eventually, the match would come down to two crucial shots – shots that perfectly illustrated the essence of the competitive relationship Ian and I would develop over the coming years.

The first came with Ian in control. Holding a 1 up lead, he was safely on 17 green in regulation but faced a tough side hill putt for a birdie. Knowing the match was on the line, I surprised him by nearly holing out a 125-yard pitching wedge that landed just inches past the pin, leaving myself with a 5 foot downhill birdie putt. Perhaps shocked at my shot under pressure, he proceeded to 3 putt and the match headed to 18 all square.

By the time we reached the final green, the roles had reversed and it was I who was in control, needing only a 2 putt from 30 feet to par the hole and win the match. Feeling confident and focused after my heroics on the last hole, I made a slow, controlled backswing, wary of slamming it past the hole on the fast greens and far from confident in my putting ability. Unfortunately, as I swung the putter forward, I first thing I hit was the ground about an inch behind the ball. Bouncing up and out of the small divot, my putter retained only enough forward momentum to knock the ball 10 or 12 feet towards the cup. Perhaps even more shocked than on the previous hole, Ian was unable to contain himself, bursting out laughing. Scott turned away, shoulders shaking, as poor Don just stared at the ground, slowly shaking his head.

"Good effort, that," Ian finally managed to get out between giggles followed by "I think . . let me see . . . yes, you're still away." That got them all – even Don – laughing again. At that particular moment, however, I was not amused, fuming at myself over the untimely mistake. As I tried to regain my composure, Ian leaned over to Scott and whispered "bet he doesn't leave this one short."

Wham! 5 feet past the hole. Stomping across the green, I could only mutter and swear at myself under my breath. Now, with what little confidence I'd had shattered, I still needed to sink what might as well have been a 15 footer just to halve the match and avoid the dreaded *lost the match on a 4-putt* scenario.

Battling my own demons, I swung the putter tentatively, pushing the ball slightly right as I tried to guide the putter head through impact, a cardinal sin of putting. Not at all clear that the ball would even reach the cup, it wobbled slightly as it gradually slowed on the slick green. Twisting and turning like a fireman holding a pressurized fire hose, I did my best to will the ball into the cup. Finally, it stopped just as it reached the right edge of the hole, pausing for one dramatic moment before gravity took over, pulling the ball down and into the cup through the side door. Bad speed, bad line, putt good. I could only shake my head in relief and embarrassment as Ian and Scott stared in amused disappointment. Staring skyward, Don breathed a sigh of relief.

Although neither of us knew it at the time, those two shots would epitomize the golfing relationship Ian and I would develop over the years as my unpredictable scrambling and occasionally great shot making would match up against his methodical consistency. Although the scales may have finished slightly in his favor, over the years, and particularly in important matches, I would get my share of wins and great moments and nothing made me happier than seeing that shocked look on his face after I'd pulled off some unexpected and unlikely shot.

The anti-climactic end to our hard fought match was quickly forgotten over a couple of beers and laughs – more than a few at my expense – before heading back to Cincinnati. As we finished our last beer and the sun was dropping low in the sky, I was struck by an unusual feeling of contentment; satisfied and happy in a way that I was unaccustomed to. I didn't want the day and its special nature to end. Here I was with friends, swapping stories and jokes as we reminisced about a fabulous day of golf. The weather had been magnificent, the course spectacular and the golf a competitive delight, cementing friendships through the intensity of a well-played match. It was the best day I'd had in a very long time and I felt *content*, a feeling I often longed for yet rarely felt.

In 1993, at age 34, I was increasingly seeing my life as empty and devoid of meaning despite success in many areas. From my youth, growing up in Madison, N.J., my life was a never ending search for something - anything - that would make me feel whole and happy, but nothing ever did. Whether it was an event, a person or a thing, high expectations would inevitably be crushed under feelings of letdown and disappointment. To escape those feelings, I dabbled in drinking and drugs in high school, an exciting diversion that quickly became an inescapable trap – and nightmare. My drug of choice became pot and by the time I was attending Bucknell University, I was smoking it every chance I got. Despite all that, I somehow graduated as a mechanical engineer.

Bad choices littered my 20s but by far the worst was one that, as always, re-volved around my endless search for self-fulfillment in someone or something else. In early 1982, less than a year after graduating, I met a cute little au-pair from Holland. With a sexy, exotic Dutch girl on my arm every night, I was living large in my hometown. So determined was I to keep this catch that when we naturally encountered some rather serious relationship problems, my solution was to ask her to marry me. Sadly for both of us, she accepted.

So off I went, hopelessly immature and stupid, eloping with a girl I really barely knew on New Year's Eve in 1982. As any sane person could have predict-ed, the realities of married life quickly set in, fires fueled by my own immaturity and relentless desire to escape from the daily humdrum. Disappointment quickly led to resentments that began to simmer and fester inside her like seeds in a hot-house. Every wife needs to feel that she is loved by her husband and that was a test I would fail at, over and over. Coming to understand my shortcomings in that area within only a few years, I sent her back to Holland but when she returned within days, claiming we had "unfinished business", I took her back to try again and our fate was sealed.

Sharing virtually no interests other than a wolf-dog hybrid who became the focal point of our relationship, we settled into an uneasy holding pattern of mutual tolerance. Having moved far from my hometown, our social lives began to revolve around friends she'd made, leading me to become ever more a loner, content to sit at home while she went on visits that were all about small talk and drinking coffee, things I had no interest in. Conversely, my obsession with sports was something she had no interest in. We drifted apart, connected only by the dog.

Finally, in 1990, we had a daughter and I made a vow to myself to stay and see her grow up. In 1992, we had another daughter but by then our marriage had reached the point of being a loveless farce, dominated by bitterness and resent-ment. With past wrongs only an ill-timed word away from being resurrected, no seed of forgiveness was ever allowed to germinate. Against this bleak existence, my need to escape through smoking pot and burying myself in work remained life's dominant force.

By October of 1993, I had somehow navigated my endlessly stupid choices to become fairly successful on a number of levels but inside I was more lost than ever, a prisoner of the empty life of narcissism and self-indulgence I had chosen. Now in my mid-30s, weeks and months sped by in mere moments, leaving little more than unrealized expectations, unfulfilled hopes and unsatisfying accomplishments. Almost always, there was the empty ache within me, longing for something good and wholesome to fill the void. More than anything, I wanted to love and be loved but I had two insurmountable obstacles: I didn't know how to love and I didn't know how to be loved. In life's big picture, I was completely and totally lost.

As I watched the glorious sunset that day at Shaker Run, though, none of that mattered. I was content, a feeling so foreign to me that I remember it striking me at the time as odd. In hindsight, the impact of that day and what it meant to my life would only grow. Within a matter of months, Ian and I would become business partners. Within a year or so we would begin going on golf trips together and, as our businesses grew through the 90s, our friendship would as well. Whatever else happened to me on that glorious October day of great friendship, great competition and great contentment, I would come to remember it most for being the day I started a lifelong friendship with Ian, a man who would teach me much in the long, slow turn back I was about to begin; a turn that would ultimately lead me towards life's great truths.

3

The Flem Cup

The Grand Strand is an unbroken arc of beautiful, sandy beaches at the north end of South Carolina surrounding Myrtle Beach, running over 60 miles from the North Carolina border down to the Pawleys Island in the south. A sleepy beach resort town in the early 1950s, the area grew to become a magnet for millions of golfers each and every year for one simple reason – value. Throughout the 1990s, with the exception of a trip to Kiawah Island in 1995, the Grand Strand was home to our annual November golf trip. Each year we would assemble, pony up some cash and compete for individual prizes like best Stableford score (a scoring system where a net double bogie or worse earns you 0 points - a 'blob', a net bogie gets you 1 point, par = 2, birdie = 3 and so on. A 36 Stableford score equals net par for 18 holes - a very good score), most skins won and closest to the pin. In 1998, though, an off the cuff suggestion by my friend Lou Flem changed things forever.

Lou was a rough-edged project engineer who worked at an asphalt refinery in south Jersey, standing about 5'-10" with slightly hunched shoulders and an ample midriff. Being a native Philly boy, Lou had a no-nonsense, straight-talking attitude to go with the heart of gold buried beneath his gruff exterior. With a golf club in his hands, Lou would have made Paul Bunyan envious. Lifting his club head up steeply and going way past parallel at the top a la John Daly, Lou would proceed to bring it crashing down into the back of the ball, often generating backhoe-sized divots. When he connected properly, the ball went a long, long way. When he didn't . . . well, it wasn't pretty. And since Lou didn't always connect so well, he always had the highest handicap in the group at about 24 or so.

When Lou suggested a team competition along the lines of the Ryder Cup, I quickly embraced the idea. Best of all, the perfect name was there for the taking, one that both honored the idea's originator and testified, tongue and spelling in cheek, to the quality of play: the Flem Cup.

There are two things that make Ryder Cup-style contests the most entertaining and compelling of all golf events: teams and match play. A fascinating aspect of match play is that it can completely change the mindset of the golfer. While your opponent in stroke play is the silent, unforgiving course, your opponent in match play is a person (or two people in a 4 ball match) and your only goal is to take fewer strokes, period. That brings previously irrelevant variables into play at various times during the match. Are you leading or trailing? What is the match score? On which holes do you give or get strokes? What is your opponent's mental state? What is yours? Where is their ball? Where is yours? Should your next shot be aggressive or safe? All these and more go into your strategic mindset, affecting both club and shot selection.

The team aspect adds to your stress level as you deal with the knowledge that others are counting on you to do your part and perform well, even if you don't win. Every shot is executed in a pressure cooker and on each hole there are three possible outcomes: win, lose or draw. In a 4 ball competition, 2 man teams compete against one another but only the lower score for each team counts. If my teammate takes 4 shots to hole out, I take 7 and each of our opponent's take 5, we win the hole. The running match score is kept based on the *difference* in how many holes each side has won so if Team A has won 5 holes and Team B only 4, Team A is 1 up or Team B is 1 down. A tie score is said to be "all-square" or "level" and once one side is up by an amount equal to the number of remaining holes (2 up with 2 holes to play), they are said to be "dormie". Going one step further, once one side is ahead by *more* than the number of remaining holes, the match is over and the final score established. If Team A wins the 16th hole to go 3 up, they've won, 3&2 (3 up with 2 holes left), and the match is over.

Modeling the Flem Cup after the Ryder Cup, we decided on 4 ball matches the first 3 days before concluding with a final day of 2 ball matches (matches between individuals played under the same rules and scoring format). My original nemesis and opposing captain for the Cup was my best friend here in the States, Jack Tanis Jr.

Jack and I clicked from the first time we met playing basketball at the YMCA in Easton, PA in the early 90s. In addition to being as competitive as me, we shared a few other character traits that quickly cemented our friendship. First, we shared an ability to find humor in pretty much anything along with an irreverent (some might say sarcastic – I prefer irreverent) way of expressing it. Second, he was a good athlete, an ultra-competitive personality and, just like me, enjoyed the mental aspect of sports. Each of us took great pleasure in coming through in the clutch in order to snatch victory away from an opponent at the last moment, including each other.

When we first played golf together, I beat Jack regularly. Whereas I was equally capable of par or double-bogey, Jack was equally capable of birdie or triple-bogey. Monstrously long, he would effortlessly hitting low, screaming drives 300 yards or more. By the mid to late 90s, though, Jack had reached parity with me and by the turn of the century, he had a lower handicap by several strokes.

We really didn't know what to make of the Flem Cup that first year. It was really just kind of an afterthought; a sideshow to the individual prizes everyone focused on. My team consisted of Ian, Jack Sr. (Jack's father) and Lou while Jack's team consisted of Terry Neal, the low handicapper in the group at 6, Jack's brother Chris and Pat Slack, a friend of the Tanis family. After 3 days of play, the score was tied 3-3. On the final day, I confidently went up against Jack Jr only to get crushed, 5&4, and his team won the inaugural event, 6-4.

But the competition had turned out to be more important – and interesting – than we'd originally imagined. The team atmosphere and camaraderie improved the entire trip, holding the interest of players who had fallen out of the individual competitions. Over a few beers at the end of the final round, everyone agreed that the Flem Cup was a success – and here to stay.

In 1999, the group expanded to 12 with Ian bringing a couple of friends from his home course of Renishaw Park: John Oates, the club pro, and Mark Nelson, the assistant greens keeper. Although Mark was an outstanding 1 handicap golfer, John was a club pro fully capable of consistently shooting under par.

With the increased interest in the Cup, I expanded the format to include 9 hole scramble matches worth ½ point each of the first three days. With the additional half-point matches and expanded group, the total number of points available grew from 10 to 19-½ and although the final score of 11 to 8-½ seemed marginally close, it really wasn't. Jack's squad, which included John, Ian, Pat, Lou and Jack Sr., led from start to finish, winning by a little bit every day and pretty much coasting to the win. Wanting some revenge against Jack for the 5&4 beat down he had administered to me in 1998, I challenged him once again in a 2 ball match but the only "revenge" I managed to get was to cut his victory margin to 4&3. With all the previous year's players returning and swapping teams, I immediately became the only player with two losses in two years.

By the following May we were once again scheduling tee times and courses for the fall trip and although neither John or Mark could return, Ian announced he would be bringing someone else: Smokin' Joe Brook, a chain-smoking, beer-drinking, middle-aged 5 handicap with a ruddy complexion, a fun loving personality and a golf swing most people would die for.

Where Ian was technical precision, Joe was natural, fluid motion. He despised practice, avoiding driving ranges like the plague, and on those rare occasions when he did venture out to the range, it was hilarious to watch his frustration build to a crescendo as he hit nothing but ground balls, duck hooks, pop ups and shanks.

Eventually he would stomp off, shaking his head and muttering about what a stupid place the driving range was.

In his younger days, Joe was a scratch golfer who played in serious amateur competitions throughout the UK. His friendship with Ian actually started in the mid-60s, when Ian was just a lad and Joe was building boats with Ian's father. It blossomed further between 1968 through 1972 when Ian caddied for Joe at high level competitions across the U.K. In 1972, Joe moved away and the two didn't see each other again until 1996 when Joe moved back to Spinkhill. When Ian was looking to move away from the nearby village of Blythe, Joe was a more than minor influence in his eventual choice. Their friendship rekindled, the two became virtually inseparable when it came to golf. Joe had wanted to come over for the Cup in '99 but couldn't make the arrangements. He made it a priority for 2000.

An interesting pair, Ian and Joe shared a love of laughter along with a passion for golf, boats, beer and wine but where Ian embraced the finer things in life, the extravagance of high society was not something Joe cared much about. While Ian loved his role as a jet-setting businessman, Joe preferred staying local (except when the travel included great golf courses). While Ian was the consummate storyteller, enjoying telling them as much as friends enjoyed hearing them, Joe was content in a support role, happy to chime in with an agreeable "quite right" from time to time. While Ian would still be entertaining the crowd right through last call and the subsequent Angel "shut-in", Joe would often be nodding off, waiting as long as possible before finally shuffling out the front door and across the street to his conveniently located home.

Although the driving range to Joe was like kryptonite to Superman, everything changed when he stepped onto the first tee. Standing behind the ball for a moment or two, he would survey his line before flicking his cigarette off to the side. Stepping up to the ball, he'd assume his perfectly relaxed stance and, after only a brief pause, begin his swing, smoothly bringing the club to perfectly parallel at the top, hands fully cocked. There was no hesitation or adjustment. It was good.

But if the backswing was good, the rest of Joe's swing was poetry in motion. His hands would come down, releasing the club head perfectly, snapping it through the impact zone with a confident precision lesser players could only aspire to before finishing with his hands high above his left shoulder, club pointed down and across his back, weight still perfectly balanced. The ball would rocket out, ideally on a long slow draw that traveled 240-260 yards, more if he caught it on the "screws". No matter what shot he was addressing, Joe was a 'feel' player and although time, beer and cigs had eroded his skills, he was still a damn good golfer, coming to Myrtle Beach in 2000 as a solid 5 handicap.

Along with Ian, Joe and me, the group included holdovers Jack Jr., Lou, Jack Sr., Chris and Pat plus Bob and Fred, a couple of previous participants who were coming again. For the first time, Jack Jr. decided to bring his son Matt, an unpolished 15-year old with a 13 handicap whose monstrous potential and monstrous drives were matched – and sometimes overwhelmed – by his monstrous temper.

The final player was the newest member of Jack's golf-playing family, AJ Karanikolas, a tall, lanky foreign currency trader on Wall Street. AJ had become part of the Tanis clan by marrying the prettiest of Jack Sr.'s children, Lauren, and his attention to the technical details of the golf swing made Ian's seem like a case of ADD. Every aspect of his swing was studied and dissected; practiced and perfected and although AJ would only play golf about 5-7 times a year, he would supplement that with an annual trip to a Nick Faldo golf school in Florida. I found it more than a little galling that despite his lack of playing time he could – and usually would – play to around a 5 handicap. But in 2000 AJ would be playing as a 3 handicap because . . . well . . . mostly because he wasn't on my team and I, in conjunction with Jack Jr., assigned handicaps for players who didn't have an official USGA one . . . and AJ fell into that category.

As in previous years, the teams were randomly chosen based on handicaps. My team consisting of Ian, Joe, Chris, Fred and Lou while Jack's side was made up of AJ, Matt, Jack Sr., Pat and Bob. Badly wanting to finally win my first Cup, my hopes were significantly dimmed when we were crushed on Day 1, managing only a lonely halve in one of the 9 hole matches and trailing 4 to 1/2 point. Facing an unprecedented deficit, Days 2 and 3 got progressively worse as Jack's team picked up an additional 1/2 point each day, building a nearly insurmountable lead of 9 to 4-1/2 with only the six 2 ball matches left. We would need to win five matches and halve the sixth to win. It seemed to be all over but the crying.

But then something strange happened.

We didn't give up.

Under one of the most interesting rules we'd implemented after the first year, the trailing team controlled the matchups. What that meant was that the leading team would issue its pairings and the trailing team would match up as they saw fit – 'setting the matches', we called it. It was a strategic advantage that allowed me to do what I loved most – strategize – and that's exactly what I did with the help of my teammates.

Right off the bat we faced a big challenge with Pat, who was leading the Stableford competition at that point. Without hesitation, Joe claimed the challenge, reasoning that consistent, solid golf by a low handicapper might make Pat crack. Out next was Bob and Fred quickly volunteered for that job, knowing his style of "in-your-head" needling could easily and effectively get under Bob's skin. Two matches were set and I liked our chances in both.

Third out for Jack's team was AJ and I'd already decided he would be my opponent. I'd always preferred getting strokes to giving them and I'd seen more than enough of Jack Jr. the previous 2 years. With Lou taking on Jack Sr. in the fourth match, we were down to their final two players, Jack Jr. and Matt, and I had exactly the two players I wanted to take them on.

By keeping Matt paired with older family members during 4 ball play, Jack had done what he could to keep the youngster's volatility under control but today, Matt would face the isolation of a 2 ball match where no advice on any match-related subject could be solicited between teammates. There was no doubt who wanted to take on the youngster – his merciless uncle Chris – and that left Ian to take on Jack. Having bested Jack virtually every time they'd faced each other over previous years, Ian felt supremely confident that his own consistency would trump any advantage Jack might have in distance. Scanning our faces, Ian's voice was steady, his gaze focused.

"Focus on your own matches, lads – this one's in the bank."

Of course, great planning means nothing without execution and five wins and a halve was, in all reality, an impossibly tall order. As we silently mulled the matches, though, I sensed a strong level of buy-in with each man liking his own chances - and that was an excellent place to start. With low expectations and no pressure, we agreed to just go out and have fun.

Singles Day in 2000 was at The Dunes, for years home to the Senior Tour Championship and one of the most well-known and respected courses on the Grand Strand. Greeted by yet another warm and sunny November morn, the first group out quickly disappeared from sight. Up next, we left the final group far behind, leaving us in complete isolation as we settled into our matches. By the time we reached the final tee, I knew only two things: Lou had won his match and I was engaged in an epic battle with AJ that stood all-square.

Our match had been well played from the start but I had gotten all the strokes I would get and I knew, in all likelihood, that I would need to par the last hole to have any chance of halving or beating AJ. Frankly, I'd have been happy with either at that point.

Although both tee shots found the fairway, I found myself in my customary position – 25 yards behind my much longer hitting opponent. With the green on 18 guarded front and left by water and the grass on the rounded banks of the green is cut short, there would be little rough to catch any wayward shots and anything short or left would be in imminent danger of finding a watery grave. The hole was cut in the back left corner of the green, only 3 or 4 paces from the edge of the green with water lurking just beyond. I ignored the sucker pin, taking aim at the center of the green.

As a surveyed my shot, I couldn't help but notice the first foursome standing and chatting on the cart path under a stand of large trees framing the right side of the green. I took that as a good sign, assuming they'd be at the 19th hole by now if the Cup had been decided. Setting myself, I focused on two thoughts as I made my swing.

Head down . . . release the hands . . .

Feeling a solid click with my 6 iron, I optimistically looked up only to find I'd bailed on it, pushing the shot towards the tree line on the right, safely away from the water. Losing sight of the ball as it dropped through the branches, Joe waved at its resting place near the cart path about 10 or 15 yards right of the green. It looked to be pin high but would be lying on the wood mulch spread around the base of the tree. I dropped my head in disgust as I waited for AJ to hit, expecting him to take full advantage of my unforced error.

Surprisingly, AJ hit his shot a bit fat. Landing just on the front edge of the green, the ball backed up before stopping at the top of the slope. He would have an awkward stance but with his short game and my difficulties, he remained in the driver's seat, having dodged a bullet when his ball stayed dry.

Arriving at the green, I found both Joe and Fred had, indeed, won their matches. Adding Lou's win, the Cup score stood at 9 to 7-½ and my shot took on a new urgency. With the unpredictability of hitting off of mulch and wood chips, it would be very dicey. The pin was on the far side of the green, 40 yards away, and I would have to keep the shot low enough to avoid the overhanging tree branches while carrying it 12 or 15 yards with enough spin to get it to check up a bit before releasing. If I hit it too hard or a bit thin, it could easily run across the green, down the hill and into the lake on the far side. Still expecting AJ to par, I was well aware this shot could make or break my Cup chances for yet another year. Doing my best to put my swirling thoughts and emotions aside, I focused.

Hands forward . . . firm and through the ball . . . strike down into the back of the ball . . .

After a half dozen practice swings, each time trying to visualize the swing that would produce the exact shot I wanted, I stepped up to the shot, taking a deep breath before swinging my trusty 8-iron.

At first, all I could see were wood-chips scattering. Then, there it was, the white ball flying, landing just past the fringe, taking two forward skips before checking up and releasing towards the hole, right on line and at a good pace. With Joe, Fred and Lou cheering it on, the ball trickled past the pin, stopping less than 3 feet away. As I allowed myself a small fist pump, I glanced at AJ's face and saw – disbelief. *Perfect*, I thought. After hitting a mediocre chip and missing his 10 foot par effort, he could only watch as I drained my putt for the pressure-packed 1-up win.

Suddenly, the Cup score stood at 9 to 8-½ and, for the first time, I began to seriously consider the possibility that we might just pull off this comeback for the ages. After all, the two matches we'd considered our best chances were still out on the course. Jumping into the cart next to Joe, I drove back down the fairway to find out if our dream comeback still had a chance of coming true. The next group had just reached the fairway.

"Can you believe it, Joe?" I said. "We might actually win this thing. That'd would be one for the record books, eh?"

"Quite right, lad. This'll be one we'll remember for sure."

On the far side of the fairway, Ian stepped out of his cart to survey his approach shot. He looked relaxed enough; surely a good sign, I thought. After Chris hit, I sidled alongside him as Ian prepared to play. Chris' face betrayed no emotion. As nonchalantly as possible, I asked the question at hand.

"So, ah, how'd you do?"

Chris shook his head and laughed, grinning sardonically. "I won 4&3."

Turning to look at Joe with a look like the cat that ate the canary, I couldn't contain my excitement, believing that Ian's win was a foregone conclusion.

"We've done it! We won the first four matches and now, with your win and Ian's, we've won the Cup! YES!! I finally won the Cup. This is AWESOME! What a way to win!!"

I was ecstatic, looking back towards the green and fist pumping to make my teammates understand that we'd pulled off the miracle comeback. Turning back to Chris with my hand up in anticipation of a resounding high-five, I saw none of the emotion that I felt; only stunned disbelief. Normally laid back, even *he* should be excited by this. I stood, waiting, hand held high.

"You're joking," he said, flatly.

"No, I'm serious. We won . . . the . . . first . . . . four"

As my hand hovered awkwardly in mid-air, my brain connected the now ob-vious dots. There could only be one reason why Chris wasn't celebrating. There would be no comeback for the ages, no celebration and no Flem Cup victory for me. Ian had lost.

Looking back across the fairway, I realized for the first time that Ian had been watching my gyrations. With a sheepish smile, he shrugged his shoulders, his hands out, palms up.

"Jack better have shot lights out," I muttered to myself, slumping dejectedly in my seat.

Well, as it turned out . . . not exactly. Jack had the 2nd worst net score of the day. Any individual would have beaten him − save one. Ian had shot not only the worst score of the day by a mile but the worst score of the entire week; a stunning 15 over par *net*. So despite the day's second worst score, Jack won easily, 5&4, and the Cup had officially ended an hour ago, on the 14th green. Regardless of how or why, I was a 3-time loser.

Ian's abysmal round and ill-fated victory guarantee would have been quickly forgotten had the rest of our plan not worked to perfection − but it did and in doing so, Ian's failure became one not quickly forgotten or easily let go of. Ironically, though, the failure would change the Flem Cup forever. Three years of tinkering had perfected the format and rules while the competitive desire to win the event had increased exponentially each year, culminating in an incredible finish where the strategic advantage of setting the matches, now a much anticipated part of the trip, had been utilized to near-perfection. In 3 years, the Cup had morphed from an afterthought into the *primary* focus of the trip; transcending the cash of the individual prizes in terms of overall importance. It had come of age before our eyes. With the quiz night meltdown 4 months later triggering Joe's brilliant suggestion of a trans-Atlantic match, the Flem Cup would be forever transformed, changing from being merely part of an annual golf trip into the centerpiece of a much-anticipated *event*.

4

The Teams

Returning home with the newly minted Cup plans in hand, I eagerly spread the word of our new task – defeating Team England. Finally, I'd be on the same side as Jack Jr. along with Chris, Jack Sr., Lou, Pat and young Matt.

In 2000, Jack Jr., Chris and I had joined a very well kept, very tough little gem of a golf course outside of Phillipsburg, NJ called Harkers Hollow. Built on the side of a mountain, Harkers' main challenges were tiny, lightning fast greens, consistently uneven lies and thick, unforgiving rough. Being a mountainside course, some of the greens were so deceptive that seemingly flat putts concealed 8 or 10 foot breaks and soon we learned to line up putts and chips based solely on experience rather than sight. Harkers' difficulty was reflected in a course rating of 71, a full stroke higher than its par of 70.

The Tanis family was a testament to the family patriarch, Jack Sr., a wonderfully nice fellow (at least *off* the basketball court) whom I'd gotten to know over the years, like his son, through basketball at the Y and golf. As I got to know him, I'd become increasingly intrigued by his fascinating life story. As a highly successful salesman with 4 young children, Jack chucked it all to attend seminary school and become a minister. While I couldn't fathom doing something like that myself, I admired anyone with that level of commitment, often wondering what sort of epiphany he'd experienced to take a leap like that into the unknown. I came to admire his deep faith, once seeing him stop angrily in the middle of a typically intense game at the Y to admonish a young man who was repeatedly using the name of Jesus Christ with an expletive inserted between names. The young man sheepishly apologized and didn't do it again. Jack commanded respect in all aspects of his life but despite his strong beliefs, he was never pushy or preachy, content to let his life be testimony to the faith I admired and envied but really didn't understand.

Although my parents had raised me and my brother in the Lutheran church, we stopped attending when I was young and I never really understood what any of it meant. As I grew older, the only services I attended were weddings and funerals, mostly at Catholic churches which left me even more confused. It all seemed cold and lifeless, filled with strange rituals and rote incantations I didn't understand. I just couldn't convince myself that with some canned prayers and occasional attendance you could somehow get in good with God. When I did ask Catholics I knew about the whats and whys, they couldn't even explain why they did what they did during a service. All in all, religion held no appeal to me and made little sense.

Over the years I'd heard empty phrases from television evangelists about *have faith and be saved* but my mental response was inevitably *in what* and *from what,* questions that inevitably remained unanswered. Have faith *in what?* God? Allah? Mother Earth? And who would save me? Jesus? Mohammed? Buddha? Confucius? Gaia? A personalized, designer god?

I found the idea of groups of people gathering once a week to shout hallelujah quite off-putting, cult-like, even, and I couldn't just fake belief in something simply because some preacher - a man like me - promised me eternal life or financial success or whatever. My logical mind was an unyielding guardian, preventing me from ever believing *anything* simply because I *wanted* to believe it. *Convince me,* my mind would scream, *prove it with evidence!* After all, I'd offered God plenty of chances over the years to prove His existence by showing up for me when I was in a jam and the results had never been impressive enough to convince me.

But although *religion* meant nothing to me, I did find myself wondering about God and life's meaning. How *did* we get here? I'd learned about evolution in school but couldn't shake my gut feeling that a God big enough to create the universe could use whatever processes He wanted to create and run the world - and that included evolution. When I was feeling philosophical, the proposition that everything around me, including my soul and consciousness, came from nothing seemed absurd to the highest degree. I would hear how science was making great strides in proving that there was no god but still couldn't wrap my head around how everything I could see and feel could come from nothing. How did every molecule in creation just randomly collect in the same spot so the big bang could even happen in the first place? On the other hand, I couldn't understand why a god big enough to create an entire universe would give a hoot about an insignificant little bug like me.

Most of the time I simply avoided such weighty subjects, content as I was with the myriad distractions I had constructed in my own little world, but what I saw in Jack Sr. intrigued me. It was a sense of contentment in who he was and what he was doing with his life. He and his family were the first Christians I'd known that really *lived* their faith and that made me wonder what it was that Jack knew that I didn't. His faith was clearly authentic, rooted in what had to be a foundational truth to him. I was sure he'd be happy to share that truth if asked . . . I just wasn't at a point in life where I cared to take that step.

Despite his gentle nature, it was easy to see where Jack Sr.'s sons and grandson got their competitive fire. In addition to his passion for God, Jack had a passion for competing – and he played to win. I'd met the whole family playing basketball at the YMCA and though I knew Jack the younger to be a deadly long-range shooter, Jack the elder was at least as good from mid-range. Slightly shorter and wider than his son (the natural long-term effect of gravity, I suppose), Senior was well into his 50s when I met him in the early 1990s but despite playing against men half or even a third his age, he usually gave better than he got. A clever passer and sneaky rebounder, his favorite move was a pivot - fake pass - pivot back - fade away - *SWISH* from about 12-15 feet. It almost always worked and if it didn't, he had a couple of variations he would employ to keep you guessing.

As for golf, Jack played off a handicap similar to mine – low teens. Deceptively long, he would, from time to time, find a groove that would garner him some impressive scores, even getting into the high 70s on occasion. He was a solid and reliable member of the team.

Chris was Jack's youngest of three sons and less competitive than his brother or dad – but that was strictly a relative term. He had the competitive Tanis fires burning; it just took a bit more to get them stoked. Having the same wry and irreverent sense of humor found in his brother Jack, Chris' was even funnier because of his serious yet unpredictably quirky side. To the endless amusement of everyone who knew him, Chris was always expounding on some secret he'd found that would unlock the vast potential of his golf game. Whether it was a different swing plane, a new grip or a new putting gimmick, he was always finding the secret that would knock 5 strokes off his score before losing it again. Whereas Jack Jr. was grip it and rip it and AJ was technical precision, Chris was a psychological spinning top, always seeing the ultimate secret to success just around the corner. In the final analysis, he played a game very similar to mine with a similar handicap.

The final piece to the puzzle was Pat Slack, a quiet friend of the Tanis family who shared their wry sense of humor and super competitive nature. Playing to a handicap similar to mine, Pat had possibly the most upside of any player on our side. Always capable of a superb round – or a dismal one – Pat seemed to be in the hunt for the Stableford title every year.

Within a few weeks, Jack gave me the disappointing news that AJ would be unable to make the trip as our eighth. I quickly recruited Terry Neal, who, like Lou, I'd become friends through business. Over the years we'd played quite a bit of golf together, including a number of Myrtle Beach and Kiawah Island trips. A quiet, common sense good-ole' boy from Ohio with a bit of a southern drawl and a bone-dry sense of humor, Terry was an excellent golfer to boot.

A few years earlier, having been laid off following a corporate takeover, Terry decided to follow his dream and go for his PGA card so he could work as a professional. In order to qualify at the time, he had to shoot 13 over par or better under the excruciating pressure of pursuing a dream at a one day 36 hole qualifying tournament played from the championship tees at a golf course set up to PGA qualifying standards. Piece of cake.

So Terry tried . . . and failed. He tried again . . . and failed. He tried again . . . and failed. Finally, on his fourth or so try, Terry finished his opening 18 holes at 11-over par. After a light lunch, he headed back out and, lo and behold, everything was working. By the time he reached 17, a par-5, he was 2-over for his afternoon round and needed two pars for his card. After a big drive, a beautifully struck 3-wood left him 20 feet from the pin and two putts later, he was in for birdie. With a par on 18, his dream of a PGA card became reality.

So our team was complete and my focus turned to my next trip across the pond for an early September training class in Chester, England, which lies just southwest of Manchester along the border with Wales. As usual, I added a few nights for a side visit to Spinkhill, a short 2 or 3 hour journey away by train. Finally, on Thursday, August 30th, I set off to Newark Airport for the overnight flight to Manchester.

After picking me up Friday morning, I accompanied Ian back to his business office so he could attend a couple of quick meetings. In true Ian-style, Monition's offices weren't next to a golf course or even near a golf course; they were built in a refurbished farm building right smack in the middle of Bondhay Golf Club – the main entrance about 50 feet from the pro shop door.

After finishing his business, we grabbed lunch over a pint before heading out for 18 holes followed by a few more pints. Having had only a few hours of fitful sleep on the flight, I'd been hoping for the customary afternoon jetlag recovery nap but with Ian scheduling a dinner date with Smokin' Joe and Phil Smith, off we went.

A quick-witted regular at the Angel, Phil was nearly as much of a fixture there as Ian. As a golfer, he was a very steady but unspectacular 13 handicap. After a couple more pints at the restaurant, we cracked the first of three bottles of good wine that Ian brought to compliment the excellent food. They would be the last detail I remembered about the evening as the rest of the night faded to black in an exhausted, drunken haze. Apparently, at some point around midnight, I was corralled standing in the middle of Spinkhill's narrow main street, mumbling something about looking for Ian, who had already driven his car home (his house was only a 2 minute walk down the hill).

As it turned out, the whole thing - keeping me up without any time to recover from the overnight trip - was set up by Ian to have some fun with me. The last laugh, though, would be had by the drunken American when I peed the mattress in Ian's guest room in my drunken stupor. Chalk one up for the law of unintended consequences.

After a morning of recovery and some afternoon golf at Renishaw, we found ourselves back at the Angel by 9 pm or so the next evening. With the Cup now looming less than two months away, it was dominating every minute of conversation with every sort of question about the trip. What are the courses like? What will the weather be like? What kind of evening entertainment is there? Are the restaurant portions as big as they say? What's BummZ like?

Before long, the door swung open and in walked a tall, dashing fellow with dark eyes and a devilish smile. After scanning the room and saying a few hellos, he had a short conversation with Ian, who led him over.

"Scott, this is Greg Matthews. He'll be coming to Myrtle with us."

Greg, who was Joe's nephew and a good friend of Ian's, was another Angel regular who loved to drink, laugh and have fun. Playing off of a 4 handicap, I immediately sensed he would prove to be a very tough opponent. Ray Mathews, Greg's father, would also be a member of Team England.

As we spoke, a curly haired, impish-looking fellow entered, immediately greeted by cries of "Swampy". Stuart "Swampy" Trowbridge had one of those friendly faces, his mouth curling up at the edges in sort of a permanent smile, possibly the result of his never resting sense of humor. A close mate of Greg's, Swampy was a wise-cracking 14-handicapper who was always up for a beer and a laugh.

Shortly afterwards, the sixth member of Team England arrived in the person of Paul "Milo" Miles, a wiry little law enforcement professional who played off a 13 handicap. Initially, he seemed a bit too mild-mannered for the regular Angel crowd but that impression quickly evaporated in light of his quiet but cutting sense of humor.

It wasn't long before the conversation turned to memorable events as Milo recounted an early Angel Golf Society trip to Wortley Golf Club, a place he described as a prototypical country club snob-a-torium.

"Well, Ian was our event sponsor that month and he'd chosen to spice up the festivities by offering prizes that included selected readings from a book he'd found called *Strokes – And How To Avoid Them*. Now, this was a serious medical book, mind you, but Ian started reading snippets he had picked out as if they were pieces of *golf* advice. Now, we were all snickering – and it was funnier than 'ell – but some club members who were sitting nearby just weren't getting it and that just made us laugh even harder. Well, eventually Ian amused himself to the point of being doubled over, nearly to the floor, laughing uncontrollably with a beet red face. By then, the looks on some of the member's faces . . . well, all I can say is that it was priceless."

While we were still laughing, in walked Mark and Paul Nelson and it was party time. The two brothers were popular local lads, great golfers and a riot to hang out with. Before long, Mark launched into another Ian story.

"I remember the time that Ian volunteered to caddy for me during the 1st Division Team Championships at Ganton. Although I was too young to drive myself, I am fairly certain that's when my lifelong love-affair with speed began; on trips as an innocent youth with old Speed Racer here."

Mark paused as the crowd laughed knowingly, quite aware of Ian's legendary driving exploits.

"Well, the 11th is a tough par 4, 430 yards littered with fairway bunkers, and I've 'it a perfect drive down the right side of the fairway. After consulting the yardage book, we agreed that I 'ad 115 to the front edge and 140 to the flag. Well, there's a bit of breeze I'm 'itting into so I'm thinking big 9 or a knockdown 8 but as I turn to ask Ian's advice, 'e's already 'anding me a pitching wedge. Well, 'e must have seen something in my face because, with 'is most serious look, 'e says,

'There's quite a bit of trouble over the back; you're best off a bit short.'

Well, the first thing I thought was *this is very un-Jennings-like* but with a bit of a smirk 'e says *'no, really'*. Now, it wasn't as if 'e was *suggesting* the club – 'e was 'anding it to me as if that were it, case closed. As I stood there considering whether or not to ignore 'im, I remembered 'e was my ride home so I 'it the damn wedge as 'ard as I could, right at the flag. Despite both of us yelling *go, go!,* it landed right on the front edge of the green – 75 feet from the damn 'ole!

Well, after slamming my club into the ground, along with one or two choice expletives, I glared at him in disgust as I start walking towards the green but as I get about ten yards away, I 'ear 'im behind me saying *'its on, in't it?'*"

Other than occasional chuckles, the crowd was silent, hanging on Mark's every word, eagerly waiting for what had to be a great Ian punchline, unsure of exactly what it could be. Scanning the faces, Mark continued.

"So 'e 'ands me the putter as we get to the green, drops the bag and proceeds to stalk round the green like an 'ungry lion, looking at my monster putt from every conceivable angle.

Finally, after taking one final look from behind, 'e brushes past me and whispers *'about an inch outside right edge'*. This is from 75 feet, mind you. *About an inch outside right edge!* 'e says!

Well, I'm still steaming from letting 'im strong arm me into 'itting the damn wedge so as 'e walks back to tend the pin, which seems to take forever, I can only glare at his back in disbelief, waiting. Finally, 'e reaches the flag and turns round at which point I finally shout *'are you sure?'*. Well, 'e just smiles that smarmy grin of 'is, points to a spot an inch off of the right edge of the cup and shouts back *'do you need it tended?'*

Well, I strike the putt on what can only be called my best guess at about an inch right of the hole and don't you know it goes straight into the cup. As I get to the hole, still shaking me 'ead in disbelief, Ian, sporting the biggest grin I've ever seen on 'is face, hands me the ball and says *'it's good you dint put it to 6 foot'''*.

Punchline delivered, the crowd exploded in laughter as Ian boyishly feigned a combination of disbelief and dismay, using his best *'What? What'd I do?'* look. Finally, as the laughter had just about died down, he quipped "it was, too – you woulda missed *that*!!" At that, the crowd roared even louder. The story was vintage Ian.

After spending the week in Chester for my training class, I headed back for two more nights in Spinkhill before flying out of Manchester on Monday. After rounds of golf Saturday and Sunday with various team members and a couple more great evenings at the Angel, I said my goodbyes. Having played with 6 of the 8 Team England players and with the Cup only 8-1/2 weeks, I knew one thing: we would be facing a considerable challenge.

Throughout the uneventful flight home, I found myself reflecting on all the friends I'd made during my England trips over the years and as I considered the list, which was considerable, the thought struck me that with the exception of a few business related friends I'd met through Entek contacts, nearly everyone I knew in England I knew because of Ian. He had a vast circle of friends and I had no illusions that he was anywhere but squarely in the center. He truly was an amazing fellow and I was feeling quite lucky to be as close to him as I was. As far as I was concerned, November just couldn't come soon enough.

Having claimed my bags, I boarded the shuttle for my remote parking lot, jolted back to reality by the frenetic activity in and around the terminal. As we pulled away, my eyes wandered in the direction of Manhattan's striking and iconic skyline. The Chrysler and Empire State buildings towered far to the north while the twin towers of the World Trade Center loomed over lower Manhattan, less than 10 miles away. Trying to stay in my "happy place" before reality impinged once again, I tried to count the exact number of days before we would leave for Myrtle Beach. Glancing at an abandoned USA Today on the seat next to me, I began to count forward from its date - Monday, September 10, 2001.

5

The World Is Changed

With my body still on England time, I was up Tuesday morning before 6. It was a beautiful late summer day and by 8:45, I was about to see my third go-round of top-10 plays on ESPN as I began putting together my expense report for the trip. Some 50 miles away, Amy Sweeney and Michael Woodward were engaged in uniquely terrifying telephone conversation.

"Something is wrong. We are in rapid descent . . . we are all over the place."

"Go to the window and try to see where you are"

" . . . . . I see the water . . . I see the buildings . . . *I see buildings!.*"

Taking a deep breath, she tried to continue calmly but panic crept into her voice.

"Oh my God . . . We are flying low . . . We're flying very, very low . . . . Oh my God, we are way too low."

Those words, spoken from her seat on American Airlines Flight 11, were the last Michael would ever hear her speak, the line going dead moments later. At 8:46 am, as a few thousand eyewitnesses watched in stunned horror, the huge jetliner Amy was riding in slammed headlong into the World Trade Center's North

Tower, vaporizing on impact in a massive fireball that instantly ended her life and hundreds more.

As Sports Center droned on, oblivious to the catastrophic events unfolding in Manhattan, I got a call from my wife telling me that a plane had reportedly flown into the World Trade Tower. Hanging up the phone, I flipped on the news, picturing a Piper Cub hanging out of the side of the Trade Center. The reality was very different.

Stunned and confused by the flames and black smoke I saw pouring from a gaping hole in the structure, I slowly absorbed the magnitude of the crash. I called Ian to tell him but he was in a meeting. I sat back, riveted by the horrific scene and unfolding drama, unable to look away. How could this have happened?

As he sat in his office on Broad Street about a half mile south of the World Trade Center, AJ, along with his colleagues, was gravely concerned. Years of working in lower Manhattan had made him immune to normal noise; traffic, construction and the like. This was different – *very* different. The entire building had been shaken by the massive boom and as he pondered the possibilities, he was suddenly ripped back to reality at hearing the sudden urgency in a colleague's voice. After a few more brief sentences, he hung up his cell phone before making eye contact with AJ.

"My wife was walking to work from Battery Park City. She saw a plane fly by – really low – and then there was a huge fireball. She said it looked like it hit the North Tower."

As crowds began to gather around the closest TV, rumors flew as news scrolls carried the story of a small plane flying into the North Tower. AJ thought back to the 1993 terrorist bombing of the WTC. Was this some sort of bizarre accident? His gut told him no, it wasn't. No small plane would cause the concussion they had felt. As sirens blared in the streets below, he waited nervously for the inevitable news reports from the scene.

"Hey" shouted a colleague from across the office. "Check this out".

Turning to look, individuals slowly drifted across the office, drawn like a hungry cartoon character wafted along by the smell of food, mesmerized by what was drifting by outside: a macabre ticker tape parade as bits of paper, large and small, carried along by the northwest breeze. Everyone understood the stark reality that only a few moments earlier, these same papers had been sitting on someone's desk.

The grim silence was broken by a shout as live TV shots came on showing thick, black smoke pouring out of the massive wound far up on the face of the North Tower. As reality hit home, thoughts bounced between the lost victims to the survivors desperately struggling to get out to the brave first responders, choosing instead to head straight into the teeth of a disaster of enormous size. As they watched the events unfold, a deathly silence fell.

Then, suddenly, with no warning and barely enough time for the live TV crews to react, it happened. As untold millions watched, United 175 flashed across the screen, slamming into the corner of the South Tower in a massive fireball. A lump in my throat grew as my mind raced in confusion. Was it some sort of gruesome graphic, a computer generated reenactment of the initial incident, perhaps even a replay? Seconds of disbelief and confusion passed before the reality hit home that what I had just seen was a second plane. *These are no accidents.*

Aware of what was coming, there was no mistaking the source when the second shock wave hit AJ's building. Even before it had subsided, a strong, firm voice rang out.

"Listen up".

It was the Head of Global Markets, an ex-special ops leader who commanded universal respect in the office.

"If you are still unsure, this is a terrorist attack. We will be executing the evacuation strategy as planned and practiced. Half of you will head for the Greenwich back up facility by car, the rest by train. You know your assignments – any questions? Go!"

As people scattered, AJ grabbed his phone, calling Lauren to fill her in on the situation. He would be in the group making its way to Greenwich via train so he would immediately be heading north to the Wall Street subway station. He'd try to keep her posted but with cell service already struggling, further contact would be iffy.

"I love you."

"Be careful" she finished, her heart pounding with fear.

As for me and millions of others, time had come crashing to a halt, a strange, otherworldly effect I would feel for weeks to come. Thoughts turned to the heroic struggles going on within the towers, innocent people trying to escape the raging infernos as confusion reigned; desperate phone calls from maintenance men, window washers, security officers, financial experts, janitors, store clerks, delivery people, newly hired college graduates just starting out, older men and women nearing retirement, executives, flunkies and countless others in various stages of desperation. I imagined the rare call getting through on the jammed circuits, a frantic loved one reassuringly saying *I'm ok, I made it out*, and the flood of relief that simple message would produce. After all, many people were already out and many more would follow, living to tell an extraordinary tale.

But many others had already died and thousands more remained trapped in darkness and choking smoke, desperately seeking an elusive path to safety while even more desperately trying to avoid the thought that there may not be one. I wondered what words I would use in their place as tears welled in my eyes. I imagined loved ones, frantic for news, waiting for a call that might never come. I imagined the pain of those who would be left behind in uncertainty, hoping and praying against the odds for the safe deliverance of a husband or wife, a parent or child, a sister or brother, a friend or acquaintance.

Suddenly, a news flash jolted me back to reality: the Pentagon had been hit. It was 9:40 am. Calling Ian again, he was out of his meeting, ready for lunch and still oblivious to the magnitude of the unfolding events. As I tried to explain what was transpiring, he seemed distracted, his thoughts preoccupied elsewhere, unable to grasp the magnitude of the situation. I knew there were no TVs anywhere at Monition and remembered my initial reaction - a Piper Cub hanging off the side of the building. As I tried to get across the magnitude of what was happening, the air was sucked out of my lungs.

"Oh my God." I gasped, unable to say anything else as my heart raced.

"What?"

"It's gone." I finally managed to get out, my voice choked with emotion.

"What's gone?"

"The South Tower. *It's gone!*"

"Oh my God"

Starting at the top, the South Tower had simply collapsed, disappearing into a cloud of dust that would become so massive that it would eventually engulf all of lower Manhattan as it slowly drifted away to the southeast, carried by the day's gentle breezes. Nothing in the area of the South Tower could be seen. Hundreds dead had surely turned to thousands as the nightmare continued with no hope of awakening.

Turning north onto Broadway about a block the subway station, AJ's crew stopped dead in their tracks, staring in disbelief at the hundreds of people racing down Broadway – straight at them. Behind the runners rose an enormous wall of smoke and debris, hundreds of feet high and growing. As they stood, momentarily frozen by the scene, it arrived – the noise. Building slowly at first, the noise grew, savage and terrible, lasting for what seemed an eternity. It was unlike anything anyone had ever heard before but there was no doubt what it was. The still visible skyline with only a single tower told them everything they needed to know. As the wall advanced towards them, the group turned and ran with the rest, heading for the east side of the island, where the East River emptied into the Upper Bay.

Glancing back periodically, they could see that the cloud was relentlessly gaining. Slowing only briefly at intersections before regaining focus and direction, an amorphous mass driven through the canyons of lower Manhattan by the unimaginable pressures and forces generated in the collapse of the huge tower.

Within 10 minutes, the group reached the East River, only a block or so ahead of the cloud as it continued its relentless advance. Staring down into the dark water below, they nervously eyed each other as they considered jumping in to avoid whatever it was that was in the cloud. After all, who knew what they were about to inhale. Chemical weapons? Biological? Faced with the option of near-certain drowning in the strong currents and murky waters of the river and bay, the group chose instead to turn north, covering their faces with whatever clothing items were handy, sucking down one last breath of fresh air before the cloud consumed them.

Realizing the subway was no longer an option, the group headed for the 34th street ferry, 4 miles up the river. From there, the plan was simple: get out of NYC. Before long, they sensed the cloud thinning out and as they trudged along the river, a gloomy, stunned silence settled over them, broken only by the gradually diminishing blare of emergency sirens in the distance and rare bursts of excitement when someone managed to connect on a cell call. Apart from the excitement of the brief contact with a loved one, the calls did little to lift their spirits. The second tower had collapsed. The Pentagon had been hit. A plane had crashed in Pennsylvania. As the miles dragged by and the sirens were slowly left behind, the sense of dread only grew. What did all this mean for them and their country? Finally, by mid-afternoon, the beleaguered group reached the dock. From there, they would board the ferry and head back down the East River, crossing the Upper and Lower Bays until finally reaching Atlantic Highlands in NJ, just west of Sandy Hook.

As the ferry emerged from the shadow of Governors Island, the immensity of what had happened struck AJ as the sight of a WTC-less lower Manhattan emerged from behind the skyscrapers, smoke, dust and debris. So many had died and so many were surely missing. Having passed lower Manhattan, he stared straight ahead, unwilling to look back again. Lauren would be at the ferry station, waiting.

It would be near midnight before AJ and Lauren arrived home. He changed his clothes in the basement, stuffing them in a plastic bag and sealing it before showering and looking in on his 1-year old son, Alex. Completely drained of emotion, he flopped into his favorite chair to catch up on the details of what had transpired. As they watched, the magnitude of what had happened continued to sink in. Finally, AJ had enough, picking up the remote and turning off the TV. Reaching for Lauren's hands, they gazed into each other's eyes in silent thanks for his safe delivery home. Then, as one, they bowed their heads as AJ began to pray.

6

Datzit Indaruf

Slowly, inexorably, life resumed its normal ebb and flow but it would never be "normal" again, at least not in the way normal had been. Life in America and other western nations would never be the same again, just as the Islamists had hoped. Despite our perceptions of the world forever changing, though, we would not live in fear. Within a few weeks, the question of whether or not the Cup would go on was answered with an emphatic yes. By late September, Ian and I had finalized the last logistical details for the Cup, including a new procedure we would use to set the matches on the first 2 days. Team England would issue their pairings for Day 1 at The Dunes, including the 9-hole afternoon scramble matches, by October 14th. We would then have 4 days set those matches. We would then issue our pairings for Day 2 at Prestwick and Team England would have 4 days to set those matches. By October 22, the first sixteen matches of the Cup worth a total of 12 points would be set. For Days 3 and 4, the losing team would hold the advantage of setting the matches.

With the excitement of events like the new match-setting format building interest to unprecedented levels, I decided we needed some sort of outlet for Cup news – a website where I could post stories and news so that players, friends and family could follow developments. Having a bit of experience in that area, I purchased the FlemCup.com domain name and got to work building it. One thing I knew from the start was that writing under my own name would severely dampen the "fun" quotient of any stories. I wanted the site and its stories to be perceived as authentic, a real news site reporting on real news and antics – including my own – from a neutral, third party point of view, knowing that would just add to the fun. With that as my goal, I set about populating an entire staff of ghost writers and editors using golf-themed names. Odam Itzindawater would be my Editor-in-Chief while Yurziz Bydatree would be my News Editor and Iva Tufshot would be my tenacious Investigative Reporter. My most important hire, though, was for the all-important position of Flem Cup Correspondent, the main contributor and writer of stories – Datzit Indaruf.

Indie, as he came to be called, would come to be alternately reviled and beloved by the website's readers, depending on exactly whose ox was being gored. Quite pleased with myself, I called Ian to let him in on the plan and he loved it, pledging support and swearing himself to secrecy.

On October 22, Indie was introduced to the world, rolling out a relatively benign article consisting mainly of actual news like the Day 1 and 2 matches and player handicaps. As a prelude to what the site and Indie would eventually become, the article also contained a few less than subtle shots designed to liven things up; items like an inspired re-telling of the story of Ian's epic failure at The Dunes the previous year, the Angel dust up and how it all led to this year's inaugural trans-Atlantic event. Unable to keep myself from stirring the pot, Indie even threw in an "official" prediction of a 13-11 American victory. At 8 am the next morning, the phone rang. It was Ian.

"What's the idea of rehashing last year all over again? I thought the website would be neutral! And predicting your team to win?!? What's that all about?"

"Well, I, ah . . I was just having some fun . . I mean, it's supposed to be . . ."

As I struggled for words, momentarily unsure of what I'd done, I heard his familiar chuckle. He'd done me.

"Oh, you bastard! You had me going."

His chuckle changed to a full throated laugh.

"Well, you certainly created a stir at the Angel last night. People wanted to know who this Indaruf fellow is but except for Joe – who I swore to secrecy – I told 'em I don't know. There are suspicions, mind you, but no one is quite sure. I think you're really on to something, 'ere. Should be great fun. Singe printed out the article and passed it round before tacking it up on the wall. I loved it. You've got a gift there, young man. I just 'ope you'll be the target of some of your jabs as well as me."

"Oh, don't worry about that. I'll be taking my share of abuse. Singe actually posted it on the wall, did he? Good. Did you give out the website address?"

"Oh, yeah. It was printed right at the bottom and I actually got a few calls asking about it. I'll 'ave to take a look myself at what you've done."

It had always amused me that Ian, a smart, sophisticated, worldly business-man, was a complete incompetent when it came to computers. He hadn't even seen the website yet, being totally dependent on others to handle the most basic of chores like opening a browser window and entering a website address. After chatting for a few more minutes, I inquired about any news. The weather was crap in England – hardly surprising for late October – and he was having a love affair with a new driver he'd bought.

After hanging up, I checked the email account I'd set up under the FlemCup domain name and discovered 21 new signups for the email blasts. Leaning back in my chair, I began to realize that Indie and the website could easily become an integral part of the Cup. After all, he would be in total control of the flow of *information* and if he didn't write about it, it wasn't news. I couldn't help but smile at the possibilities. Hard facts were fine – they would be duly and accurately reported on – but rumor, innuendo, embellishment and hyperbole were far more fun. With our conversation fresh in my mind, I decided to engage in a little fishing expedition about some of the info Ian had innocently revealed. Within 20 minutes, I had everything I needed for my next article. It would post on Thursday the 25th.

Illegal Clubs Stir Up Flem Cup Brew

By: Datzit Indaruf, Flem Cup Correspondent

MYRTLE BEACH, Oct 25 – In a devastating discovery, Captain Ian Jennings of Team England has been found conspiring to use a non-conforming club in the upcoming Flem Cup, sparking controversy on an unprecedented scale since the rule requiring USGA compliance was implemented in 1997. Curiously (or perhaps brashly), Captain Jennings freely offered the information during a conference call with Team U.S. Captain Scott Dow two days ago. Despite the clear breach of rules, there has been no official acknowledgment of a rules violation or any indication the England captain will abandon use of the illegal club – quite the contrary. Reached for comment, Jennings said:

"Well, I thought I'd let him [Dow] know as a courtesy. Then, if he had a problem, I'd use it anyway."

Dow, not surprisingly, had another take on the issue.

"It's not the club that bothers us – Lord knows he needs the help. It's the attitude. He has basically said 'screw you, you low-life American bastards. We're going to beat you like the rented mules you so closely resemble - even if we have to cheat.' Well, that attitude is not quite as gentlemanly as we would like."

Manufactured at an undisclosed location in the English Midlands by a shadowy outfit named "Integro", the driver's name – "Victory" – may well betray the company's apparent "win at all cost – rules be damned" mentality. When our undercover reporter, Iva Tufshot, attempted to phone up the company for comment, she got a only disconnect signal. Checking the USGA website, Tufshot found the Integro driver not listed at all, either as a conforming or non-conforming club. Inquiring further, she found that the USGA's senior equipment rules official, Doanbee A. Cheetur, was quite familiar with the manufacturer and the driver.

"Ah yes, the Integro Victory. We know of the club but haven't been able to obtain one for testing. I can tell you that the last driver they manufactured was made of some secretive space-age material that had a spring-effect like a cannon. The first ball we hit went right through the side of our building, leaving a hole the size of my fist. We sent them a bill along with the non-conforming ruling and that was the last we heard from them. Apparently, they seem to cater to people who simply do not respect the integrity of the game of golf"

The Americans find it highly suspicious that Jennings, after using only name-brand clubs such as Ping and Calloway for years, suddenly switched to this little known manufacturer – a switch that suspiciously coincided with the end of a nearly 2 year golfing slump, a slump brought on by Jennings' last known public attempt at any physical exertion, a brief but disastrous tennis match during his 1999 Majorca golf trip that not only ruptured his Achilles tendon but also caused incredibly far reaching consequences. Although a full accounting of those consequences would require more space than this web site can possibly afford, the Cliff Notes version includes (1) ramming his 17-meter luxury boat directly into a 30-foot high cement wall in Oostende, Belgium (providing unforgettable entertainment for hundreds of vacationers), (2) forcing American Captain Dow into several years of intensive psychotherapy, and (3) being a leading factor in the wound dressing bull-market of '99.

What is undeniable is that with the acquisition of the Integro Victory driver, Jennings' drives suddenly became straighter and longer, enabling his game to revert to its pre-injury level of excellence. The Americans suspect it is more than a coincidence, even voicing concern that the foul play runs even deeper. Unsubstantiated rumors from disgruntled partners and opponents alike accuse the England Captain of carrying undersized balls in his bag, yet another serious rules infraction. Speaking on condition of anonymity, a source close to the matter had this to say:

"Ian wants everyone to think he has regulation-sized balls in his bag but they are actually undersized. No one has ever been able to check because he never leaves them lying about. He only takes them out when he is ready to play with them so he gets away with it but one night, while he was asleep, I measured one and I can assure you: it was quite undersized."

The American side, reluctant to turn the controversy into an international incident, is considering requesting a full, independent inspection of Jennings' balls upon arrival. When asked about this development, Jennings' response was both diplomatic and revealing.

"It really depends on who they choose to inspect them. I've no problem complying with USGA standards but I'm not going to let just any American go inspecting my balls. It has to be *someone with some level of authority – preferably wearing a spiffy uniform, dark sunglasses and carrying a big nightstick."*

With uncertainty on so many levels, the question remains: does Jennings have the balls – and driver – to be in compliance with USGA standards. For its part, the USGA continues to try to defuse the international issue by obtaining an Integro Victory driver for testing. The closest they've come was a few nights ago when a USGA official was approached on a dark street by a man in a trench coat.

"Psssst, buddy - you need a watch? . . some jewelry? . . an Integro Victory Driver? I got the good stuff!"

Unfortunately, the deal was nixed when a voice from the shadows yelled "Cheese it . . . it's da golf feds". The mysterious man disappeared into the night like a wraith.

If the USGA is successful, the whole issue may well blow away like the fall leaves before the teams arrive in Myrtle Beach on November 1. If not, temperatures may be running a bit hot in South Carolina next week.

***

The next day, having heard nothing from Ian, I decided to throw him – and England fans – a bone with an article that posted on the 27th.

Team USA In Complete Disarray

By: Datzit Indaruf, Flem Cup Correspondent

MYRTLE BEACH, Oct 26 – In a stunning development, Team USA apparently has descended into chaos at the worst of all possible times – on the eve of first trans-Atlantic Flem Cup – with news of a wild conference call between Lou Flem, Jack Jr. and Captain Scott Dow where Dow ended up offering to resign after being accused by his teammates of being afraid of Team England.

According to unnamed sources, Cup namesake Flem kicked off the festivities by pointing out Dow's tiresome and never-ending warnings Team England's golfing abilities. In his usual no-nonsense South Jersey manner, Lou got right to it after one too many warnings from Dow.

"Yo. All we've heard since you'ze got back from your trips has been all dis crap about how well Ian was playing, how great Greg Matthews is, how consistent Milo is, how cute Phil is, how our <u>only</u> chances are poor ole' Ray Matthews and this pathetic sounding Swampy fellow. Then you go off on how committed they are, how sweet Joe's swing is, how much fun quiz night is, how well-mannered the English are, blah . . . blah . . . blah . . . . blah, blah, blah, blah. I mean, ya know what I mean? I'm sicka dis crap. I mean, if they're so freakin' great, why don't you'ze just move there and start talking like dem insteada da right way, like us?!?"

Apparently, co-Captain Jack Jr. concurred.

"Look, Scott . . . I know you can be a pretty good player – except when you're playing me, of course – so let me put it this as delicately as I can. If you putt like you've been shooting a basketball lately, we're dead. I mean D-E-D dead. You shoot scared, you lose. You play golf scared, you lose. You need to suck it up and stop being such a pathetic weenie. I mean, for the love of Pete - they're ENGLISH!"

Drama-queen that he is, Dow responded by offering to resign as Captain. While Lou was immediately agreeable, Jack reminded him that a change of that magnitude should be a team decision, especially on the eve of the Cup. By the call's end, Dow remained Captain – for now.

The tumultuous call provided a clear juxtaposition against Team England's rallying to their Captain Jennings' side in response to the recently leveled charges of a non-conforming driver and playing with undersized balls. Emails from England supporters have been running approximately 107 to 1 in defense of Jennings, some even going so far as to accuse the Yanks of dulling their spikes in preparation for the Cup, an oblique and somewhat pathetic reference to the 1999 Ryder Cup celebration when Justin Leonard made his monster putt. [Editor's note: Get over it, already, will you please?]

In a sudden and unexpected role reversal, it is now Dow who is in the hot seat. The only good news for him is that other than Lou and Jack, the American players seemed strangely ambivalent – oblivious, even – to the controversies. Chris Tanis, for instance, offered only a blank stare before replying,

"Yeah, whatever."

Defending Stableford champion Past Slack, on the other hand, had a number of unanswered questions.

"We have a Captain? And he's the guy who's never won?? What the . . . ? When is the trip again? Do we come back Monday or Tuesday? Who am I driving with?"

Terry Neal, a man of few words, was characteristically terse.

"Terry, are you concerned about Team U.S. morale and its overall mental state?"

"Yup"

"Well, do you agree that Dow's conduct is grounds for dismissal?"

"Nope."

"Is there anything Dow can say to help the situation?"

"Doubt it."

"What are your thoughts on the Jennings small balls controversy?"

"That dog won't hunt."

Young Matt, who was contacted while doing his homework, said only:

"Hey, I'm getting out of school for 4 days and a free golf trip – what do I care who the captain is?"

When Jack Sr, was contacted for comment, he ignored the controversy entirely.

"I'll have to check on the genealogy of 'Jennings' – could be quite interesting. Could be derived from lemmings"

Returning to Jack Jr., the question was posed as to his thoughts about the team's appalling ignorance of the issues and seemingly apathetic attitude. Shrugging his shoulders, his only reply was,

"I don't know . . . and frankly, I don't care."

Finally, the U.S. Captain himself was questioned over the sad state of affairs. Asked why he'd offered to resign, Dow said

"Well, it appears I've lost their confidence, their loyalty, and their will to follow me wherever I lead - so I wanted to let them decide whether they want me to continue leading them. It's up to them."

When told about his comment, Lou let out a derisive snort.

"He never had any of those things – how could he lose 'em?"

At the end of the day, Dow's offer to resign was a non-starter. Terry spoke for most.

"Then we'd have to do all this stupid organizing and paperwork. Does it look like we just fell off the turnip truck?"

Asked about the original accusation of being afraid of Team England, Dow's normally calm, cool demeanor seemed to finally crack, a flustered look appearing on his face.

"Ok, ok, I admit it. Anyone who has spent time with them simply has to be impressed. That's what my teammates don't understand. The Brits just have this incredibly elegant, graceful aura. That's why their people do the most infomercials. They're kind of like, well, "Chantilly Lace" people. The way they talk and always sound so smart even if they're dumber than a box of rocks, the way they pile mushy peas on the back of their forks and don't spill any; the way they gather for quiz night so serious-like; the way they watch a cricket match and actually care; the wiggle in their walk, the giggle in their talk, it makes my world go round. They make me act so funny, make me spend my money, they even make me feel real loose like a long-neck goose - oooh baby, that's a-what I want. Magnificent pagan beasts - that's what they are."

As news of these recent developments leaked out, bookmaker odds have shifted dramatically in favor of Team England, moving the Brits from a 6:5 underdog to an 8:5 favorite as millions of pounds and dollars have been dumped on the England side.

In light of the highly unorthodox state of the US team, their obvious lack of focus and their apparent lack of commitment to practice, FlemCup.com is now changing its prediction to a hard fought 12-½ to 11-½ Team England win with a bullet: it could easily be much worse for the Americans.

***

Over the next few days, six more articles would be posted, including one concerning attempted murder charges and another alleging secret, war-like messages being sent but by October 31, all the posturing and talking was done and by the next day, we'd all be heading for Myrtle Beach. While everyone else was taking the 11 hour drive from northwest N.J., Chris and I would fly to Raleigh-Durham, rent a couple of mini-vans and pick up Team England after they arrived on a direct flight there from Manchester. By tomorrow night, we'd all be sitting in BummZ, sucking down beers and getting a headache from laughing in preparation for Day 1 at the Dunes. Like a kid on Christmas Eve, I went to bed early, too excited to sleep.

7

And So It Begins

At around 6:30 Thursday night, the arrivals screen announced Team England's flight had landed. Having been belatedly cut off somewhere over Nova Scotia, Ian and Joe emerged feeling no pain, having consumed untold quantities of wine, beer and mixed drinks. Staggering into the terminal, the two were in rare form, greeting us with far more flair than normal and giggling like a couple of school girls. Others were in only slightly better shape. Once everyone and everything was collected, we headed south with spirits high and three hours, one beer stop, two speeding tickets and one narrowly avoided encounter with an inmate named either Bubba or Tiny later, we were all in BummZ, laughing and drinking beer as Greg distributed the assortment of Nike team golf shirts he'd had made up. With everyone tired from the long day of travel and well aware of our early tee-times, the evening ended relatively early with everyone retiring by midnight.

Day 1 dawned picture-perfect. Against the backdrop of a piercingly blue, cloudless sky and with fifteen fellow Flem Cup golfers looking on, the first shot of the 2001 Flem Cup was struck by Dave Richmond and the first match of the inaugural trans-Atlantic Flem Cup was on, pitting Dave and Phil Smith against Jack Sr. and Lou. Right out of the gate, the two Brits jumped on top, never looking back in an easy 5&4 win.

In the second match out, Terry and Chris faced off against Ray and Greg Matthews in what began as a tight match. After making the turn all-square, though, the Brits caught fire, winning 3 of the next 4 holes before coasting in with a second England win, 3&2.

Perhaps the most interesting match of the day was the third out as Jack Jr. and Matt took on Ian and Milo. The memory of his collapse on the same course against Jack had been kept alive in Ian's mind (mainly because I kept it alive through the website) and the pairing was no coincidence. My strategy would work even better than I hoped.

Despite starting out with a winning par, Ian's game quickly fell apart as he bumbled his way through the next 12 holes in 14 over par *net*. Milo, in essence, would be playing solo, a hopeless task against Jack and Matt, and by the time Ian got his game back on track, the 6&5 beat down was long over.

In the morning's final match, Pat and I took on Joe and Swampy and after battling our way to a 2 up lead after 8 holes, we proceeded to halve the next seven holes before Pat won the 16th to close it out, 3&2. After the first four 4 ball matches, the Cup score was 2-2.

After a quick lunch, we headed out for the 9-hole afternoon scrambles and when Lou dropped in a 3-foot bogey putt to clinch a win in the final match of the day, he finished off a nearly perfect afternoon – 3 wins and a halve – that gave us a 3-3/4 to 2-1/4 point lead after Day 1.

By the time the group got back to the hotel, it was about 5:30 and Ian headed off to a team meeting he'd called for 6 pm, promising to meet me at BummZ afterwards. Although it was way too early to gloat, I was relishing the opportunity for just a bit of trash talk. Unfortunately, by the time the door to BummZ swung open and Team England walked in, it was around 9:30 and I had spent two hours or more in an increasingly foul mood, having been stood up. Ian just laughed and smiled, feigning confusion about any "plans" we may have had.

"Hullo, lad."

"Where have you guys been? Weren't we meeting here after your meeting?"

"Oh, were we? I'm sorry. The boys wanted to get away from pub food and 'ave a nice big juicy steak so we took cabs to Carolina Roadhouse. Couldn't find you. Been 'ere long?"

"No, not too long." I lied unconvincingly. "Here, have a seat."

After a few lame attempts designed to get a rise out of someone – anyone – concerning the day's events, I realized the Brits were impervious to the barbs, perfectly content to bask in the warm glow of their consumption. Brushing aside the day's golf, they were much more interested in discussing the fabulous food, the huge portions, the great service and the sexy little waitresses with the southern accents.

Moving on to the Day 2 matches, I did my best to impart my own healthy respect (fear?) for Prestwick, a much sterner test of golf than The Dunes. That, too, went nowhere, leaving me no option but to slump dejectedly in my chair as the group continued their varied assortment of stories and jokes, laughing and carrying on without a care in the world. By midnight, flush with beer and food, we all retired. With 27 holes on the docket, it would be another early start.

Saturday dawned as Friday did – warm and sunny with a crisp blue autumn sky. After warming up, we convened on the first tee, peering down the narrow, tree-lined 10th hole (we would start on the back) with pockets of dense underbrush and out of bounds on both sides. *Oh yes*, I told myself. Prestwick would provide a much different – and more difficult – test than The Dunes.

While most areas under the trees at the Dunes were open enough to allow you to knock any wayward shots back into play, Prestwick frequently offered no such opportunity. Heavy foliage, meandering streams with steep embankments, large lakes, tight fairways and fast, undulating greens guarded by deep, menacing bunkers made Prestwick one of the toughest courses in Myrtle Beach and a great test of golf. Indeed, scores would skyrocket.

The first match out pitted Pat and Lou against Dave and Ray and with the score knotted after 7 holes, an unexpected bogey win by Pat on 8 triggered a run of good holes that eventually resulted in a convincing win for our boys, 4&3. Unfortunately, that would be our high water mark in an otherwise dismal day.

In the second match out, Jack Sr. and Terry took on Ian and Swampy in a well-played match. All-square after 11, Swampy's net birdie gave England a lead it would not relinquish and with Ian's net eagle win on 14 followed another net birdie win by Swampy on 16, England would prevail 3&2.

In the third match, Greg and Phil took on Jack Jr. and Chris. With England in control at 3 up after 8, the two brothers stormed back, going birdie, eagle, par to get back to all-square. The Brits would grab control once again with wins on 13 and 14 to go 2 up before Jack's net birdie brought us back to 1 down but we would get no closer.

Our final hole, the 9th, is a long, tight par 5 that gradually bends left around the large lake. To the right, beyond the mounds next to the cart path, lurks out of bounds all the way down to the green. The tee shot must be struck on a well-judged line across part of the lake. Left or short and the ball will find a watery grave. Too far right and you are O.B. There, in the only match to reach the last hole, Phil stepped up with a perfectly played par net birdie to win the hole and close out the match in style, 2 up.

In the final match, young Matt and I went down without so much as a whimper to Smokin' Joe and Milo, 5&4. Sadly, it could easily have been worse. Trailing from the very start, our loss was so lopsided that Milo's 1 over par net (35 Stableford) – which was the day's best score – beat our *combined* Stableford score of 28 by an astonishing seven full points.

As we licked our wounds, everything I'd been worried about the night before had come true in spades, especially for me, but there was no time to sulk – we still had 9-hole afternoon scramble matches to play. England had erased our 1-1/2 point lead and claimed a 1/2 point lead of their own with the morning win. We knew we would need to find some way to staunch the bleeding but it would elude us.

With Ian leading the way, almost singlehandedly earning a halve in the first afternoon match out against Jack Jr. and Pat, England continued to dominate. Hole 8, a long, narrow par 5 with O.B. right and a meandering stream running its full length down the left before cutting across directly in front of the green, would prove a disaster for us. In each of the four matches, the Brits would walk off the green with a win, twice ending the match there, once going dormie and once drawing level heading to the last hole. It was, for us, a graveyard.

Finally, with the shadows lengthening and a chill creeping into the air, the first 12 players sat sprawled about the mounds in back of the final green, waiting and watching as the final match approached. Sitting just below Ian, I watched in silence as he laughed and joked with his teammates, victory cigars already lit in celebration of the day's dominating win. In the distance we watched the final group tee off, a sure sign their match was still going.

Joe's drive was the only one to find the fairway and when he followed that with a crisp 4-iron to the center of the green, he had only 12 feet for birdie but when Terry's 25 foot last gasp par putt ran past the hole, Joe's putt was conceded and the day's carnage was complete. Team England broke into songs of celebration, standing atop the mounds surrounding the green and high-fiving one another. Soaking it all in as he puffed on his victory cigar, Ian laughed and smiled as he surveyed his team, reveling in the day's complete dominance. It was a perfect scene for the lads from Spinkhill.

There was little solace for us in the wreckage of Day 2. England had won 6 of the 8 matches and halved another. Our 1-1/2 point lead from the morning was a distant memory, turned into a 2 point deficit, the Cup score standing at 7-5. Our only consolation would be the advantage of setting the matches for Day 3 at Marsh Harbor, where we would need to pick up a point or more to give us any realistic chance to win on Monday. Failure to do that would leave us needing to win 5 points in the eight 2 ball matches just to tie, a difficult proposition at best.

Casting a long shadow over my team's state of mind was the unspoken but inescapable conclusion that we'd been dominated in every facet of the game. Lou and I rode back to the hotel in glum silence as our load of Brits happily regaled each other with stories of great shots, clutch moments and funny incidents. Finally, I looked across at Ian, riding shotgun.

"I'll need your pairings as soon as you figure them out. We need to set the matches."

"All right, just give me a chance to talk to the lads. I'll drop them at your room by 6 or so. What do you want to do for dinner tonight - your choice."

Reminded of the previous night's shenanigans, I turned again to find a subtle smirk on Ian's face. It was unmistakable in its meaning - I'd been done the previous night and done good. I'd let myself be distracted and upset over the perceived slight and I'd paid the price. Although perhaps I'd struck the first blow in the mental warfare battle by doing everything I could to highlight Ian's failure at The Dunes, he had retaliated with a direct hit. I had no anger left at him, only myself for falling into his trap. After all, it was all part of the game.

"*Bastard*" was all I could say under my breath as I turned my attention back to the road, shaking my head and smiling. Ian laughed his hearty laugh.

"I am sorry about last night, lad."

"No you're not" I immediately shot back, smiling. He laughed again.

"No, I suppose not, at least based on today's results, anyway."

From the perspective of our friendship, I knew he was sorry. From the perspective of this match, he was well pleased with what he'd accomplished - and I couldn't blame him. I suspected he'd been playing me at the time but let myself get upset anyway and it affected my focus. How much it affected me was another question. The other piece of the equation was Prestwick, a course I usually struggled with. It was one of my favorite courses, beautifully designed and maintained, yet it constantly brought out the worst in my game for whatever reasons. The combination of last night's anger and my subconscious dread of Prestwick created a toxic mental cocktail. As I drove on, I vowed to never let myself be so distracted again. Steady and focused would be the rule, steady and focused; one hole at a time played one shot at a time.

The mental aspect of golf has a stunningly small margin of error, particularly for important matches. Anything that puts your opponent off focusing on his game is useful, at least within the bounds of respectability and rules of etiquette. We loved the mind games, Ian and I, and when an opportunity presented itself, either of us would take full advantage. In that regard, one thing was for sure as we headed into Day 3 of the Cup – the gloves were off. Despite that, my mind kept returning to our situation, facing an opponent as we were who was outplaying us. We would definitely need some sort of spark moving forward but I didn't have any idea where that might come from. I would need some sort of miracle.

8

Karaoke Night

By 6:30 or so, I had posted the day's results on the website along with some brief commentary. As I was typing, Lou, Jack Jr. and I had discussed and set the next day's matches and after including that information in my post, I clicked send and the three of us headed down to BummZ to join the others. I'd paired myself with Terry against Joe and Ian in what would be the day's feature match, adding an extra bounce to my step as we entered BummZ on the Beach.

BummZ was a perfect hangout for the teams, a well-kept little oceanfront bar sitting right next to the Breakers. With a sheltered outdoor patio on the beach side and lots of tables, it was perfect for groups. With an excellent pub menu, reasonably-priced pitchers of beer and cute, friendly waitresses, it was ideal for *our* group.

After grabbing a glass and pouring a beer, everyone quieted down as I read off the matches for the Day 3 at Marsh Harbor. After finishing, we raised our glasses.

"Here's to great matches and good luck" I offered.

"Here, here" came the reply as glasses clinked and beer flowed.

The Brits, having arrived nearly an hour earlier, were already finishing off the sandwiches they'd ordered. Realizing that we, too, were hungry, Lou, Chris and I looked over the menu as Jack Jr. and Pat headed off to meet Jack Sr., Matt and Terry for a quiet dinner and an early night, their normal routine. England's attention, on the other hand, had focused in on the serious business of celebrating the day's big win with copious quantities of beer.

About 8:30 or so, a stocky little fellow resembling Burle Ives strode in, speakers and assorted electronic equipment in tow, and began setting up at the table right next to us. Evidently, it was karaoke night, Buddy was in the house – and Team England was primed to *go*.

By 9, Buddy kicked off the festivities with pair of Jimmy Buffet songs that first exposed the growing crowd to England's sing-along style of karaoke, a style only intensified by the celebratory state of mind of the now thoroughly inebriated Brits. As *Margaritaville* struck up, off went the England players, singing right along with Buddy - and with at least as much gusto as the surprised host.

Having finished his second song to a smattering of applause, it was time for the show to begin in earnest as Buddy, reaching into his basket of requests, called out a name. Walking up confidently, a fellow grabbed the mic, turned and pointed straight at Team England.

"This is fer y'all. You look like yer havin' a gooood time!!"

Approving whoops and whistles emanated from our corner as the opening words flashed:

"Yeow . . . I feel good"

Immediately recognizing James Brown's famous opening lines, the Spinkhill lads didn't miss a beat, their unified voice booming out the *Na-na-Na-na-Na-na-Na* horn parts. As the song progressed, England's rowdiness only grew and I couldn't help but be impressed by their single minded focus on celebrating. Smokin' Joe was parked in the corner, his back to the ocean, cigarette held perfectly still in his left hand while conducting the music with his right (except when sipping on his pint). Phil, trapped between me and Joe with his back against the north wall, was dancing in place, enthusiastically belting out the song as he made wide, sweeping gestures over the table, seemingly auditioning for the role of lusty backup singer.

Across the table, Dave and Swampy were downing beers like BummZ was running out as they attempted to out shout-sing each other. Behind those two stood Greg, bopping around while pumping his fists like Tiger Woods and occasionally glaring at me with as demented a look as he could muster. To his right was Milo, who, despite being the least animated of the lot, was singing along and enthusiastically jabbing his fist into the air every few stanzas. Finally, there stood Ian, at the far end of the table between Joe and Milo, back to the ocean. Dancing his little signature dance, he was simply singing along with the rest, smiling and laughing the whole while.

As the song progressed, the Brits were becoming more and more animated, cranking up the volume and intensity of the grand sing-along. Then, from nowhere, we realized Lou had joined three ladies on the dance floor, showing off his finest South Jersey barn-stompin' dance moves to shouts of *"Go, Lou, Go!"* The rest of the crowd, now upwards of 40 or 50 people, was growing increasingly rowdy as well, clearly amused and energized by the spectacle of the group of fun-loving Brits.

Each time my eyes met Ian's, he'd mouth some words, make a funny face or flash me some unknown sign and throw his head back in laughter, fully expecting me to understand what the hell he'd said over the noise. I just nodded and smiled. Finally, with the song beginning its long wind down and the energy in the small bar reaching a fever pitch, the crowd began cheering wildly for both the singer's and the crowd's impressive performances. His energy spent, he finished before turning once again in our direction.

"Thank you. Y'all have fun, now!"

As the wild cheering continued, I found myself surveying the scene with a mixture of awe and amusement. I couldn't tell if the girls at the bar were cheering the singer or the Brits. *These boys know how to celebrate*, I told myself.

Then, out of nowhere, the thought first entered my head. It was an evil thought. A wonderfully, deliciously evil thought. As the thought percolated and grew in my mind, a nudge from Phil snapped me back to reality.

"That was nuts!" he yelled over the cheering.

"Yeah, it was." I shouted back. "You guys are pretty pumped. I'll be right back."

With that, I headed off to the men's room as a woman began to belt out Aretha Franklin's *R-E-S-P-E-C-T* (and nearly as well as Aretha herself). Clearly, this was no ordinary karaoke. This was some sort of Super Karaoke and Team England was going off the rails, meeting each song with more enthusiasm than the last. Behind me, I could hear Phil doing his very best to match the diva's range with his own fabulous falsetto: *"R-E-S-P-E-C-T"*.

Making my way back to the table as the Monkees' *Daydream Believer* blared, I had to stop and laugh out loud as I spotted Ian using his hand as a frilly hat whenever the line "homecoming queen" was being sung. Shaking my head, I continued to laugh to myself as I made my way back to the table. Before long, three buxom beauties from the bar area approached the Brits, introducing themselves and carrying a tray of shots.

"Hello Boys" began one in a lilting southern drawl. "My name is Laura Lee, this is Tammy Mae and that's Shelly Ann. Y'all just are soooo much fun. I just love the way y'all get soooo into your singing. Y'all are just great and . . . well . . . we wanted to see if you'all wanted to do a shot with us?"

Greg didn't hesitate, blurting out "Sure" as he eagerly looked around for other takers.

"What's this?" inquired Swampy, eyeing the amber-colored liquid.

"Why, that's Jack Daniels. Do y'all have this in England?" replied Laurie Lee, smiling.

"Oi, Oil ave un o'dem", Dave slurred, snatching a glass from the tray. Immediately, the rest followed suit.

Lifting his glass, Ian shouted "To Team England" over the din.

"To Team England" the players responded, downing the shots quickly.

After some more small talk, the girls returned to the bar as the karaoke continued with an unbroken line of outstanding singers, the Brits gregariously joining in at exactly the right spots. After a great rendition of Right Said Fred's *I'm Too Sexy,* the girls showed up again, tray of shots in tow. This time the glasses, containing a clear liquid, were accompanied by a couple of salt shakers and a pile of lemon slices. It was tequila time.

"Oi ent gittin anudder drink aught uenn be drinkin too" Dave hollered.

Through the din, I heard Greg shout "To Queen and Country" as the Brits raised their glasses and drained them, unconcerned with protocol as the lemon, salt and tequila were pretty much randomly sequenced. After about a half an hour, the girls returned again with lemon drops, a vodka drink. About 30 or 45 minutes after that, they showed up again with test-tubes of a wicked drink alternately known as a Jersey Devil or Red Death. Containing vodka, triple sec, southern comfort, sloe gin and amaretto along with some lemon mix, lime juice and orange juice, I knew from personal experience that it was incredibly potent.

Finally, with the evening winding down, I slipped away for yet one more trip to the men's room only to find a tray of Old Grand-Dad awaiting my return. As inconspicuously as possible, I tried to slip into my seat only to hear Ian's voice calling out my name.

"SCOTT"

Looking up, I saw him gesture for me to join the group. Leaning across Phil to try to hear him, he pointed to the tray of shots, shouting "Why don't you join us?"

"No, thanks, I'm not much of a bourbon drinker."

Gesturing again, I strained to hear Ian.

"No, I'd like you to join us. I got one more just for you."

With no dignified way out, I made my way to the back wall as the shots were being distributed. Raising his glass in the air, Ian looked me straight in the eye as he made his toast.

"Here's to doing whatEVER . . . is necessary . . . to win."

"'ere, 'ere" England players responded as they once again drained their shots. Ian's glass, however, remained frozen in place as he held my gaze. I stared back, equally unwilling to relent. Finally, we both smiled, our glasses clinking them together lightly before draining our drinks. I sensed the jig was up but that was ok – my work here was done. Moments later, the lights came up and Team England players poured themselves onto the sidewalk for the short stagger back to the hotel. Ian and I lagged behind, both quite drunk.

"I've got to 'and it to you, that was pretty slick." he began as we followed the others out.

Unsure of what or how he knew, I gave him my blankest, most innocent look.

"What?"

"You pay for those shots?"

"What?!? Where would I get that kind of money?"

"Uh huh. You know, I saw you talking to those girls outside."

"When?"

"A little while back. You went outside and they followed you. Then they came in and you followed them. Then you ducked into the men's room. I saw the whole thing."

I continued to play it coy as Ian searched my gaze for any sign of guilt. Finally, he laughed, shaking his head as we joined Joe and Lou at the elevators.

Having done my best to conceal my efforts, I was only partly disappointed to discover Ian had noticed. No matter, I thought with a smile. With an early tee-time in the morning, I'd maximized our chances tomorrow – and we'd need all the help we could get. The clock read 2 am and although I'd only had one shot, I had consumed far too much beer to expect no consequences. With an 8:45 tee time and a 45 minute drive to the course, I knew it would only be a few short hours before a cruel alarm clock would be ringing in my ears.

9

Marsh Harbor

Slowly, I came out of my drunken stupor, finally recognizing the evil sound I'd been hearing for what it was: the alarm clock. It was 6:15. Sitting up on the edge of the bed, I felt like I'd been broadsided by a sledgehammer, a wave of nausea rising in my throat. Lying back down, I offered Lou first shot at the shower. Twenty minutes later, I tried again, knowing I needed to get ready for the day's matches. Staggering into the shower, I stood there, motionless as the water beat down on my head, hoping against hope and all previous experience that the water would somehow cure my pounding hangover. Suddenly, memories started flooding back . . . *karaoke . . . girls . . . money . . . shots . . . oooh, my head . . . I need coffee and . . . something.*

Forcing myself to keep moving out of necessity, I gathered my things before heading downstairs to see what I could possibly stomach for breakfast. Moving straight to the buffet, I searched in vain for something - *anything* - that looked the slightest bit appealing.

Toast? . . . maybe . . . grits? . . . blecch . . . banana? . . . no . . . orange juice? . . . hmmm . . . what else? . . . waffles? . . . better not . . . eggs? . . . just a spoonful of eggs? . . . I need something . . . is there ketchup at the table? . . . oh good, coffee is there . . deep breaths . . deep breaths . . oohhh, my head hurts . . . this sucks . . .

Circling the buffet twice, I imagined the smell, taste and texture of each buffet item but nothing was appealing. Finally, I piled a few bites of scrambled eggs and a piece of toast on my plate to go with the coffee I'd ordered. After forcing what I could down and grabbing a banana for later, I headed outside to retrieve the van only to be greeted by a cold, biting wind that was whipping down the street. After briefly considering returning to the room for additional layers of clothing, I assured myself the buildings were funneling the wind, making it colder, that it would be better at the course and that it would quickly warm up. Reaching the van, I jumped in and got it started, urging it to warm up. Pulling up to the curb outside the hotel, several players were already huddled about, bouncing up and down in a vain attempt to warm themselves. The Tanis family was there along with Terry, Pat, Milo and Ray. Jack Jr. walked over to the window as I cracked it.

"So, ah, word on the street is that you had some girls buy drinks for the England guys last night." he asked with a slight grin. Since I'd borrowed (confiscated might be a better word) $40 from Chris for the last of round but hadn't told him why, I assumed Jack knew but felt committed to my strategy of plausible deniability, at least for the time being.

"Nah. I don't have that kind of money."

"Uh huh. And exactly what kind of money would that be?" Jack said, shaking his head and laughing as he walked away.

Sensing my best option was to keep the mouth shut, I just smiled. Looking at the clock, I saw we were running 10 minutes late and several England players were still missing. Finally, Ian and Joe showed up. Walking up to my window, Ian peered in from behind his dark sunglasses.

"I've told everyone what you did."

"What do you mean?"

He stared at me for a moment before shaking his head and walking away as Greg and Swampy emerged, followed by Dave moments later. When they saw me sitting in the van, they gave me their best dirty looks while simultaneously declaring themselves to be #1 - with both hands. For a moment, I felt quite proud of myself but just as quickly the nausea returned and I re-focused on taking frequent deep, cleansing breaths and massaging my forehead.

Finally, everyone piled in and we began the long, quiet ride north to Marsh Harbor, arriving at the course just after 8am for our 8:45 tee-times. Although it was another gloriously cloudless morning, any idiots would have known that the cold, biting wind at the hotel was just the appetizer - any idiots other than terribly hung over ones, that is. A cold front had moved through overnight and it was far colder and windier than what we'd briefly experienced at the hotel. In fact, with the early morning temperature in the low 50s and a steady 20-25 mph wind, it was borderline brutal. Players capable of coherent thought and planning were properly outfitted and prepared but the rest of us - the karaoke ten - were pitifully under dressed. Barely capable of simply remembering our clubs and shoes, we'd been oblivious to weather reports and our own physical senses, showing up in the same shorts and light shirts we'd worn the first two days. Big mistake.

It was bad at the hotel but we were able to retreat to the warmth of the building or our vehicles. Once out on the golf course, there was no place to run and no place to hide. The relentless north wind had us wandering about, teeth chattering, with only a thin layer of light fabric separating us from the cold as our pounding hangovers magnified every sensation. Not surprisingly, the three most heavily suffering Brits were the three most celebratory: Greg, Dave and Swampy. At one point, standing behind a rack in the pro shop, I overheard Dave say to Greg *"Oi, moi 'ed er boundin'. Oil kil dat bastard Dow. Oooo me 'ed"*. I quietly slunk away.

Swampy, meanwhile, seemed to spend most of his time in the men's room, apparently close to giving up what little breakfast he'd managed to swallow but trying his best to hold out. Greg mostly sat in the grill area, head down on the table as he waged his own private battle against nausea and a pounding head. My own claim of a raging hangover, not surprisingly, garnered zero sympathy but I had other problems more important, like trying to stay warm and walking in a straight line.

With our match out first, Terry would be low man with a 4 handicap; meaning Joe would get 1 shot, Ian 2 and I would get 5. Surprisingly, the match would turn out to be one of the closest, best played matches in Cup history. Three times Ian and Joe would grab a 1 up lead on the front only to see an immediate reply from Terry and me on the next hole. With the match still standing all-square on the 13th tee, all four drives found the fairway.

Although the 13th green at Marsh Harbor looked large on paper, the actual target area was much smaller thanks to a massive ridge, easily 4 feet high, that separated the front half of the green from the back half in the shape of an arc. The pin this day was located on the front half, just at the bottom of the ridge. An ideal approach shot would be to use the ridge as a backstop and let the ball trickle back down towards the pin. If you went too far, leaving your ball on the upper tier, you would be virtually guaranteed a 3 putt.

Playing first, I hit my 6-iron well but pulled it badly, leaving my ball 25 yards left of the green on a bed of pine needles. Terry, playing next, left his ball pin high on the left fringe, leaving a very tricky putt across the ridge. Joe hit next, knocking his approach into a trap at the front right of the green, leaving a short, uphill sand shot. Up last, Ian hit his approach shot right over the pin, hoping to accomplish what we'd all failed at – landing it on the ridge and letting it feed back down. The ball landed slightly long, hopping just at the top of the ridge and checking up. We all stared, fully expecting the ball to start its inevitable journey back down the ridge at any moment. As we watched, though, the ball just sat there, precariously perched on the ledge.

"You're joking" Ian cried out in frustration, staring futilely as the ball remained in place, defiantly holding its ground against the relentless pull of gravity. Putting from there, he would be lucky to keep it within 10 feet of the hole.

Like Ian, Terry faced an impossible putt but his was across the face of the ridge, causing it to break sharply right and accelerate as it approached the hole. The further up the slope he aimed, the more speed would be generated and the further it would break. Joe's straight forward bunker shot from an uphill lie suddenly had him in the driver's seat.

Then, of course, there was my less than ideal position. Sitting pin high but 25 yards left of the green, I surveyed my options. If I hit my shot just a hair too far left, I'd leave it on the upper tier and be facing a 3 putt double bogey. If I hit it just a hair too far right, the ball would hit the ridge and kick hard right off the slope and run downhill, quite probably right into the bunker with Joe. The only line with any sort of chance at success was a very narrow path right along the ridge, a line perhaps a foot or two wide with a miniscule margin of error. I would need a healthy dose of lady luck.

But every once in a while, in moments that I positively lived for, I was capable of summoning the right combination of imagination, skill, execution and luck needed to produce an incredible recovery shot – and thankfully, this would be one of those moments.

Standing well away from the ball to avoid the possibility of moving it through the pine needles, I took a dozen or more practice swings, seeking to gauge the exact feel of the swing the shot would require. Swing after swing, I tried to visualize one that would generate the exact ball flight I needed for the right distance. Finally, I stepped up to the ball, addressed it briefly and took a full swing with the face of my lob wedge laid open.

As the pine needles scattered, I looked up to see the shot flying 30, 40, 50 feet in the air. Glancing at the bunker, I could see it was on about the right line and seemed to have enough distance. As I watched, it landed on the fringe just past the bunker, hopping forward before disappearing from view. Unable to see the surface of the raised green, I bent down to pick up my putter and headed for the green, pleased I had kept myself in the hole and executed the difficult shot.

Coming off the loose pine needles, the ball had little spin and released quickly, rolling past Ian's mark as it tracked along the top of the ridge, following its curvature as if it knew where it was going. Finally, having slowed to a crawl about halfway across the green, the ball's forward motion gave way to the pull of gravity and it began to curl right, down the ridge and *back towards the pin.*

Oblivious to the drama unfolding on the green, I watched the three heads follow the ball's progress, the direction of their eyes providing the only evidence of the ball's location. Finally, about the time the forward momentum ceased and gravity took over, Terry called out over his shoulder.

"Yer gunna like this,"

Another moment and his chuckle turned to a full-throated laugh.

"Yer gunna *really* like this!"

It was just about then that the green surface came back into view just in time to see my ball trickle past the hole and stop about 3 feet below the cup. I would have a straight uphill putt for a par.

Smiling from ear to ear, I looked up at Ian. He was also shaking his head but he was not laughing or smiling. Between his bad luck and my good luck, I could tell he was steaming. Not surprisingly, none of the other three could get down in two and when I drained my short par putt, Terry and I had our first lead at 1 up.

Like the previous ones, our lead was short lived and by the time we reached 16 tee, the toughest hole on the course, the match was all square. With all three of us getting a stroke from Terry, 16 would prove another pivotal moment, this time with Ian providing the fireworks. Both Terry and Ian played the hole perfectly, hitting big drives and solid approach shots to about 25 to 30 feet above the hole on the small, heavily-sloped green. With the pressure on, Terry did what he had to do, draining his long downhill putt for an impressive birdie but Ian was not to be denied, topping Terry's birdie by draining his own birdie putt and with the stroke he was getting, the Brits were 1 up with 2 to play.

The signature hole of Marsh Harbor was the 17th, a fantastic par 5 that played over, through and around the marshes that bordered the course and gave it its name. After narrowly avoiding disaster with a so-so tee-shot that was pulled along the trees down the left, leaving me on a hardpan lie, I played my second and third shots perfectly, knocking a 4-iron onto the green and leaving myself with a 30 foot birdie putt. With Terry and Joe out of the hole, it was left to Ian and me to settle the issue.

Buoyed by the birdie on 16, Ian had ripped a perfect tee shot followed by what he *thought* was a perfect second shot. Unfortunately for him, it took one roll too many, just trickling over the edge and down into the marsh at the far side of the second landing area. Once again he stewed, pacing back and forth like a caged tiger in a vain search for his ball.

Finally, after reluctantly taking a drop, Ian hit his fourth to the green, leaving himself about 25 feet for par. After lagging up to about 3 feet, I could smell the win but Ian once again had other ideas, again dropping his putt to guarantee a halve, making England dormie 1 and tightening my collar considerably in the process. After managing to sink my knee-knocker for the halve, we headed to the final hole where Terry took things into his own hands, nearly holing his approach shot and leaving himself a kick-in birdie for the win that brought the final score to an appropriate all-square.

With the anti-climactic halve in the extraordinarily well played match in the books, I headed back out to see how the rest of my side had fared – and whether the substantial price I'd paid for today's advantage had paid off.

The second group out featured Jacks Sr. and Jr. facing off against two of the biggest partying and most heavily suffering Brits, Greg and Dave. Their heads hurt, their hands hurt from the cold, noise hurt, sunlight hurt, swinging a golf club hurt, reading a putt hurt and bending down to pick up a ball or stick a tee in the ground hurt - and that didn't include the nausea. Barely able to focus, by the time the two joined the match, it was far too late. Throughout the ordeal, they were more interested in plotting revenge against me than hitting golf shots and by the time they reached the last hole, their only focus was on getting a little *"hair o' the dog"*.

As for the golf - or lack thereof - the two Brits managed only two net bogies over the first five holes and were incredibly fortunate at that point to be only down 2. A mini-rally by Dave, who pieced together 3 pars in 4 holes, kept them only 2 down at the turn but they never seriously threatened our boys and steady play by the Jacks produced a deceptively easy 3&2 win.

The third match saw Pat and Chris facing Phil and Milo, two Brits who had weathered the evening's shenanigans better than most. With the match see-sawing throughout the day, England reached the final hole 1 up. There, Phil's clutch par, his second on the closing hole in two days, produced a similar result, closing another one for England at 2 up.

The day's final match started as a terrible mismatch. Stuart, like Dave and Greg, was suffering from a pounding head, double vision and a queasy stomach. Paired with Ray, the two had the challenge of facing young Matt, who was determined to make up for his previous day's poor play, and Lou. Solid, consistent golf on the front allowed us to make the turn 4 up without losing a single hole but Swampy rallied on the back, breaking through with par wins on 11, 15 and 16. Suddenly, England were alive at 1 down with 2 to play but it was too little, too late and Matt's routine par win on 17 was enough to close out the match, 2&1.

As I'd hoped, we'd made up a crucial point, winning the day 2-1/2 to 1-1/2 and drawing to within one overall at 8-1/2 to 7-1/2. Sitting on the veranda of the clubhouse, the tone of my previous night's victims was changing from the morning's vitriol to one of grudging admiration, my little stunt beginning its inevitable ascension to legendary status. Now that the morning's pain had passed, more than one glass was being raised in my direction.

Driving back to the hotel, though, I kept replaying Ian's long putts on 16 and 17, putts that prevented Terry and I from winning the match and squaring the Cup.

"I still can't believe those back to back putts on 16 and 17. You guys really dodged a bullet."

Ian, understandably, saw things a bit differently.

"Yeah, maybe, but c'mon. That shot on 13 was . . . I don't even know what to call it. Ridiculous?"

We laughed at our newest memories. Although my play was outstanding, producing the best Stableford score of the day, he was right about the shot on 13. Given a hundred chances, I'd be lucky to pull off that shot once. Finally, looking at me with a smirk on his face, the previous evening's shenanigans came up.

"You 'ad a big chance today, lad. We were ripe for the picking."

"I know. I wanted to pick up 2 points but that's ok – now we still get to set tomorrow's matches."

"That was some stunt last night."

"When did you catch on?"

"By the third round I'd got my antenna up, thinking something was just a bit off. But I din't catch on 'til I saw you 'ead outside with that one girl – Laura Lee, was it? When she came back in I waited and, sure enough, another round of shots showed up. That's when I realized it was you so I 'ad to invite you to join us with that final round . . . as my guest, of course."

"Yeah, that's what I figured. But I paid for it, too. Man, I felt like crap this morning. I would have loved to keep it secret but, oh well. I guess that won't work again!" I laughed.

"'Ow much did it cost you?"

"$140. I had to borrow $40 from Chris."

"$40 from Chris, eh? I'll 'ave to get 'im back for that."

"He didn't know what it was for. I just asked and he gave it to me."

Throwing his head back, Ian laughed his heartiest laugh, straight from his gut, the one that made everyone else laugh.

"Well, all I can say is well played, lad, well played. Will you be putting the story up on the website?"

"Oh yeah. It's already written in my head. I'll get it done and posted when we get back."

Having played only 18 holes, we arrived back at the hotel by 3 pm, plenty of time to crank out an article guaranteed to drop jaws over at the Angel. After posting the day's match results, scores, I got to work on the lead story. By 5 pm, it was up.

American Captain Dow Accused of Bribery, Corruption; Locals Back Up England Captain Jennings' Accusations

By: Datzit Indaruf, Flem Cup Correspondent

MYRTLE BEACH, Nov 4, 2001 – Coming off an impressive Day 2 beat down of the American side at Prestwick, explosive bribery and corruption charges have been leveled against Team U.S. Captain Scott Dow. In a stunning allegation, England Captain Ian Jennings has claimed that Dow paid local women to buy shots for celebrating members of Team England. At the presser prior to today's 4 ball matches, Jennings, wearing dark glasses, holding a large container of ibuprofen and talking softly between frequent deep breaths, laid out his case.

Now, despite Dow's repeated denials, any benefit of the doubt he may have gotten at the start of the day is long gone, along with all credibility. With the teams out on the course, investigative reporter Iva Tufshot landed an exclusive interview with Laura Lee Sugarbuns, one of the young ladies in question, and the full scope of Dow's unquenchable appetite for victory has been exposed. After showing Ms. Sugarbuns a picture of the dastardly American Captain to insure no case of mistaken identity could occur, the interview began.

###

Iva Tufshot: *Laura Lee, how did you get involved with this fellow, Scott Dow, last night?*

Laura Lee Sugarbuns: *Well, we was just a-sittin' theyuh, minding our lil' old bizness when this feller – Dow, you called him? – well, this Dow feller poked his old head 'tween*

Tammy Mae an' me an' asked us if he could talk at us out front – so out we went. And do you know what he asked us? He asked us if we wuz patriodic 'mericans! Can you 'magine? Well, we said we shur wuz, mister.

Anyway, he says he needs our hep cuz America's losing 'n we cud be a big hep in beatin' back the English hordes. Well, I said I thought they wuz our friends but he laughed and laughed and asked us if'n we'd heard of the Revolutionary War'n all? Well, I said sure and he said you heard of the war of 1812 or something and I said no and he said we fought 'em agin. Well I had no idea!

So then he says this is a different kinda war and he needed us to take some money and buy them cute England fellers some shots – and to mix 'em up reeeal good – cuz it'd really hep America out. Oh, and most important, he says, was to leave him outta it.

Tufshot: *So what did you do?*

Sugarbuns: *Well, I don't know 'bout no war but dem England fellers sure wuz nice and they wuz easy 'nuf to find, what with dem funny accents n' singing out loud n'all. So we did it.*

Tufshot: *How much money did he give you?*

Sugarbuns: *Eighty bucks. First, we bought them cute Englishmen some 'ole Jack Daniels. An' I got to meet Greg, you know, the big, dark, handsome feller. What a stud-muffin HE iz! Oooh my, he was dreeeeamy. Oh an' that Ian . . . mmmmmm. He wuz just smooooth as molasses, he wuz. And that cute 'lil Phil – I just wanted to pick him up and take him home! Then later we got 'em shots of tequila, and I got to meet that Swamp-feller. He was so funny . . . and cute! And then we got 'em lemon drops – those'll waste y'all in a hurry, honey! I just luv them, don't you?!? And then, well, we wuz outta money.*

Tufshot: *So you spent the $80? Then what happened?*

Sugarbuns: *Well, then that Dow feller come back and gave us sixty more bucks and asked us to keep doin' it cuz we wuz doin' great, hepin' America an' all, but by then I din't care nothing 'bout America cuz we wuz having so much fun! If them fellers is the enemy, I wanna be captured, ya know?!?*

Tufshot: *So you bought two more rounds?*

Sugarbuns: *I reckon. I lost count when I wuz staring into Greg's eyes. Mmmmmm.*

###

Following today's round, Chris Tanis, as a matter of personal conscience, admitted to unwittingly funding some of Dow's shenanigans. Denying any knowledge of what the money's true purpose was, he said Dow claimed it was for "an insurance policy . . . for tomorrow."

"I feel terrible! I thought he was going to the driving range. THAT would have been worthwhile! But it was after midnight and $40 would never have been enough – how foolish of me!"

After Jennings made his suspicions known this morning, England players were not a happy bunch and Dow not a popular man. Swampy, in particular, was highly upset at what he referred to as "lower than a snake's belly behavior", mumbling something else about the deed being the "most despicable, 'orrible, unsportsmanlike be'avior I can even imagine. I don't think I can bring meself to even talk to 'im today. Ooooh, me achin' 'ed."

With Captain Jennings reportedly looking into legal action, Dow had no comment when confronted with the developments, mumbling something about "all's fair in love and war and golf" before fleeing to his room and slamming the door.

***

With Indie's work done, I couldn't help but smile as I headed over to BummZ to get Ian's pairings before getting together with Jack and Lou to set the next day's matches. Walking in, I was greeted by Ian, Phil, Greg, Milo, Joe, Dave and Ray working on a couple of pitchers of beer. Only Swampy was missing, still recovering from his ordeal. With my cover now officially blown, my defense shifted to blaming the victims. After all, no one *forced* them to take anything and as the beer flowed, Team England's appreciation of the opportunistic stunt grew.

Eventually, the discussion turned to the next day's pairs. After helping to engineer last year's near-miraculous comeback, I was confident we could make up a 1 point deficit and capture the Cup. Anxious to get the England pairs so I could get together with Jack and Lou to set the matches, I was taking a sip of beer as Ian turned to me.

"Umm, do you mind going over there for a few minutes while we talk?"

After delivering my best *are you kidding me?* look, I retreated to the bar as the Brits huddled. Being only a few feet away, it wasn't hard to eavesdrop on most of the conversation.

"Phil and Milo" Ian began, turning to address the newly anointed dynamic duo. "I think we ought to leave you lads together."

No surprise there I thought to myself.

"Yeah, fine" Phil responded as Milo nodded his agreement.

Before Ian could go any further, normally quiet Ray interrupted.

"Look, Cap'n, I know I aven't been playin' well. Why don't you just play the same groups as today? You and Joe obviously played well today and so did Phil and Milo."

Looking at his son, Greg, a smile crept in.

"I know Greg and Dave will be up for a bit of revenge."

He paused as the group chuckled, nodding their agreement at the understatement. Greg and Dave just glared and nodded, each with just one goal in mind - a punishment of whatever unlucky soul they would each draw. Finally, as things quieted down, Ray continued.

". . . and they usually play well together. So put me with Stuart again and we'll do our best - you can be sure o'that - and let the chips fall where they may."

Ian scanned the table, gauging the response to the sensible and selfless offer, before turning back to Ray.

"OK, if that's what everyone wants. I'm not sure who Scott will send against Swampy – maybe Chris or Pat – but I'll bet Jack Sr. will take you on. 'Ow do you and Dave fancy playing together again?" he said, turning towards Dave and Greg. "Up for a bit of revenge?"

Dave leaned forward, eyes blazing, veins popping, jaw thrust out even more than usual. He'd suffered greatly today and was not one to let go of a good grudge. He wanted revenge on someone and any Yank would do.

"Aarrgghh. Oi'd loike da kill dat bastad Dow. Oi'd teke me alarg en bane oi'n bangin' 'im inna 'ead, oi' will" he growled, speaking so intensely that I could see flecks of spittle flying Ian's way. Nonchalantly sliding one hand over his beer while grabbing a napkin with the other, Ian leaned as far back as he could to avoid as the incoming missiles. Greg was a picture of intensity as he tried to figure out what Dave was saying.

"Roight!" Greg finally shouted, done with his best go at interpreting Dave. Turning back towards Ian, he said. "Tosh, who do you think they'll send against me?"

For quite a while, almost since I knew him, *Tosh* had been a commonly used nickname for Ian, one I had come to understand had affectionately been given him by Greg. The first time I heard it I'd assumed it was some flowery English phrase alluding to culture and sophistication, like 'pish posh' or something like that. It was another few years down the road before I discovered the true meaning of the nickname: 'crap'; as in 'full of'.

"I'm not sure. Maybe he'll take you on himself. He likes getting strokes."

"Oh, if only . . . I will beat his ass!"

Smiling, Ian turned back to address the full group again.

"So that's it then? We're all agreed? We'll leave all the groups the same? I'm certain . . . . faaairly certain . . . . [Ian's spread hand would always waggle slowly back and forth in situations like this to reinforce his uncertainty] that Scott will put Jack Jr. up against me and Terry against Joe."

Looking around the table one last time for any questions or disagreement, there were none.

"Roight, then. Our only change will be to reverse the order. We'll send Swampy and Ray first, Milo and Phil second, Greg and Dave third and Joe and I last. Ok?"

Again, nods all around. With that, I was invited back from the bar. Not wanting to give away my eavesdropping, I eagerly asked "So, whatchya got?"

Patting his shirt pocket where the secret cocktail napkin lay, he gave me a sly grin.

"It's right here. I've just got to let Swampy take a look and then you can 'ave it."

"Oh, come on. Where is he?"

"Sleeping. Let me give him a call."

Pulling out his cell phone, Ian dialed the Breakers and asked for Swampy's room.

"Swampy . . . it's Ian . . . 'ow ya feeling, boy? . . . Roight . . . Will you . . . uh huh . . . I did . . . yeah, we're at BummZ . . . uh huh . . . will you . . . yes, 'e's 'ere . . . will you be down . . . Well, we've got to give 'im the pairings and wanted your . . . roight . . . uh huh . . . . yes . . . I know you don't want to see . . . yes, it was, I know . . . . OK . . . . roight . . . . we'll be here . . . . 10 minutes? Roight. Cheers."

Before long, Swampy walked in, looking vastly improved. After stopping to glare at me for a moment, he burst into his familiar grin, sticking out his big paw to congratulate me on my stunt. Personal suffering aside, no Brit appreciated an underhanded, devious scheme more than Swampy. Finally, after another 10 minutes (9 of which were spent by Ian and Swampy haggling over the number of hot wings they would be splitting), the food order was placed and Ian asked me to retreat once more to the bar for another 'secret' team strategy meeting, this time solely for Stuart's edification. It was all I could do to bite my lip. Perhaps seeing my annoyance, Swampy called out to the waitress for one more beer - for me.

"Yeah, yeah. That's fine. Whatever is best for the team, you know that" I heard Stuart say as I stood at the bar, explaining to our waitress why I kept being exiled and telling her I really didn't want the beer. Finally, Ian called me back to announce what I already knew - same pairings as today in reverse order. After solemnly scanning the list, nodding and harrumphing for show, I turned towards the door. Before I'd taken 3 steps, I heard Swampy's voice call out.

"I just ordered you a beer."

"I know but I already cancelled it. I want to get together with Jack and Lou."

"Come on. After what you did last night, the least you can do is let me buy you a beer."

Shaking my head and seeing the smile on Swampy's face and faced with the rising catcalls from the peanut gallery, I relented, heading back to the bar to reinstate my order before pulling up a chair alongside Swampy. Before long, the waitress arrived with a tray full of pints. Raising his beer in appreciation, Swampy was effusive.

"Scott, I've got to tell you, that was brilliant. Simply brilliant. We'll be talking about that one for a long time. When did you come up with that?"

Despite my eagerness to get upstairs and get the matches set, I couldn't help but enjoy basking in Swampy's admiration for my underhanded trick, spending the next 10 or 15 minutes detailing the bare details of the night as Swampy – and several other lads – took turns laughing and shaking their heads at the details of my hastily hatched plot. Life had returned to normal for the Brits after the first taste of beer crossed their lips. They were, after all, a hardy lot when it came to drink and too much one night rarely affected the next.

At the far end of the table I could hear speculation as to who we'd match up against whom. At my end, Ian had begun to recount, for the umpteenth time, my improbable shot on 13, the perfect setup for the epic tales of his own heroics on 16 and 17 and, ultimately, Terry's fantastic match saving approach on 18. Sensing my cue to leave, I downed the rest of my beer and headed off.

I found Lou and Jack already in the room, wondering where I'd been. After filling them in on the pairings, we got down to business. Jack Sr. would, as Ian predicted, take on Ray but we would be sending out Matt take on Swampy to round out the first group. With Phil and Milo out next, we faced two very tough competitors. With the duo playing so well, we decided to throw out Lou and Chris, respectively, and hope for the best.

Before going any further, I looked at Jack.

"I know you may be expecting me to pair you up against Ian again."

"Doesn't matter to me" he responded blandly, sensing I had an angle.

"I'd like you to take on Greg. I want Ian."

His eyes flickered as he grinned. "I thought you might. That's fine."

"And Terry can take on Joe. That'll be a good match."

"Fine. That leaves Pat to take on Dave. I think Pat can take him."

As the words exited Jack's mouth, the phone rang. I reached to pick it up.

"Hello"

"I'VE SHIT MESELF AND MY NOSE IS BLEEDING. Get down 'ere NOW." Click.

Hanging up the phone, I had no words to express how I felt about what I'd just heard. The voice was Ian's but the words were beyond anything I would ever have imagined I'd hear him say. So I sat there for a few moments, sitting and staring blankly as Jack and Lou wondered what the heck was going on. I mean, how *does* one react to a phone call like that, I asked myself. I was in uncharted territory. Although it seemed longer, probably only a few seconds had passed before Jack spoke up.

"Who was that?" he asked apprehensively.

"It was Ian." I replied blandly, finally looking up.

"Yeah . . . and what did he say?"

"He's shit himself . . . his nose is bleeding . . . and we need to get down there now."

I stared blankly at Lou and Jack who stared blankly back at me before turning to stare blankly at each other. Then, it hit me, the answer to my question of how to react. Apparently, the others had come upon it much more quickly.

We rose as one, almost immediately breaking into a run down the hallway towards the door, jostling for position like jockeys coming out of the gate in a race to the elevators.

10

The Hot Sauce Incident

Swampy, seated at the end of the table facing the ocean, was on Ian's left when the waitress plopped down the large plate of wings they had ordered. The nap and a few beers had perked him up considerably and he was feeling rather hungry. Sharing a love of Buffalo-style hot wings, the two ordered them naked with the sauces on the side. Being connoisseurs of the hotter sauces, they'd ordered a few – mild, hot and very hot – for the sumptuous feast of fat wings awaiting them.

Next to the wings were three dipping bowls; the standard creamy bleu cheese dip, a hot honey mustard sauce and a third containing a thin reddish-brown liquid, no doubt the hottest of the three judging by looks. After picking up one of the juiciest looking wings, Swampy dipped the bottom half for just a moment in the bowl of reddish-brown sauce, deciding to play it safe until he could gauge just how hot it was. The conversation resumed.

"Tosh, I think Scott may send young Matt against me" he said before expertly vacuuming the meat off the bone in a single suck. Ian, who had picked up a wing of his own, began waving it about absent mindedly as he once again ran through his various predictions for the next day's matches, more interested in his own thoughts than what was happening to his wing-man.

As his eyes widened, Swampy's mouth involuntarily formed the shape of an 'O' as he smacked his open palm on the table once or twice, turning his head to the side as the burn continued to grow in intensity. The table smacking distracted Ian for only a moment, merely adding to his anticipation of a nice, hot sauce before he continued to lay out his analysis. What he didn't notice was that Swampy's breathing was becoming increasingly labored, little "whoas" emanating periodically. Through it all, Ian remained oblivious to his friend's gyrations.

"Wow, that's hot" Swampy finally managed to get out in a hoarse whisper, a massive understatement concealing the fact that he was struggling to simply draw a breath. Finally looking Swampy's way, Ian could only admire his friend's delightfully delicious discomfort as he prepared to take that magical first bite of a much-anticipated meal.

"Do you mind," Ian said, gesturing towards the same bowl Swampy had dipped from. Swampy shook his head, a sign Ian naturally assumed meant "No, I don't mind, go right ahead." Only later would Swampy be able to tell him the true intent was to say *"NO! DON'T!"* A few others had been watching the developments in Swampy's plight but they, too, remained unaware that he was careening towards a state of panic, uncertain of where, exactly, the experience was going. Ian was not looking at Swampy's eyes, nor was he listening to his labored breathing. The sweaty brow and running nose were, after all, merely the inevitable – even desirable – consequences of a nice, hot, spicy wing sauce. Ian was looking only at the thin reddish-brown dip.

Hardly an impetuous man, some of the effects he'd observed in Swampy had penetrated enough to cause Ian to approach the sauce with respect – but not fear. He had seen enough to err on the side of caution, deciding to just coat the bottom bit of the wing with a brief dip before raising it to his lips for that first delicious bite. Swampy, seeing the mortal danger his Captain was in, made one last futile effort to form words as Smokin' Joe, who'd been watching the events closely, jumped in.

"That's too much!"

But Ian paid no heed to Joe's warning and a moment later, it was too late.

As Swampy's final attempt to warn his friend died on his now numb lips, Ian bit into the wing. It took only a fraction of a second for the process to begin to repeat itself. Ian's eyes widening as the dab of sauce began to work its magic.

"Bloody hell that's hot . . . ."

Turning his head a bit, Ian entered phase 2, his mouth reflexively going circular as his breathing became labored.

"Bloody hell that's HOT . . . ."

Grabbing his beer, Ian drained what was left in a gulp. Slamming it back down, he waited to see if it would have a calming effect. It didn't. His voice was now a hoarse whisper.

"BLOODY hell that's really, SERIOUSLY F#*%ING HOT"

By now, Swampy had resorted to drinking beer straight from the nearest pitcher rather than wasting time filling his glass. Greg, seeing two of his closest friends in the throes of self-induced agony, began laughing hysterically as the rest watched in silent disbelief, unsure of what, exactly, was happening.

Knowing that beer does nothing to quench the burn from hot peppers, Ian vaguely recalled being told that sugar would help so he began grabbing nearby sugar packets, ripping them open and pouring them straight onto his tongue. Desperately hoping Ian knew something he didn't, Swampy followed suit and the two quickly exhausted the immediate sugar supply.

With relief nowhere in sight and the heat still climbing, Ian naturally assumed that the problem was simply that hadn't used *enough* sugar yet. Spinning around, his eyes were wide with panic as he frantically searched neighboring tables for more of the sweet balm. Almost immediately, his gaze settled on a well-stocked condiment holder on a neighboring table where a 60-something couple, doing their best to ignore the nearby ruckus, were enjoying the last bites of their meal. Sliding his chair across the floor as hard as he could, Ian overshot his target, crashing into their table before reaching across and digging into their condiments, focused only on his own desperate need, oblivious to their confusion and terror.

Sadly for all, it was during that sequence – the moment of maximum exertion and its immediate aftermath – that the chemical reaction going on inside his body reached critical mass, veering into the territory where the rare and fearful phenomenon known as a *Spinkhill Special* lived.

There were but a handful of Angel-regulars who had the ability to generate a dreaded *Special*. Until now, it was believed that a precise set of gastrointestinal conditions were required: namely some spicy Indian curries, lots of beer and at least 48 hours of fermentation (i.e. constipation). Delivered late at night in the Rave Cave surrounded by hard core Angel patrons, successful delivery invariably resulted in an explosion of relief to the deliverer and abject misery to anyone inside the blast zone.

On this day, however, Ian managed to reset the bar, surpassing all previously recorded *Specials* by so great a margin as to enter into the territory of "unbreakable record". His momentary effort, combined with the highly destructive chemical reaction occurring within his body, caused him to blow the largest, hottest, wettest, most repulsively stinky *Spinkhill Special* that has ever been blown. More slurry than gas, it was a true weapon of mass disgustion.

But there was more to it than even that.

What really made this the *Special* against which all future *Specials* would be measured was that in addition to the gastrointestinal explosion, a momentary spike in blood pressure caused him to hemorrhage through his nose. With his blood flowing and the dead zone growing, the poor woman at the table could only hold her hand up to her mouth, blurting out "Oh My" as she and the gentleman jumped to their feet, fleeing BummZ as quickly as they could, bill unpaid.

Oblivious to everything other than his own desperate condition, Ian grabbed the napkin she had dropped on her plate of mostly eaten food, jamming it up his nose in an effort to staunch the blood flow but the real damage has been done.

Like a daisy cutter bomb, the blast zone spread rapidly as patrons retreated down the hallway or out onto the patio amid cries of "ahhh, man!!" and "dude!!"

Within seconds, Ian and Swampy were alone in the bar. Standing behind the kitchen door, the waitresses, cook and bartender peered through the porthole windows like trapped rats, waiting for some courageous person to give them the thumbs up that the dense gas had dissipated but like sulfur after a fireworks display, it hung defiantly in the air, clinging to whatever it touched as it burned the eyes, nauseated the senses and defied all efforts to force it outdoors.

So everyone waited, watching as Swampy and Ian ate sugar, drank beer and slapped the bloody, napkin-strewn table, oblivious to everything but their own anguish. Finally, after about 10 minutes, a few brave souls ventured back in, covering their faces with clothing or napkins just in case. Finally, the all clear was given and as things slowly returned to normal (well, as normal as the aftermath of an episode like that *could* be). Soon enough, their waitress timidly ventured forth from the kitchen with a look of fear and trepidation to ask if they were all right. Knowing it was a truly dumb question, what else was there to ask?

Looking at her, Ian bit what was left of his tongue before deciding upon taking the high road.

"WHAT . . . is . . . THAT?" he began, pointing to the dish of sauce. "Because THAT . . . nearly KILLED us."

Pausing, he looked at the poor, speechless waitress before continuing.

"Now . . . Oi've 'ad 'ot sauces . . . and THAT . . . is THE 'ottest sauce . . . I've EVER 'ad . . . Stuart? . . . Wouldn't you say . . . that THAT . . . is THE 'ottest sauce . . . you've EVER 'ad?"

Poor Swampy, looking pathetic, could only nod vigorously as the befuddled waitress bent down, examining the dish nervously without touching it.

"I . . . I don't know what that is but I'm so sorry. Hang on, hon."

Disappearing into the kitchen, she reappeared moments later with the cook, looking equally submissive. Bending down, he smelled the dish cautiously, eyes widening as he bolted straight up.

"Good Gawd! It's *Da Bomb*. We put a drop 'er two o' dat in when someone wants some super hot wings 'er whatever. But this ain't even cut – it's straight *Bomb*! DON'T touch that dish – 'er yoursef – y'all better go wash yer hands! And DON'T go to the bathroom first!"

Recovered enough to grasp the implications of what he was saying, Ian and Swampy headed down the hall to the men's room as the cook headed for the kitchen, returning a moment later with goggles and heavy-duty rubber gloves. Ever so gingerly, he picked up the dish as Ian and Swampy returned.

"Can't spill none o' this stuff. This is whatcha call pure, distilled habanero pepper sauce. That's just about the hottest pepper in the whole world, that's all. I hafta call the EPA if I spill this stuff. Normally I get full-suited up but this he'yar is a mergency n'all."

Apologizing profusely, the waitress quickly brought two fresh pitchers of beer, assuring them their beers and food would be free. After she left, Ian looked at Swampy, then Joe, then Greg. Perhaps for the first time in his life, he was speechless, having absolutely no idea what to say as he continued to recover from the painful incident. Finally, he asked the question on everyone's mind.

"How the 'ell could this 'appen? How could they have given us that uncut?"

Shaking their heads, no one had a clue. Suddenly, Greg's head lifted.

"Did you see Scott talking to the waitress before he left?" he blurted out as the memory of my time at the bar flooded back. All heads turned his way.

"What?" Ian asked.

"Scott! Remember? 'E spoke to the waitress for a while after you had ordered your wings, right before 'e went back to the Breakers; when we were telling

Swampy the pairings. And then 'e spoke to 'er again when Swampy bought 'im a beer. And 'e didn't want to hang around after that, remember?"

Torn between disbelief and the memories of what had happened the night before, Ian pulled out his cell phone, dialing the Breakers.

"Scott Dow's room, please."

Deep breath.

"I've shit meself and my nose is bleeding. Get down 'ere now."

Flipping it shut, he wiped it off and slipped it back into his pocket, unsure of what to think. Moments later, out of breath and eager to find out what had happened, the three of us walked in.

11

2001 Singles Day

After retelling the story of what had happened and waiting patiently for us to stop laughing, Ian wanted answers. Recognizing a new and completely unexpected opportunity to expand my newfound reputation for skullduggery, I decided to play into their wild insinuations, stating over and over, whenever asked or "interviewed", that I could neither confirm nor deny rumors of any involvement or lack thereof in the incident. After what I'd pulled the previous night, who could blame them if they smelled a rat – and that was fine with me. I couldn't help but laugh to myself as Ian grilled the poor waitress, who was clueless. All she could do was offer blank stares, repeated denials and sincere apologies and eventually Ian gave up, perhaps realizing that no restaurant staff would do something as clearly dangerous as that as a gag. I, on the other hand, continued to drop hints, eager to take advantage of a totally unplanned yet golden opportunity to feed Team England's new-found paranoia and my growing reputation as a "stop at nothing" opponent.

Feeling rather satisfied with all the commotion and all laughed out, Jack, Lou and I went to find a secluded table and finish discussing the matches. Before long, the rest of our contingent walked in, eager to find out who they'd be playing tomorrow. After spending the better part of 30 minutes listening to Ian recount the hilarious story once again (it just didn't get old!), we ran over our choices with the rest of the team. Everyone satisfied, we rejoined the Brits.

"I've got your number tomorrow, boy!" Swampy growled upon learning that Matt would be, as he'd predicted, his opponent, glaring at the fuzzy faced youngster with his most menacing look (which was more comical than menacing).

"Bring it, old man!" Matt laughed, unsure what the strange look was intended to inspire.

Unlike Swampy, there was no doubt what the looks from Greg and Dave meant as they offered a polite but frosty "good luck" to their opponents, Jack Jr. and Pat, respectively. From the look in their eyes and the set of their jaws, I knew our boys would need all the luck they could muster.

As the next to last match was announced, I watched as a brief look of surprise flashed across Ian's face upon realizing that I, the only remaining American player, would be his opponent in the Cup's final match.

"Good . . . very good." he said, smiling as he raised his glass to mine.

"Here's to doing whatever it takes to win" I offered with a smile.

"Here, here. And to a great match. Good luck, lad." Ian replied, smiling broadly.

"And to you"

The next morning we headed out bright and early for the 45 minute ride to The Heritage Club, a magnificent old-style plantation golf course draped in Spanish moss on Pawleys Island. Heritage remains, without a doubt, one of the finest courses on the Grand Strand and beyond. Noted for its large, wildly undulating greens, long water carries and magnificent scenery, we'd long considered the back nine to be one of the finest nines of any course, promising lots of drama and nearly always delivering.

Needing to win 4-½ of the 8 points available to tie, our first group got us off on the right foot when Jack Sr. jumped out to a huge lead on Ray, making the turn at 6 up. Matt, however, saw his early 5 up lead nearly evaporate as Swampy came charging back to win the last 4 holes and make the turn only 1 down.

In the second group out, Milo stayed hot, shooting a solid 2 over par net on the front side and making the turn 3 up over Chris, who was struggling to find an answer to the wiry Brit's monotonous consistency. Lou, meanwhile, stormed out to a 3 up lead against Phil only to see the determined Brit rally back to make the turn all square.

The third group was, as I'd feared the night before, a disaster for us as both Brits came out loaded for bear. Greg jumped all over Jack Jr., playing mistake-free golf in winning 4 of the first 6 holes – and that was the closer of the two matches. Dave was even more dominating, standing at 1 under par *gross* (4 under par net) through the first six holes and leading Pat, 5 up. Despite our boys rallying a bit down the stretch, Greg and Dave each made the turn at 3 up.

In the final group, Terry and Smokin' Joe each came out solid as a rock but it was Terry who was just a tad better, his even par net good enough to make the turn 2 up over Joe, who was only 1 shot behind. Meanwhile, my Captain's match started as a train wreck as my nervous, wobbly start was contrasted with Ian's confident, solid one. With easy wins on 1, 3 and 4, Ian jumped to a quick 3 up lead and I was on the ropes, perilously close to a complete meltdown.

Standing in the 5th fairway, I was staring a 4 down deficit in the face after watching Ian put his second safely on the green in regulation, 20 feet from the pin. Focused on making a solid strike to get my game going, I made solid contact but pulled it, my 6 iron heading 30 feet left of the pin. After watching the ball disappear behind a yawning bunker on the left front, safely on the green but miles from the pin, I disgustedly slammed my club into the ground, knowing I'd have a long, difficult putt. Looking up again, I was stunned to see the ball had reappeared, running across the wide, sloping green straight towards the pin. Having landed on a ridge hidden behind the bunker, the ball kicked right, running all the way across the green before stopping 4 feet below the hole with a straight, uphill putt. It was a stunning break and just the medicine my game needed. After watching Ian 2-putt for a par, my birdie putt brought me back to 2 down.

Ian remained focused, determined not to allow another lucky break by me de-rail his otherwise stellar play and when I led off the par-3 6th by chunking a fat 3-iron about 10 yards short and left of the green, he smelled blood, hammering a crisp 4-iron onto the upper tier and leaving himself a makeable birdie putt from about 15 feet. With a renewed bounce in his step, he was confident his lead would once again be 3 up as he surveyed the very delicate little 25 yard chip shot I faced.

Sitting left and short of the green, I would need to run my ball up the 6 foot high ridge on an awkward angle, breaking right all the way until it reached the top where it would straighten out. As usual, I chose an 8-iron to pitch and run the ball, a shot I was very comfortable with. Striking the ball crisply, everything was right, the ball breaking just enough to the right to be running straight at the hole by the time it reached the top, burning the edge before stopping only a foot or so away for a conceded par. Like the day before, the look on Ian's face was pure disbelief and when his birdie putt slid by the hole, the halve felt like a win to me and a loss to him. He should have been 4 or even 5 up - and we both knew it - but the lead was only 2 and I had dodged another bullet.

Still holding the tee on 7, I laced a perfect 1-iron straight over the bunker on the corner of the dogleg, leaving a short iron from the middle of the fairway. My game was back on track, my confidence was growing and I knew Ian couldn't play mistake-free golf forever. Sure enough, a pair of unforced errors on 7 and 8 al-lowed my two pars to level the match and despite a careless bogie loss on 9, I felt good about making the turn only 1 down.

About the time we finished the front 9, Jack Sr. was polishing off Ray by winning the 11th hole for a lopsided 8&7 win and Lou was back to 1 up against Phil after winning the 10th hole. Unfortunately, that would be the last good news we would receive for about an hour or so as the floodgates were about to open - with a vengeance - in England's favor.

As we played our way down 10, Milo and Dave were stretching their leads to 4 up over Chris and Pat, respectively. By winning 10, Smokin' Joe cut Terry's lead to 1 up and by the time we'd teed off 11, Phil was leveling in his match with

Lou. By the time we reached the 11th green, Greg was back to 4 up on Jack Jr. while Super Dave had gone 5 up against Pat. As we teed off 12, Phil had taken a 1 up lead against Lou and by the time we'd reached that green, Dave was dormie 6 and Milo was 5 up. Finally, the floodgates closed as we played 13 but only after Phil had gone 2 up on Lou and Dave had finished off Pat in another blowout, 7&5.

For Team U.S., the 4 hole stretch – 10 through 13 – was a complete and total disaster. Combined, the eight Yanks had lost 12 of the 32 holes and won only 1. Only Matt, Terry and I came through without losing ground and despite a Cup score of only 9-1/2 to 8-1/2 in favor of England, our hopes were dimming fast. Only Matt (1 up) and Terry (1 up) led for us while Greg (4 up), Milo (4 up), Phil (2 up) and Ian (1 up) were each leading for England.

Before too much longer, Greg (5&4), Matt (3&2) and Milo (3&2) closed out their matches, leaving 3 on the course and England with a lead of 11-½ to 9-½. We would need 2 wins and a halve to tie for the Cup, a tall order for three tight matches but when Lou grabbed 15 to get back to only 1 down against Phil, a glimmer of hope remained.

But as our group traversed the back 9, we knew nothing of the results ahead, only that we were engaged in tough matches that each of us wanted very badly to win. Wins on 13 and 14 extended Terry's lead to 3 up before a par halve on 15 ended his match with Joe, 4&3, in a match that was a lot closer than the final score indicated. Meanwhile, my match with Ian had finally turned my way and with wins on 14 and 15, I grabbed my first lead of the day and with it, all the momentum. Ian had clearly been the better and more consistent golfer throughout most of the day yet here he was, once again frustrated by my ability, with a few well-timed doses of lady luck, to scramble and escape disaster. Another opportunity to frustrate him on 16 resulted in a perfectly executed little bump and run that bounced once in the greenside rough, leaving the ball just enough momentum to barely reach the green and trickle down the steep slope past the pin, leaving me with a 4 foot uphill par putt. This time, however, I failed to convert, providing Ian the opening he needed and when he drained his tricky little 3 foot side hill par putt, the match was level once more as we headed to 17.

As we teed off, knowing our match would now reach 18, all conversation had ceased, the two of us completely focused on the job at hand. Terry and Joe, their match now ended, had faded into the background, spectators and fans watching our now epic Captain's match play itself out.

Knowing I'd be getting my last stroke on 17, a hard dogleg right par 4, Ian tried to cut a 3 wood around the corner but hit it dead straight, dribbling it into the fairway bunker on the far side of the dogleg. Hoping to take advantage, I slapped a weak 1 iron down the right side along the tree line, failing to clear the corner and leaving myself with no chance of reaching the green in regulation.

Knowing I was getting a stroke and Ian was in a fairway bunker with a very tough approach shot to a well-guarded green, I took my medicine and punched my second shot safely back out into the fairway, leaving myself 75 yards or so to the pin. With no other choice, Ian went for broke, ripping a brilliant 200+ yard fairway wood that landed just on the front of the green, dead on line with the pin and perfectly splitting the narrow opening between two deep, nasty bunkers that guard the approach (a few years earlier, I'd taken 5 shots to get out of the one on the right, eventually having to give up on advancing my ball towards the green and playing out sideways).

After executing his magnificent shot, Ian engaged in a bit of gamesmanship, driving up to the green and standing to the side as I prepared for my approach. With my only option a little 2/3 pitching wedge, I pulled out my last dagger, landing the crisply struck shot a couple of inches right of the hole and leaving it only 2 feet away. One last time, Ian looked sick, staring up at the sky in disbelief, perhaps asking the golfing gods what he had done to deserve this. After missing his long birdie putt, I knocked in my short putt for a net birdie to go dormie 1.

What we didn't know at that point was that pride was all we were playing for. As we had been putting out back on 16, the Cup had ended when Phil's par on

17 was good enough to win the hole and close out Lou, 2&1. Although he had been a bit erratic, carding five double-bogeys or worse, Phil more than made up for it with solid play on the other 13 holes, carding two birdies, three bogeys and eight pars.

But pride was enough for the two of us as we headed for the final tee.

The 18th at Heritage is a simply magnificent finishing hole, a 550-yard par 5 dogleg left with out of bounds to the left and water all the way down the right and nearly surrounding the peninsula green. A perfect tee shot is right to left, wrapping around the cluster of large trees guarding the corner. With a mighty blast and a favorable bounce or three, you can go for the green with your second shot (if you have the stomach for it) or lay up for a short third. The green slopes back left to front right and is bordered by a bulkhead wall that starts on the far left side, about 6-8 feet above the water level on the far left and quickly lowering to a height of only about 3 feet around the middle and wrapping all the way around the back. Almost always, it is a 3-shot approach.

Still riding the emotional wave of my success on 17, I crushed a 1 iron right down the gut, finishing about 250 yards out in the middle of the fairway. Knowing Ian was still reeling from my shot on the last hole, I wasn't entirely surprised when he pull-hooked his tee shot onto the roof of a house, out of bounds left. Despite the break, I managed to allow him back into the hole by shanking my routine 7 iron approach into the lake, a brain fart that forced me to make a 5 foot knee-knocker to match his double bogey and win the match, 1 up, bringing the final Cup score to 12-½ to 11-½ in favor of England.

As we got out of our carts at the final green and discovered the Cup result, the emotions Ian and I had been experiencing in our match were quickly reversed, my joy turning to dismay as Ian's distress turned to joy. After all, winning the Cup was what really mattered and as England players milled about the final green in jubilation, we could only offer our sincere congratulations for their hard-fought win before gathering off to the side, commiserating with one another.

"Well played, lad, well played." Ian offered we walked off the green.

"That . . . was an awesome match - unbelievable." I replied as we shook hands and embraced. "You got the big one, though. Congratulations on the Cup win. You guys were just a bit too much for us."

As the greenside celebration abated and players began drifting back towards their carts, Ian pulled me aside.

"This was everything we'd hoped for, wasn't it?"

Stepping back, I looked at his sun-drenched face, warm and smiling. I turned to look at the two teams, meandering back in random, mixed groups of friends, teammates and opponents alike, the competition now officially ended.

"No, it wasn't. It was better. Miles better. This week was simply awesome."

Feeling a hand on my shoulder, I turned to find Jack Jr. there, hand out.

"Great match today. Sorry I let you down."

I laughed. "Well, I think you paid for what I did the other night. From what I've heard, Greg was a beast today. Sorry about that."

"Well, it was fun. Kind of."

With that, he laughed and we moved off, talking, congratulating and commiserating, making our way back to the bag drop before heading to the clubhouse for some lunch and beers.

As we ate and drank, I could feel that miserable feeling creeping in, knowing that, for all intents and purposes, it was over. Not the golf, although that was sad enough. Our time together was rapidly coming to an end. Refusing to give in just yet, I pushed it down, knowing we had one last round the next day for individual prizes; one last hurrah before the emptiness and loneliness took over again.

The award dinner that night was a festive party for the Brits. Ian broke out a flag emblazoned with the Cross of St. George to celebrate, the team breaking in song and celebration. Phil, who had captured 4-1/2 out of 5 points, was awarded the Most Valuable Flem prize and the Flem Cup trophy was unveiled for the first time: an antique, hand blown greenish glass spittoon sitting on a wooden plinth. It was quickly acknowledged to be a perfect trophy, a fitting tribute to our event.

With the sides now alternating each year as "home" team, Ian concluded the evening by presenting his tentative plan for the 2002 Flem Cup - Ireland. In order to accommodate the unpredictable Irish weather as best we could, we would move the Cup to early October. As he reviewed the details, everyone was salivating at the prospect of playing courses like Ballybunion and Lahinch.

By early afternoon the next day, the final round of golf was complete, Milo had won nearly everything and we found ourselves once again saying sad good-byes, first at the golf course to our teammates and then at Raleigh-Durham airport to the Brits as Chris and I prepared to fly home. At the end of the line, I reached Ian.

"Goodbye, pal," I said, eyes misting up as I tried to keep my voice from cracking. I'd never been good with goodbyes and today was no different. Ian looked into my eyes, smiling.

"Goodbye, lad. You know, I've been thinking. We've had quite some fun since we met in Cincinnati. This was an incredible trip – absolutely incredible. Thanks for everything; I know you put a lot of work in and everyone appreciates it. You take care, now, and work on that golf game. Lord knows, if you can just put some skill with all that luck you have, you'll be unbeatable . . ." his voice trailed off into his trademark giggle.

"Yeah, it was a great trip. And as I've told you before, it's not luck." I claimed, my best mock outrage emphasized by my finger wagging in his direction.

"Oh, that's right. Sorry. It's "sporadic skill", is it?" Ian chuckled. "Sure you're not interested in our January ski trip? It's a blast."

"I'd love to but I can't. What else do you have coming up? Any interesting trips?"

"No, nothing exciting. A doctor's visit next week . . . that's as exciting as it gets before the ski trip. Then our ski trip in February and our golf trip to Majorca in March. You know, if you're interested, I can find you a spot."

I smiled, knowing I had no chance of making either happen. "I know, I know. One golf trip a year is all I'm good for. What's the doctor's visit for?"

"Oh, just a few lumps to be looked at. Nothing serious."

"Really? I'm getting some minor surgery done – they're removing this thing" I said, touching the lump on my left temple.

"Yeah, I'd noticed that. Does it bother you?"

"No, but it seems like it's been growing. They'll be doing a biopsy on it. The doctor doesn't think it's a problem, though. Some sort of a fibrous mass but nothing to worry about."

Checking the time, I reluctantly opened my arms for a final embrace. "We need to get going. You take care, now. Say hi to everyone back at the Angel and I'll see you soon."

"And you, lad, and you. You take care."

With a last slap on my shoulder, Ian turned to head off with the rest of Team England. Our plane was already boarding by the time we reached our gate and I plopped down into my seat, already engulfed in depression now that our incredible week was over. Like the first year of Enteract in Cincinnati, this past week had been one of those times in life that you just knew would never – *could* never – be duplicated no matter how hard you tried. The spontaneity . . . the new friendships . . . the drink buying scandal! . . . the hot sauce incident! Thinking of them made me laugh out loud once again. Ireland would be fun but it would be different and, frankly, I just couldn't imagine it living up to all this. The trip had been better than I'd ever imagined and the depression of seeing it end and my friends depart had only just begun to sink in.

12

The News

By the time Thanksgiving had passed, I'd spoken to Ian only once, an ill-advised phone call that caught him on a Friday night at the Angel surrounded by friends and teammates, each of whom wanted a turn describing how fantastic the Flem Cup trophy looked sitting atop its new perch on the mantle in the Rave Cave. It would, indeed, be a long 11 months. Finally, in mid-December, my office phone rang early one afternoon, an unusual time for a call from England considering the time difference of 5 hours. Picking it up, I was greeted by a familiar voice.

"Mr. Dow."

"Mr. Jennings! What a surprise! How is merry old England these days?"

"Fine, England is fine."

His subdued tone made my antenna go up.

"Hmmm. Doesn't sound fine. Is something wrong?"

An uneasy silence only heightened my concern. Finally, he continued.

"Actually, something is wrong. I had a visit with the doctor the other day."

"Really? Nothing serious, I hope."

I offered the words casually but a sense of dread hung in the air.

"Do you remember the tests I went for after getting back from Myrtle Beach? Well, they took biopsies of some lumps . . . . . . I 'ave non-Hodgkin's lymphoma."

My mind went into scramble mode, unsure exactly what that was or meant, leaving me only the uncomfortable option of asking.

"What does that mean?"

After another long pause, he continued.

"It's cancer in your lymph nodes." He paused again as my mind raced. Knowing my next question and dreading the possible answer, I was unwilling to utter the words. Finally, he confirmed my worst fears.

"It's incurable. . . I've been given 1 to 5 years to live."

Incurable? My word exploded in my mind. This had to be some horrible, cruel joke – perhaps a nightmare. 1 to 5 years? It just couldn't be. Ian was only 45, far too young for something like this. My only experience with death was with older relatives – this couldn't be right. I scrambled for something to say, a coherent, helpful thought, but nothing was there, my mind swirling wildly in disbelief. Finally, a question bubbled up.

"Have you gotten a second opinion?"

"And a third. It's been confirmed."

I went numb as the word echoed through my mind. *Incurable.* Through the shock and dismay of the moment I did my best to be positive, perhaps more for me than Ian. Finally, with nothing more substantial to offer I went with a few empty clichés about people beating it, the rapid advances in medical science and how miracle treatments could be just around the corner. Ian half-heartedly went along, having already heard it all.

Incurable.

The word continued to reverberate, obliterating any positive thoughts I tried to conjure. Silence set in and as my emotions began to overtake me, tears welling in my eyes. I struggled for words, knowing I wouldn't be able to verbalize them without losing what little composure I had left. Finally, after what seemed an eternity of silence, pure and honest words broke through the raw emotion of the moment.

"You know . . . . you're . . . . my best . . . . friend."

With the final word, tears were unleashed, breaking in a torrent as I vainly struggled to control myself. I'd never heard Ian's voice crack from emotion before, let alone seen him cry, but I heard it now as he struggled to get out a reply in a low voice, barely a whisper, his voice cracking.

"And you, lad . . . . . . and you."

Over the days that followed, I kept returning to my own fleeting brush with mortality, one that ended with a benign, fibrous mass being removed from my temple a week or so after we'd returned from Myrtle Beach. The question soon began to haunt me . . . *Why Ian? Why not me?* I had no answers.

Incurable.

As hours, days and weeks dragged by, I did my best to stuff it deep into the recesses of my mind but it was always there, lurking, waiting for any excuse to leap back into my consciousness. Christmas and New Year slid by slowly and uneventfully as the shock slowly faded. On New Year's Eve, I got my annual call from Ian from the deck of his rented chateau in Austria, celebrating the holiday with his ski trip friends as they shot off fireworks. He sounded great. The doctors had warned him against any major lifestyle changes lest he waken the disease from its slumber and Ian was fully compliant, moving into an uncertain future living with all the gusto he ever had, pulling his friends and loved ones right along. No one would have suspected a thing from his attitude, his conduct or, I was sure, his appearance.

In February, another body scan showed the disease remained dormant, encouraging the doctors to continue their cautious wait and see approach. After another good scan in early May, the doctors throttled back the scan schedule to bi-annual instead of quarterly and I indulged myself in a tiny bit of optimism. Perhaps he would beat this. Others had, why not a man like Ian?

A June trip to Chester for a training class provided my next chance to spend some time with Ian during an extended side trip to Spinkhill and we had a wonderful time on his boat, travelling around the Broads in eastern England. The trip happened during the 2002 World Cup so we would stop every few hours at a pub to watch whatever game was coming on over a bite to eat and several pints. Between boat excursions, we managed a few rounds of golf on some terrific courses. On my next to last night, we stopped at a restaurant near Sheffield on an absolutely perfect evening, choosing to eat on the patio as the sunset began its nightly work of painting the sky in ever-changing colors. Having finished our meals, we sat back to enjoy the last bit of sunset as we sipped our beers. Before long, the conversation turned to future plans.

After receiving the bad news late in the fall, Ian had immediately set about retiring as Managing Director of Monition and although he was still in the process of winding up his affairs and consolidating his assets, he was far enough along to focus on his future as a man of leisure, specifically his hopes and dreams for the next few years. Ian had always had a crystal clear picture of where he wanted to go in life, what he wanted out of it and how to get there. Whether he truly believed he would beat this thing or not, he surely understood the importance of a positive mental outlook and he was determined to maintain one. In his mind, nothing about his future had changed except the timeline.

As he spoke, his bleak prognosis faded to irrelevance as I closed my eyes, the cool breeze wrapping itself around me like a refreshing blanket. Like a master artist, he painted vivid pictures of the life he and Caroline would someday embrace in a small village in southeastern France where he had already purchased a couple of building lots for houses he intended to build, one for investment and one for his new home.

"They're on the east side of the village, which is just up in the foothills of the Alps. We'll build the houses facing west so we can watch the sunset across the valley. It's just so beautiful – you must come and visit when we have it built. From where we are, the foothills gradually roll away, down to the valley, it's like some sort of endless painting that continually changes throughout the day. The sunsets are just spectacular. And, of course, to the east we have wonderful views of the Alps, which are just amazing. And the village is a lot like Spinkhill – very quaint, very old-world-ish. Old stone buildings that sit right on the cobblestone streets. There's a local pub and lots of very good restaurants. It's very nice."

"Oh, I'll be coming to visit, that's for sure" I offered casually, knowing how much more difficult a trip like that would be with no business interest to make it happen. "How close is the skiing?" Ian smiled.

"We can be skiing in an hour and there are some very picturesque golf courses nearby. We've already met some of the villagers and they seem very nice. And of course we'll keep the boat somewhere nearby, probably on a river where we can get down to the Med. I'm not sure where yet. We're planning on taking the boat down to the Med sometime this summer – maybe next – and just explore a little bit. We've submitted the building permits and everything looks good but you know how these things go – never as smooth as you'd like. I just love the culture over there. 3 hour meals at 9 o'clock down at the pub and wonderful wine . . . . "

As Ian continued to paint the canvass of his future, I found myself swept away in the images he was conjuring, picturing the quaint little village they would call home, the spectacular sunsets they'd watch nightly, the Mediterranean ports they'd visit on his boat, the Old World culture and lifestyle they would embrace. I had no doubt Ian would quickly improve on his already passable French and suddenly the image of him holding court in the village pub popped into my head, a thought that made me laugh out loud, interrupting his stream of consciousness. Turning, he looked at me with a surprised look.

"What? What's so funny?"

"I just imagined you telling your jokes in French!"

Throwing his head back, Ian erupted in laughter.

"Yeah, that will be something, won't it? Mon dieu!" he chuckled after we settled down.

Ian went on to speak of Caroline, of how wonderful she'd been and how she'd left her job so they could spend all of their time together. His affection for her was palpable, something I'd never sensed in him about any other woman I'd known him to be involved with. I'd always had the feeling that she truly loved him and found myself hoping that he felt the same way; that they'd found true love in each other. If the doctors were right, she would need more strength and courage than I could even imagine to handle the ordeal they faced. She would have to become his rock, refusing to give in to despair or fear while supporting him unconditionally, his safe harbor against the coming storms.

I had often wondered to myself why Ian had never considered moving to America. Business opportunities were limitless compared to England, living was cheaper and there were so many things he loved. Despite all that, he was never the slightest bit interested in the prospect. Tonight, the light bulb in my head finally went on. The reason was simple: the village pub.

We Americans live our lives, for the most part, alone in our big suburban houses. Ian had no interest in living that way because he knew himself too well. He was an entirely social creature, one who enjoyed *nothing* more than evenings at the Angel, surrounded by friends, laughing and drinking. For Brits, that sort of lifestyle is virtually embedded in their DNA and although he loved visiting America, living in a small village with a cozy pub where he could, on a nightly basis, laugh and drink with friends and neighbors was far more important. Combined with the old world culture he so loved, living in the U.S. was a non-starter.

The depth and details of Ian's dreams struck me profoundly, his vivid descriptions carrying me away to a little Ian-world I was creating in my head. He knew exactly where he wanted to live and why, down to the precise environment and lifestyle, and sitting there on a beautiful summer evening looking at the optimistic twinkle in his eye, I found myself gripped by optimism that he *would* beat his cancer, that he would be not a victim but a survivor. It could end no differently. *Incurable* was momentarily banished from my mind.

Gazing off into the distance, I was carried away by the breeze, the sunset, the stories, the jokes and the dreams about Ian's future life. Everything seemed perfectly balanced. Suddenly, though, I realized he'd gone silent, staring off into the distance, finished with his portrait painting. After taking a sip of his pint, he turned and looked me straight in the eye.

"'Ow about you?"

The question snapped me back to the moment feeling like a student who'd been caught daydreaming by the teacher; not only unprepared but without the faintest clue about the subject matter at hand. While Ian spent his life cultivating his answers to those questions, I'd spent mine ignoring them, too unsure of myself to muster the courage to even try to answer them in anything more than the most generic terms. Yet here they were, laid squarely at my feet – and I had nowhere to hide.

Unlike Ian, my life had been spent living moment to moment, always chasing the next self-gratifying distraction while forced to live with the consequences of previous poor decisions, each rooted in the same self-indulgent quest. Unlike Ian, whose roadmap was clear, I was lost in life, mired in an increasingly poisoned marriage more focused on selfishness, bitterness and resentment than selflessness, love and forgiveness. Like it had for so long, life seemed purposeless. For me, even the good things - wonderful times like the Flem Cup - were transient, momentary pleasures on the river of life, a river filled with empty feelings of disappointment and unrealized expectations, the pain of broken relationships and, somewhere in the future, the ultimate uncertainty that death represented.

Despite our ongoing problems, my marriage kept moving forward, one day at a time. In 1995, we added a third child – a son – and I re-committed myself to remaining married for my children's sake, focusing my energies on doing what my father had done – being a good provider. I was earning enough to pay all the bills so my wife could stay home with the kids. Wanting to improve on what I had gotten from my father, I also vowed to be as involved in my kid's lives as possible in whatever ways I could.

As selfishness continued to drive my life, the seeds of resentment and bitterness grew and grew within my wife. By 2002, resentment over some past grievance I'd committed was never more than an argument or comment away from bubbling up to the surface, a condition that began to manifest itself in incredibly destructive ways. There was also the fact that her own upbringing was diametrically opposed to the old school American parenting philosophy I was raised with.

When I did try to do things for and with my kids, I was accused of doing it only for selfish reasons. Coaching the kid's sports teams or trying to spend time teaching them something I loved like golf would only result in accusations about how selfish I was or how I was pushing them into something that only I wanted. Whenever my priorities around the house were not hers, I was being lazy and those two words – lazy and selfish – would be used openly, frequently and indiscriminately, even with the children right there.

Having naively thought that we would never involve the kids in our differences, I would beg her not to say things like that in front of the children. *They were innocent little sponges*, I would say, knowing they absorbed anything they were exposed to, good or bad. After any argument, I would inevitably come out the bad guy to the kids; the one with the louder voice and angrier face, the one who would sullenly retreat to the basement while Mommy packed them up for a visit to a friend's house, a place where she would continue to vent about me in front of them. There were even times when her resentment spilled over at social events, in front of friends, acquaintances and even family members. My resentment and bitterness grew but it was no match for hers.

Not knowing what to do, I did nothing beyond continuing to numb myself against what was happening, constructing a wall of indifference towards her, convincing myself I didn't care, that the things she said didn't matter and that I would only stay until the kids were grown.

What I didn't realize yet was that I had already lost them.

No matter what I did or what I said or how I tried to be involved in a positive way in my children's lives, the distance between us was inexorably growing, a chasm filled with increasing disrespect and apathy over my role in the family. They had been taught that a father was of no value, irrelevant to the family, other than financially, of course, and in that regard I could never provide enough. The kids viewed the things I loved and cared about as unworthy of respect so why should I be any different? It was a chasm I had no clue how to cross and as it grew, I became more and more of a basket case, torn between my urge to escape into a shell and my desire to stand up for myself and my relationship with the kids. The shell usually won. My addictions and obsessions were consuming me as I watched the truly important things in my life drift away, powerless to stop their inexorable progress.

Spiritually, I was just as lost. Over the years, I'd come to the belief that there had to be *something* out there – but what? I still had little use for religions and the rules and rituals and blind belief they required yet couldn't get past the beauty and complexity of the world around me. I simply could not bring myself to believe it had all come from nothing. I vaguely believed in some sort of higher power, a belief that, like shifting sand, I could make of what I wanted.

No one knew of the secrets I carried; not my mother or my brother or Jack Jr. and certainly not Ian, for whom I always wanted to put on my best, most "together" face. After all, my entire life had been spent making people believe I had it all together and I had become rather good at it. One of my escapes from the hopeless circumstances of my own life was living vicariously through Ian and his dreams, an exercise now shattered by his innocent question. I was in a panic, caught between the risk of unleashing a web of lies and the bitter truth.

As I frantically pondered my response, Ian offered the question again, thinking perhaps I hadn't heard him. Searching one last time for some semblance of a viable future dream or hope, I came up empty.

"I . . . . . don't . . . . . . know."

Dropping my head to avoid his gaze, I shook it slowly, feeling his eyes upon me. His silence offered me time to amend my pathetic answer but when I finally looked up, I could only shrug my shoulders, silently announcing that it was, indeed, my final answer. As the awkward silence that ensued lingered on, Ian picked up his beer for a sip. Swallowing, he looked at me once again with what I interpreted as a sad smile on his face.

"Sounds like a good plan."

Had I said it, it would have sounded snarky, snide and sarcastic but Ian never sounded that way, regardless of how he meant it. In his words I heard a profound sense of sadness. From his perspective, I was sure he had to be wondering how anyone could be so lost in life. Perhaps he was even slightly resentful, his own prognosis always there on the fringes of his consciousness. Staring back at him for a moment, I smiled, chuckling as I shook my head again, reassuring him that no offense had been taken at his uncomfortable attempt at humor. How could there be? His innocent question had simply exposed the truth of my life, tearing away my facade and laying bare the consequences of what I knew to be my own foolish choices; consequences that had led me to nothing but emptiness, loneliness and hopelessness. Needless to say, the conversation quickly shifted to another subject.

The next night would be my last before heading home and we spent it back at the Angel with Ian holding court. With Greg, Smokin' Joe, Milo, Phil and Swampy adding their wise-cracking abilities to the evening's festivities, it was a riotous evening. I even met Super Dave's replacement, Gary Jarvis, or "Jarvo" as he was universally known. An 8 handicap, Jarvo added his own terrific sense of humor, including a spot-on imitation of Ian, a talent that would bring tears of laughter to our eyes more than once.

Like the England side, our team for Ireland would include only a single change from 2001 but it was not the one everyone had expected. Matt, the anticipated casualty, would be returning (thanks to his outstanding grades in school and a large cash infusion from dear old Dad) while Terry would not, a victim of personal issues. When he let me know he would not be coming, we quickly went to the obvious choice to replace him - AJ - and he gladly accepted. With my trip over and anticipation of the '02 Cup building, I had a new future date to focus on.

Over the rest of the summer, I would speak to Ian every week or two, always fishing for storylines for the website. Determined to improve my game for the upcoming Cup, I was also playing golf more than ever but the results were, at best, erratic; at worst, highly disappointing. With high hopes, Jack Jr. and I entered the Harkers Hollow match play championship in late August only to be trounced in the first round, 4&3, in a match that wasn't even as close as the lopsided score indicated. Even more concerning was the fact that we were not alone in our futility. The entire team was playing infrequently and, with the exception of Matt and AJ, poorly. Although our hopes were high, genuine optimism was not.

The news story side was little better. Despite my best efforts, Team England remained silent. Finally, I deployed Indie and the power of the press, posting a couple of stories containing references to empty promises of a reliable England correspondent who would periodically submit news. Finally, I got an email from Swampy, perhaps seeking to stir things up a bit on his end. Not so coincidentally, it arrived right after Europe had decisively won the 2002 Ryder Cup.

An Open Letter From Swampy

It is that time of year again. The leaves are dropping from the trees, Team Europe has once again reminded America why she rarely plays international team sports and we are but a few days away from the 2002 Flem Cup.

As a recap, Team England beat the Yanks like rented mules in 2001, kicking their arses all over the silky-smooth greens of Myrtle Beach. The Yanks had no reply to the tight knit unit representing these ancient and historic isles, collapsing into a pathetic, quivering mass of hooks, slices, duffs and missed putts when it mattered most. It was no surprise to us when we claimed victory with nearly half the matches still out on the course.

Now I am sure that the Yanks have been practising hard in an attempt to put up a better showing this time around. Frankly, that shouldn't be hard. For our part, we must err on the side of caution and assume that they will be greater than the sum of their parts. Again, that shouldn't be hard. I'm told bookmakers won't even take any action on our side - we are considered simply too much of a sure thing! How very sad - for America.

My only hope is that the '02 Flem Cup can be played in a more sportsman-like manner, with both sides displaying all the honourable qualities expected while giving or receiving no quarter. Unfortunately, with Captain Dow leading our foes that may be little more than a pipe dream. Still, our hope - like the Flem Cup in the Rave Cave - remains.

Finally, with all due respect to Jack Tanis Jr., a fine man and honourable foe, I would like to assure everyone that when it comes to golf, I AM young Matt Tanis' daddy and when we are paired again, as we inevitably will be, it is I who will be victorious this time round.

Swampy . . . . . OUT!

***

By late September, the matches were set and the Cup was ready to go except for one news article I'd been crafting for a week or so. Designed to divert England's attention from the task at hand, it was timed for maximum impact, published only two days before travel day. At its core was one of the truly marvelous aspects of the game of golf: the handicap system. A single handicap stroke can change the result of a close match and, in doing so, conceivably alter the outcome of the entire Flem Cup.

We had long known that a problem existed in correlating English and American handicaps since they are calculated under different methodologies. For Ireland, Ian had unilaterally decided to use the English R&A system rather than the American USGA system and although no one disputed his right to do so (England was home side) or the logic behind the change (Irish courses operate under R&A guidelines), I'd found an angle to exploit in my never ending quest for an advantage.

On a whim, I had decided to compare the handicaps of the players under Ian's system with what they would have been had we used our normal methodology. The results were so striking that I immediately set about compiling - complete with charts and graphs - a detailed impact study which I titled: *Impact Assessment for the New-Assignment of Strokes System* (IAN-ASS for short).

The report showed how various Yanks would gain strokes on each of the first two days - 6 strokes total - over what they would have gotten using our old methodology in what Indie termed a "stunning and significant development". A list of affected holes and matches was published and in an "interview" I graciously allowed, I announced that I'd instructed my affected players to state "this is a Jennings Stroke Hole" on the tee of any of those holes. Within hours, I began receiving emails concerning the article, each one recounting how the Angel Inn had been in a complete uproar the previous night - with Ian forced to defend his perfectly reasonable action.

"Remember now . . . they still have to actually WIN those holes . . . and knowing them they won't" he protested with as much confidence as he could muster.

Swampy, for one, was particularly impressed with the detail of the study provided.

"This is classic journalism. The best article ever by a country mile! Is it all true? It is so complicated I can't work it out with my brain!"

I smiled to myself, agreeing with Swampy on both the quality of the article and the limits of his brain. Having already decided that Indie would go dark until our arrival in the Emerald Isle, I left the data to fend for itself, knowing Ian was right about one thing: the extra strokes would only matter if we took advantage on those specific holes - and that was a big if. Even less likely was the hope that one of the holes would affect the outcome of a match. Despite those details, I was satisfied that the effort had served its purpose - to disrupt and distract the Brits on the eve of the Cup.

13

Ireland

Following uneventful trips, the two teams arrived at the Woodstock Hotel just outside of Ennis, Ireland around lunchtime on Thursday, October 3. After settling in, we broke into groups and played a practice round at the hotel golf course. The normally conservative and mild-mannered Chris had done his part in the psychological war by dying his hair blonde for the trip and it took about a millisecond for Swampy to dub him Sven, a moniker that would be around far longer than the dye job. After a few pints of Guinness and some dinner, we all retired, weary from the trip and knowing that Lahinch, probably the most difficult test we would face all week, awaited us in the morning.

The official term "links" refers to a course built on the sandy land that links the bedrock of solid land to the sea. Great links courses embrace the natural contours of the land; featuring holes that wind their way over, around and through the dunes. Greens, fairways, bunkers and perhaps a small strip of intermediate rough are the only parts maintained by human hands with the rest being left in its natural state.

Beyond any intermediate rough lies the long, wispy fescue grasses, often concealing a heavy, thick underlayment of rye grass. Even when it is fairly sparse, seemingly innocuous fescue can wrap itself around the shaft during the downswing, twisting the club and sending the ball who knows where. When there is a thick grass underlayment, it often simply swallows the ball whole. Trees, on the other hand, are rare and, frankly, unnecessary, the long grass being a more than adequate penalty for any wayward shot.

Some courses feature gorse, the most ruthlessly efficient ball eating bush ever devised by nature, and all have fiendishly evil bunkers that might as well be black holes, sucking in any balls that get too close and forcing a sideways or even backwards recovery shot. With sandy soil providing excellent drainage and the constant wind sweeping away any residual moisture, the hard, dry, undulating fairways encourage balls to roll for great distances, an invitation to end up in all sorts of nasty and unexpected places. With the greens nearly as hard and unreceptive as the fairways, the *fire at the pin* strategy commonly used in the U.S. is taken completely out of play.

The most feared element on any links course, though, is the wind. Prevailing winds of 15-25 mph are enough to turn a controlled fade or draw into an out of control slice or hook, knock a seemingly well struck approach shot into a pot bunker short of the green or send it bounding long into whatever trouble lurks beyond. Elements like rain, heat and cold can be handled with the right preparation and equipment but wind is different, a physical force that changes ball flights while altering golf swings through the fear it generates.

It was against this backdrop that we arrived at Lahinch, universally considered one of the finest links courses in the world. With an idyllic location at the east end of an inlet on the west coast of Ireland, the combination of prime real estate and the architectural brilliance of Old Tom Morris and, years later, Dr. Alister MacKenzie, made Lahinch a world-class track.

Two exquisite examples of the brilliant marriage between course and nature are the 4th and 5th holes. The 4th is one of the great par 4 holes in all of golf, one that requires pinpoint accuracy, abundant courage and, perhaps most important, a bit of luck. From a slightly elevated tee, you gaze across a sea of long, rippling fescue to the fairway's edge about 180 yards away. From there, the fairway angles away from the tee at about 1 or 2 o'clock, making your choice of line absolutely critical. Going at the nearest point in the fairway brings the far side (and a near certain lost ball) into play and effectively turns the hole into a par 5. Aiming further right increases the distance you need to carry to reach the fairway and brings the right side into play. The optimal tee shot will be long with a left to right trajectory but danger lurks everywhere and any slight misdirection – short or long, left or right – is a potential lost ball.

About 280 yards from the tee, the fairway turns doglegs back to the left before abruptly ending at the base of Klondyke Hill, a massive sand dune 120 yards wide and 100 feet high that simply rises up out of the fairway. Covered in tall grass and a few swatches of open sand, the monster looms in the distance from the tee. With no way around Klondyke, the only option is to go over it, guided only by a V-shaped mound on top for an approximate line to the green.

Once clear of Klondyke, the fairway runs gently downhill to a large green that not only slopes front to back but is guarded close behind by a stone wall that marks the course boundary – out of bounds. Shots that reach the green on the fly have little chance of stopping before they reach the wall. The best chance for success is to land your ball well short of the green, leaving its fate to the vagaries of the rolling fairway. A bogey is a good score on the truly remarkable hole.

The following hole, the 5th, is the course's signature hole and, like the 4th, it has remained unchanged from Old Tom Morris' original design. Named "The Dell", it is a short, blind par 3. With the hourglass-shaped green set in the midst of several high, sprawling dunes, even the flagstick is completely obscured from the tee box and although it measures only 140-160 yard, the prevailing wind usually makes it play longer; sometimes much longer. The highest of these dunes stands squarely in front of the green, a white marker stone just right of its peak the only guide for your line. Missing the green will likely cost you your ball since the dunes are covered in fescue and a thick undergrowth of rye grass that permit only the luckiest bounces to reach the bottom – and safety.

Exiting our coach upon arrival, we were greeted by strong winds of 30+ mph blowing in from the west. Everywhere we looked there was nothing but tall fescue, waving and beckoning in amusement. I cocked my head, wondering if that was faint laughter I heard. As I scanned the beautiful yet forbidding landscape, I knew there would be no place to hide.

Ever the showman, Ian was reveling in his first chance to host the Cup, even going so far as to arrange with the club pro to hit a ceremonial first shot to kick off the 2002 Cup in style. After all, this was a serious international competition and, as such, worthy of the respect of all serious golfers. After posing for pictures, we all gathered to the side of the tee as Ian and I solemnly shook hands, wishing each other the best of luck as cameras snapped. Photo-op complete, I walked across the tee to join the others as Ian prepared himself to strike the ceremonial first shot of the 2002 Flem Cup. *This is it*, I thought; my favorite moment of the entire year.

Over my shoulder, I noticed the club pro stepping out of his office to observe the solemn moment, a moment he, himself, had sanctioned. Tradition is important but nowhere is it more revered than in these ancient isles. Behind the pro, additional staff paused to witness the ceremonial first strike, unsure who these golfing giants were or what important international competition they were witnessing yet drawn by the pomp and circumstance of the moment. Driver in hand, Ian solemnly stepped behind the ball, gauging his line as the flags above the clubhouse snapped taut in the breeze. We all stood silent, cameras in hand.

Ready to hit, Ian stepped up to address the ball, assuming his familiar stance. With his feet set wide for balance and stability, his face was all business as he focused on the task at hand. *Better him than me* I thought, remembering how nerve-racking a shot like that, with dozens of eyes watching, could be.

Finally, his familiar little heel bounce announced his swing was about to start. Sure enough, an instant later the club began its graceful arc, back, away from the ball and up until, hands held high, the shaft reached parallel to the ground, perfectly positioned as he paused for a moment. Then, the driver head began its return trip, his hands coming down and around, releasing the club head, now just a blur, through the impact zone as we heard – POOF.

Although I could see most heads turning, instinctively, searching against the grey sky for any sign of the ball, my eyes remained on Ian, transfixed by the curious cloud of smoke created by the impact, a cloud that was rapidly expanding as it was carried towards us by the wind. Ian stood motionless, perfectly silhouetted behind the cloud, hands held high in follow-through. By the time we were engulfed, we had all caught on to the gag and everyone was howling with laughter, having witnessed a simple exploding ball trick carried out in incredibly dramatic fashion. Brilliant! Simply brilliant!

The club pro, on the other hand, did not seem amused, scowling as he turned and stalked back to the clubhouse, clearly unappreciative of being taken in by Ian's false sincerity. His retreat allowed the young staff members, unsure of how to react in their boss's presence, to let loose and they quickly began howling with laughter at the brilliantly conceived and perfectly executed gag.

With the tension broken, we could now get down to playing some real golf, if that's what it could rightly be called. With the exception of a pair of excellent rounds by Ian and Greg, his playing partner, who each managed a 4-over par net, the *average* score for the rest of us was 13 over par *net*. With some late clutch putting, the dynamic duo of Milo and Phil continued being a thorn in our collective side in Match 1 by knocking off Jack Sr. and me, 3&2. In Match 2, Swampy's shot a normally pedestrian 28 Stableford but in the challenging conditions, his score was good enough for 4th best of the day and he dominated the group as he and Ray topped Lou and Pat, 4&2.

Match 3 was the most anticipated match of the day, pitting Ian and Greg against AJ and Matt, the four low handicap golfers off of 6. AJ and Matt, however, were thrashed by the two Brits, 4&3. The match was actually well played on both sides, featuring no fewer than 9 natural birdies, but Greg dominated the front-9 and the Brits held a 3 up lead at the turn. When Matt chipped in for birdie on 10, he and his uncle had hopes of putting on a charge but when Ian followed by draining a 20 foot birdie putt for a halve, that hope was dashed and the Brits coasted home from there.

With England having a perfect day, we badly needed a point out of the final match. Having played in the first group, I was drowning my sorrows on my second beer by the time Ian's group strolled in and although we already knew their result, the big news was an update on the final match: Jack Jr. and brother Sven were dormie 3. A win would make it 3-1 and I felt much better, knowing that tomorrow we had set the matches.

Unfortunately for us, Smokin' Joe had other ideas.

After winning the difficult 16th with a par, he'd followed up with another par win on the equally tough 17th to keep England's hopes for an unlikely halve alive. Finally, on the final hole, an uphill par 5, he hit a knockdown 9-iron from 110 yards, drawing it into the stiff crosswind and landing on the front of the green as we watched from the veranda. Taking one big bounce, the shot checked up perfectly, spinning to a stop 6 feet below the pin. By now, word had spread through the clubhouse of the international match and the veranda crowd had been swelled by locals who, naturally, were rooting for the England side. With Joe's great shot and the loud roar of approval that followed, even more emerged from the grill room, eager to find out what was happening.

After conceding Jack's short par putt, Joe stalked his putt, examining it from every angle before settling in. I had no doubt he would drain his birdie putt to get England the unlikely halve and when he did, an even mightier roar went up from the crowd, now three deep at the rail. Officially it was a halve but to us, it might as well have been a loss, an unexpected body blow that left us 3 points behind rather than 2. *So much for handicap analysis* I thought to myself. Jennings' Stroke Holes? What Jennings' Stroke Holes?

The day had been an unmitigated disaster for our side, our scores *averaging* a dreadful 21 Stableford, or 15 over par net. The top five net scorers were Brits while the bottom five were Yanks. The only bright spot, I told myself, was that we had time to fight our way back into the match, one point at a time. I was confident in the matches we'd set for Day 2 at Ballybunion, knowing I had once again threatened the line of good sportsmanship by unilaterally arranging for caddies for my team. Although I didn't know if Ian had done the same, my strong suspicion was that he had not. I also had no idea if caddies would be readily available whether reserved or not but I had made sure we were prepared when I'd contacted the course months earlier with an email requesting caddies be reserved for four pairs of Americans, a request Ballybunion had happily obliged. I then kept the tidbit to myself, leaving the issue of caddies aside throughout the run-up to the Cup.

Bumping down the Irish roads, I thought back to England's big win on Day 2 in 2001, harkening back to the other advantage I'd discovered that night. Team England could be, and often was, their own worst enemy, especially after a dominating day like this. With plans in place for a welcome dinner followed by a night out in Ennis, I had high hopes for some help in our comeback quest and sure enough, by the time we returned to the hotel the following afternoon, I'd pieced together enough snippets of what had transpired the night before to write the hilarious recap. Leaning back in my chair as the article posted, I smiled to myself as I imagined the tears of laughter that would surely follow at the Angel.

Wild Night in Ennis, G. Matthews Implicated in Slush Fund; England Players Find Themselves With More Than A Wee Problem

By: Datzit Indaruf, Flem Cup Correspondent

ENNIS, IRELAND Oct.5 – In the first controversy of the 2002 Flem Cup, charges have been leveled against Stud-Muffin Matthews concerning a rather large "drinking" fund he accumulated before disappearing, cash in hand, into the seedy Ennis nightclub scene. Being a bilateral issue, players on both sides were upset at the loss of important drinking funds but as the night unfolded, those charges paled in comparison to the far more weighty shenanigans that would follow.

Like the now infamous karaoke night of 2001, the evening began with Team England celebrating the day's domination of the overmatched American side. Advertised as a "wel-

come dinner", all eight Brits and five of the Yanks (everyone not named Matt or Jack) hit the town of Ennis as Greg quickly solicited a drinking fund of €20 per man (about $25). After collecting the money, he suddenly decided he was not hungry, bowing out of the planned dinner at 8:30 with unindicted co-conspirators Jarvo and Sven in tow. As the other players looked on, the three disappeared into the Ennis night.

It was shortly after that, sometime between the starters and main course, that Father-of-Stud-Muffin Ray went missing. Initially, it was suggested that he might be part of a father / son scam but that possibility was quickly dismissed as calmer heads recalled that Ray was not, by any stretch of the imagination, the type of party animal who would attempt such a dastardly deed. Eventually it was assumed he was tired and went back to the hotel, allowing the meal to proceed, sans Ray.

Unexpectedly, as the meal wound down, Greg returned, wild eyed and raving about a nightclub called "Queens". Brushing off questions of his father's whereabouts, Greg latched onto American Captain Dow, Swampy and Pat Slack before heading back out into the night, recruits in tow. Immediately thinking better of their decision, Scott and Swampy broke away, opting for a cab back to the hotel but Pat, in a decision he would later describe as "one of the worst of my entire life", forged on. Finally, with most of the crowd gone and the restaurant preparing to close in 30 minutes, the dinner party dispersed.

It was around 11pm that the cleaning crews entered the rest rooms only to find someone lagging behind in a men's room stall. After pounding and yelling failed to roust the sluggard, concern set in and the police summoned. Jimmying the stall lock, the cops slowly pushed the door open only to find an older man slumped over and non-responsive, sitting on the bog, head on his knees, pants around his ankles.

Fearing tragedy, the policeman reached out to gently nudge the man. No response. Another gentle nudge gave the same result. Finally, as the assemblage feared the worst, Ray Matthews slowly stirred, lifting his head, squinting and blinking as he tried desperately to connect where he was with what he was doing and who all these people were. Finally, as consciousness slowly crept back in, Ray started answering simple questions that the police asked, assuring them that he had simply fallen asleep and, other than his disorientation, felt fine.

Having put their concerns to rest, Ray started to rise – but something was holding him back. He tried a second time, still unable to move. Once again, the police and cleaning crew became concerned. Was it a locked up back? Legs fast asleep? Equilibrium thrown off? No one was sure but 2 hours on the bog couldn't be good.

Ray, however, knew exactly what the problem was. Over the time he'd sat there, his butt had slowly become one with the toilet seat until a near-perfect seal had formed between them. Now, having also forced enough air out of the cavity to form a bit of a vacuum, the pressure differential was enough to hold him firmly in place. Realizing this, he began rocking back and forth as his fingers tried to pull his butt skin away from the seat, slowly breaking the seal and allowing air to seep back in. Finally, after 30 or 40 seconds of rocking, enough air seeped in to release his cheeks. Then – and only then – could he begin to deal with the other problems of a sore back, sleeping legs and distorted equilibrium. It would be near midnight before England's Ringbearer would get back to his room at the hotel.

In the meantime, unconfirmed paparazzi reports from the nightclub Queens had Jarvo and Greg spending inordinate amounts of time and money, their attentions being lavished on a "young blonde Swedish-looking man" later identified as one "Sven Dover". A fourth man, reportedly Sven's much older and less attractive brother Ben, was also with the group but there was no doubt as to the primary object of the Brit's attentions. Finally, the hard-partying foursome returned to the hotel, heading off to bed around 12:30.

But the night was not over. Not by a long shot.

It was around 1 am that Ray was woken up to the sound of grunting and banging in the room. Turning on the light, there was Greg, naked as a jaybird as he vainly tried to open the window.

"Whatchya doing?" Ray asked blearily.

"Gotta wee", Greg grunted, continuing his efforts.

"No, no, you drunken git. That's the window. Bog's that way" said Ray, pointing towards the bathroom. Annoyed, he rolled over to go back to sleep but as he lay there, he heard the *door latch click followed by the door opening and then banging shut. Through the fog of being half asleep, Ray took a moment to realize that the noises he'd just heard didn't sound like the bathroom door. Not at all. Rolling back over, he opened one eye only to see the bathroom door open, the light out – and no sign of Greg.*

Sensing the hotel would frown on two naked men running round their hallways, Ray frantically threw on some pants and a shirt before racing after his son. Flinging the door open, he half expected to find Greg peeing right there in the hall. No dice. He looked left. Nothing. He looked right. Nothing. Finally, a loud ding from down the hall signaled that the elevator had arrived.

In a panic, Ray took off, racing towards the elevators at top speed – but it was too late. With the doors closed and the elevator slowly starting down, Ray flew down the nearby stairwell, taking two and three steps at a time in hope of beating the elevator to the lobby. Fully awake and engaged at this point, Ray's imagination ran wild with the possible outcomes of the dire situation – and none were good. A quiet, dignified man much like Jack Sr., he was mortified at the thought of his son in this condition. Finally, with one last leap, he reached the ground floor.

Bursting through the door to the lobby, Ray was enormously relieved to find he had, indeed, beaten the lift down. Hopefully, he could just slip in and get Greg back to the room with no one the wiser. 'Don't be peeing, Greg. Just don't be peeing' he thought to himself as the lift came to an agonizingly slow stop.

It was just about then, with his desperation at its zenith, that Ray first heard the crowd coming down the hall behind him. With a renewed sense of urgency, he did his best to mentally will the elevator down and the doors open, whispering C'mon, C'MON *out loud as it inched to a complete stop. Finally, as it settled and the doors began to open, Ray allowed himself a slight head turn to peek, fearful of who, exactly, was approaching.*

The entire wedding party had come to see the happy couple off for their wedding night, 40 people, maybe more, heading towards the lift and the grand sendoff. As Ray watched the crowd approach, mortified, the wedding party stopped as one, mouths wide open in return. Only they weren't looking at Ray; they were looking past him, fixated on what was happening behind. Ray closed his eyes, hopes of a dignified exit dashed. He didn't need to turn round to see what was happening behind him. He could hear it.

Head back, feet splayed wide and back arched, there was Greg, silhouetted in all his glory, a mighty stream unleashed against the wall of the lift. Like heavy rain on a tin roof, the sound was unmistakable. Finally, Ray collected himself, calmly walking over and spreading his shirt as wide as possible to cover his naked son as best he could as the intensity of Greg's pee slowly diminished, dropping in volume as the stream slowly lowered down the wall. Oblivious to the watching crowd, Greg finished the only way one can – with a loud "aaahhhhhh".

Everyone in the wedding party plus a couple of hotel staff who had wandered by was frozen in place, unable to speak or move as they watched the situation play out.

"Sorry" Ray called out over his shoulder. "'E's drunk and sleep walking. I'll get this cleaned up."

With the realization that Greg was, indeed, sleep-walking, the crowd, led by the bride breaking the ice by collapsing in a heap, broke into complete hysterics, leaning against walls and each other's shoulders, tears coming down more than a few cheeks as they laughed. Ray, now in the elevator with Greg, could only wave meekly as the elevator doors closed. As for the wedding party, they would take the stairs.

***

It was during breakfast on Day 2 that Ian learned of Greg's previous night's escapades despite Ray's best efforts to keep it on the down low. The hotel staff knew what happened, who did it and what group he was part of so it didn't take long for the story to come out and once it did, it spread like wildfire. Adding to the morning's comedy was that upon arriving downstairs, Greg, who was horribly hung over, had no clue as to what had happened. Immediately upon seeing his friend show up, Swampy pounced.

"I understand you 'ad a wee problem last night?"

Greg just stared, red-eyed and expressionless, futilely trying to attach meaning to Swampy's still oblique reference. We snickered, fully understanding the state he was in.

"something 'bout an unauthorized leak . . . . . ?"

Shaking his head, Greg finally shrugged and moved on, clueless about the meaning behind the comments. Even Ray, who had come to terms with the secret having gotten out, couldn't help himself by now, chuckling and shaking his head as he smiled.

Ian's initial amusement turned to concern, though, when he realized his playing partner, Jarvo, was possibly in worse shape than Greg. It wasn't until departure time that Jarvo finally staggered downstairs, zombie-like, lumbering slowly towards the bus, dark sunglasses doing their best to protect his eyes from the pain of light. Lou and I would be their opponents in a Captain's match and this was a problem Ian didn't want or need.

For the rest of us, the most disconcerting part of Jarvo's condition were the *Spinkhill Specials* he was unleashing. Three times he managed to clear the entire bus before launching a fourth as we were driving away, trapped us like rats. Windows flung open, we gasped for fresh air between threats on Jarvo's life and desperate pleas for mercy. Jarvo, however, remained, to all appearances, not only unresponsive but entirely lifeless. Finally, after an hour or more, we reached the picturesque village of Ballybunion, home to one of the best known courses in all of Ireland and the world: Ballybunion's Old Course.

Like Lahinch, Ballybunion is a true links course. Located in the Shannon estuary, the most memorable hole is probably the 11th, a brutal 450 yard par 4 that runs south along the top of the seaside dunes. From the tee, the narrow, segmented fairway appears as a small, green oasis in a sea of long, rippling fescue. Only two well-judged and executed shots provide a reasonable chance at a routine par and the small, pear-shaped green bordered by the grass-covered dunes and beach beyond make the approach shot a true knee-knocker.

Unlike the previous day, the weather was surprisingly sunny and warm with only a light breeze. Entering the clubhouse, I joined Ian at the counter to ask about our caddies. Taken aback, Ian looked at me with what I could only describe as a look of shock, clearly taken off guard by my one-sided advance planning. After being assured our caddies were ready and waiting, Ian addressed the gentleman behind the counter.

"Do you have any more caddies available?"

"I'm sorry sir but no." came the terse reply. I smiled as Ian shook his head and walked away.

In the first match out, Jack Jr. and Matt came out strong against Joe and Ray, intent on making up for the previous day. Making the turn 4-up, the two would coast home with a 4&2 win.

Ours was the second match out and we, too, jumped out quickly, claiming a 2 up lead after 3 holes. At that point, inexplicably, we both collapsed, providing Ian with virtually no resistance as he personally reeled off six wins on the trot to grab a 4 up England lead at the turn. Reeling from the onslaught, we fought to regain our composure and slowly cut into the lead, managing to claw our way back to only 2 down after 14. On 15, a 200+ yard par 3, I struck perhaps my best shot of the day, sending a 1 iron straight at the pin and leaving myself 15 feet for birdie. Back to 1 down and charging, another par on 16 was thwarted by Ian's matching par and when my second on 17 sliced up onto the dunes, another of his routine pars was enough to close us out, 2&1.

The third match pitted Jack Sr. and Pat, who played brilliantly against the still-suffering Greg and Swampy. Despite outstanding play from our side, the Spinkhill lads hung around, refusing to succumb as the two ham and egged well enough to somehow reach 17 tee all square. At that point, though, Jack Sr. took the match into his own hands, finishing with a pair of pars to win the match 2 up.

The final match of the day was crucial for us and to get it Sven and AJ would have to knock off the seemingly unbeatable dynamic duo: Phil and Milo. Talking to Sven before the match, he passed along a cryptic yet prophetic comment concerning how the day might unfold:

"They may be Batman and Robin but AJ is Superman and I'm Lois Lane".

Wondering what the hell really *had* happened at Queens the night before, it was all I could do to walk away - quickly. Sure enough, after making the turn 2 up, our lads coasted in with a hard fought 3&2 win. Milo and Phil's reign of terror had been officially ended and the day's 3-1 margin brought the Cup score to 4-1/2 to 3-1/2 in favor of England. Just as I'd hoped, our Day 1 debacle was nearly made up for – and slightly ahead of schedule. It was, once again, a dogfight.

The untold story of the day was the difference the caddies had made in providing local knowledge, club choices, putt reads and the exact time of day to within 3 minutes without a watch. Talking to Ian later over a pint, he took my long range strategic planning in stride, unable to resist the accompanying dig.

"I 'ave to give you credit, lad. The caddies clearly made a difference. Too bad about you, though, but even a great caddy can only do so much . . . you know?"

Shrugging off his cutting humor, I was just happy to get as close as possible but still retain the advantage of setting the next day's matches, an advantage that history was proving to be significant. With five days of 4 ball matches over the past two years in the books, the team setting the matches had won each of the days, often decisively. Except for it being my loss, the day's outcome was perfect.

Ian had his own reasons for being pleased. His team leading, he had won both his matches and he was leading the Stableford, two points clear of Jack Sr. and Matt and four clear of AJ. As the bus cruised home, the Team England brain trust huddled to sort out the pairings for the next day at Adare, a wonderful inland course built around the striking centerpiece of Adare Manor.

With their aura of invincibility pierced and their winning streak ended, Ian decided to split up the dynamic duo of Phil and Milo, taking Milo as his own part-ner. England's other pairs were Ray and Phil, Joe and Swampy and Greg and Jarvo. The power pairing was clearly Ian and Milo, each of whom was playing solid, steady golf. Once back at the hotel, Ian settled into a comfy chair, sipping on a pint of Guinness and puffing on a Cuban cigar as Jack Jr., AJ and I huddled to discuss the matches and decide how to set them.

We decided we would try to steal one against Ray and Phil, choosing Jack Sr., who had been playing very well, and Lou, who had not. As our own power pairing, we decided to pair Pat and AJ, both coming off solid rounds, against Smokin' Joe and Swampy while Matt and Sven would face off against Jarvo and Greg. That left Jack Jr. and I to take on Ian and Milo in another Captain's match. After announcing the matches, we settled in for a meal and a quiet evening, discussing the events of the day as we sipped on pints of Guinness and smoked Cuban cigars. By 10pm, we all headed up to bed.

The next morning dawned another surprisingly nice October morning – warm and sunny with only a light, refreshing breeze. Arriving in plenty of time for our tee times, we wandered through the magnificent grounds of Adare Manor as well as the massive Gothic-style house itself, built by local town villagers for a wealthy nobleman during the 1830s at the height of the great potato famine. Amazingly, we were told there is a different chimney for every week of the year and a different leaded glass window for every day of the year. With no driving range, we eventually made our way to the putting green as our tee times approached.

The first match out, AJ and Pat against Joe and Swampy, would turn out to be the lowest net scoring match of the week. Swampy played the role of underachiever despite a very solid 32 Stableford while Joe and AJ tied at 35 and Pat fired a still standing Cup record of 40 (4 under par net), breaking the previous best by 3 full shots and keying our deceptively easy 4&3 win.

The second match was our Captain's match and, like the day before, I came out focused and ready, eager to avenge the loss at Ballybunion, a loss in which I'd thrown away holes with sloppy, careless mistakes and concentration lapses. Despite my superior tee to green play early on, Ian would parry every one of my thrusts. After my routine par on 1 was halved by his 15 footer, he followed with an 8 footer on 2 to halve my bogey and a 20 footer on 3 to again halve my par, keeping the match all-square. Each putt he made only added to his confidence and my frustration, each of us knowing that soon enough, the worm would turn.

Heading to 7 with the match still level, the worm had done its thing and Jack and I were scrambling while Ian and Milo had settled into solid, steady golf. Having been unable to turn our solid early play into a lead, we would now pay the price as our opponents flawless play led to five wins over the next six holes. Suddenly, the match was as good as done with the Brits standing at dormie 5.

Worse still, by the time we'd reached 14, I'd become little more than a cheerleader, unable to make a solid ball strike or sink a putt. It was all on Jack and, with the Brits feeling supremely confident, he suddenly came alive, winning 14, 15 and 16 to keep the match going. On 17, he alone reached the long difficult par 4 in two and for the first time, I allowed myself a glimmer of hope about reaching 18 still alive, trying to re-focus myself and get my head back into the match. Unfortunately, Jack slid his birdie attempt about 4 feet past and lipped out coming back, allowing Ian's bogey to halve the hole and end the match in England's favor, 2&1.

Having split the first two matches, I was eager for news from behind. The latest I'd heard was that Sven and Matt were on their way to a lopsided win in the third match while Jack and Lou were 3 up against Ray and Phil on 14. If we could somehow hang on to those two wins, the resulting 3-1 margin would give us a 6-1/2 to 5-1/2 point lead going into Singles Day – a terrific turnaround considering where we were two days earlier.

Unbeknownst to us, though, Ray and Phil had suddenly turned things around. With wins on 14, 15 and 17, the match was level coming to the last hole, Adare's magnificent signature hole that finished at the foot of the Manor Castle.

Teeing off straight at the Castle, the Maigue River, a top-notch trout river, runs along the fairway all the way down the left side and past the green, which is located on the far bank some 500+ yards away. A massive drive would allow the boldest to try to get home in two, a feat no one in our group would attempt. No matter the length or angle of the approach shot, the target and its surroundings is a living work of art, framed magnificently by the lazy Maigue drifting by in front, a massive, sprawling Lebanon Cedar to the right, a high, impenetrable stand of trees on the left and a 10 foot high stone and brick wall topped by the lush, perfectly manicured Manor gardens behind. The final piece of the scene was Adare Manor House itself, towering over the regal scene as if placed there for that very purpose.

With Lou in for a net par, Ray was faced a 20 foot putt for par net birdie. Standing atop the garden wall, I was confident Ray's 2 putt would gain us a halve. Ray was having none of it, plunging a dagger into our hopes by draining his putt to win the match in dramatic fashion and send a cheer up from his teammates.

The Brits had stolen another match we'd thought we'd won, this time outright, and their lead was back to two with one match remaining. Fortunately for us, that one had ended long ago with a dominating 7&6 win by AJ and Matt, a match so lopsided that England did not capture a single hole. Particularly inexplicable was Greg's lackluster play. So many times in life, though, things that seem to happen for one reason or another occur for entirely different reasons and, as Paul Harvey would say, we were about to find out the *rest* of the story.

Standing in the pro shop, I was listening to Jarvo recount the circumstances of the elbow injury he'd sustained the previous night while hoisting his 10th or 11th pint of Guinness when something behind him caught my eye. Through the window I could see Greg standing perfectly still on the walkway next to the main building, looking out towards the car park as if someone were approaching. As I watched, he suddenly knelt down, opening his arms wide. My curiosity piqued, I headed outside just in time to see a small boy race up.

"Daddy, Daddy" he cried excitedly, flinging himself into Greg's arms and squeezing. Greg held him there for a long time, eyes closed, whispering into his little ear. I stood frozen in the doorway, transfixed by the spectacle, not wanting to move lest I disturb the moment. Others were similarly frozen as they watched the situation unfold.

Greg's divorce had been finalized earlier in 2002 but shortly before the final decree, his soon to be ex-wife moved back to Ireland to be closer to her family, taking their little boy, Charlie, with her. Only Greg's family and closest friends had known that today would be the first time Greg had seen Charlie in many months.

Like me, Greg had been a young man when he was married but unlike me, he had soon become a father. His marriage, however, had quickly soured and one of his ways of dealing with it was to escape. While my vehicle was pot, his was booze. In Myrtle Beach the previous year, he'd still been seeing his son frequently as he and his wife worked through the divorce details. Now, in 2002, everything had changed and the "golf" trip meant far more to Greg than just golf, turning his focus more and more to the few precious moments he'd be spending with his beloved son. Suddenly his wild behavior and sub-standard play made a whole lot more sense.

Charlie's voice sank to a whisper as he became aware that he was being watched. Suddenly feeling awkward at my intrusion on their moment, I and the others turned away so the family reunion with Dad, Grandpa Ray, Uncle Joe and good friends Ian and Swampy could play out. As our coach arrived, the two headed off to spend a few hours together.

As we started our drive back to the hotel, the coach was quiet. I, for one, was consumed with what I'd just seen, my thoughts turning to what was truly important in life. Staring out the window, the Irish countryside rolled past as I considered the emptiness of my own life. In my own family I felt like an outsider, someone whose presence was tolerated – but nothing more – yet I couldn't imagine the pain of Greg's situation, separated from his son by the Irish Sea. How I could have known so little about someone I'd considered little more than a happy go lucky friend literally minutes before. How could I be so disinterested, not even bothering to get to know the person behind the fun and the good times?

Really? I asked myself. *Who had I let in on my secrets?*

No one, the answer came back, *not a soul.*

I thought about the hopelessly ingrained resentment that dominated my marriage. Although I missed my wife, I knew from experience that the feeling was nothing more than an illusion. I knew she was filled with resentment and bitterness over my past lies, my indifference towards her and my inability to show her the love she wanted and needed. She couldn't forgive or forget those things, much less get past them.

I thought about my own children, of how they seemed to be drifting away from me, carried by the tide of the indifference and disrespect they'd been taught from birth – and I couldn't forgive *that.* So there we were, trapped in a bitter, angry and resentful marriage. Without forgiveness or an understanding of what a commitment to marriage is, nothing would ever change. Deep in my heart, I knew our marriage would never be anything more than what it had been for too long; loveless and bitter, broken beyond repair.

I thought back to Ian's question about hopes and dreams, wondering what I would have to focus on and care about once the Cup was over in 2 days. I dreaded that day with every fiber of my being, knowing the emptiness that waited. I shook myself, refusing to give in to my self-loathing and pity. Not yet, I told myself, not yet. We were still only one point down and this was still a match. There would be plenty of time to be depressed – why get a jump on it?

Looking around, Swampy and Smokin' Joe had joined Ian to discuss tomorrow's pairings. With the Cup score standing at 6-½ to 5-½ in England's favor, we retained the advantage of setting the matches but unlike last year, there was no chance of a playoff for the Cup. In case of a tie, England would retain it. That meant 4-½ of 8 would not be good enough. We would need 5 points to carry the Cup back home, a steep but surmountable hill. I leaned back in my seat, staring out the window as the lush, green Irish countryside slid by, shifting my thoughts to what our matchup strategy would be.

14

2002 Singles Day

By the time we'd reached the hotel, I had England's pairings in hand. Ian had just smiled that smarmy smile of his when he handed them over and I could tell he was brimming with confidence for himself and his team. Who could blame him? He'd won all three of his matches and led the Stableford by 7 full points over second place AJ and 15 over Milo, who stood third.

Heading straight to the lounge, Jack, AJ and I each ordered pints of Guinness before heading off to a secluded corner to discuss the matches. AJ spoke first.

"We need to go right at them. Strength for strength. Let me take on Ian."

Jack and I looked at each other, knowing each other's thoughts without saying a word. We simply could not afford a loss by AJ and although he *might* win, it was simply too risky.

"We know you want the challenge but we've got to do what's best for the team." Jack began. "You're playing really well and you may even beat Ian . . . but the way he's playing there's also a good chance you won't. We need five points and we need you to bring home a win."

"For the moment, let's concede a likely loss to Ian." I offered. "I think our strategy should be fairly simple. Based on Stableford scores, their four best players are Ian, Milo, Swampy and Joe. We need to beat their four worst golfers and hope for one other win. If we send our three worst golfers, the ones who have the worst Stableford totals so far, against their three best, we can set the most advantageous matches in the other five."

After scanning their faces for any sign of disagreement and finding none,I continued.

"Going strictly by Stableford scores, our three worst are me, Jack and Sven. But before we get to that, let's talk about attacking their weaknesses. Jack Sr. crushed Ray last year – that's a mental advantage. Let's redo that match. Despite his heroics today, I don't see Ray beating Jack."

Jack and AJ nodded at what seemed an obvious choice for first match out.

"We also need to beat Jarvo. He hasn't been playing well at all. What do you guys think of sending out Lou and trying to steal one? I know Lou hasn't been playing too well but he'll be getting nine shots and I don't think Jarvo will be up that. We know Lou is capable of anything and hopefully tomorrow he'll be good."

Knowing a win against Jarvo was a must have, Jack and AJ exchanged glances. Lou hadn't been shooting lights out but Jarvo hadn't either and if Lou could beat him, our chances would be boosted considerably. After a bit more discussion, we all agreed. Two down.

"OK. Let's move on to another must-have match," I continued, "Phil hasn't been playing well and we absolutely have to beat him. Suggestions?"

AJ wasted no time.

"Pat. The way he played today, he should kick Phil's butt."

Jack and I nodded our approval.

"All right, that's three down. We have one more must-have match to decide on before moving on to the tough ones: Greg. We all know what he went through today and, frankly, he may well be a basket case tomorrow but we can't afford to take him lightly. I've seen him shoot lights out – you saw him do it two days ago, AJ. We know how tough he can be."

I glanced in Jack's direction before continuing.

"Last year, we worked Matt in carefully, keeping him away from the really tough matches. It's clear he is ready for primetime. I'd like to put him against Greg."

Jack didn't hesitate.

"Absolutely, I agree. There's no doubt Matt's ready. Give him Greg."

"Oh, yeah - he'll be fine." Added AJ, having seen Matt up close today.

"OK. That's it for our four must-win matches. Let's move on to their top four players – Ian, Milo, Swampy and Joe. AJ, what do you think about taking on Joe? You'll actually be getting a stroke, which I love. Although Joe's a very tough match, I know you can beat him."

AJ, now on board with the strategy, quickly agreed.

"OK, I'll take him down. How about putting Sven up against Swampy?"

"That's exactly what I was thinking." Jack agreed, nodding. "He's played well the last two days and I think he can beat Swampy, or at least give him all he can handle."

"That leaves you and me to handle Ian and Milo, their top two guys." I said, looking at Jack. "We'll have nothing to lose and maybe we can catch a break. What do you think?"

"OK, I'll take Ian. I think I'm inside his head and if I can get off to a quick start, I think can beat him."

There was grim determination in his eyes. I couldn't tell if he was just trying to convince himself of his chances but I did know that with Jack, you never knew. He was as competitive as anyone I'd ever known and would give it his best shot. I'd seen quite enough of Ian's big Irish golf adventure the previous two days so I'd take on Milo, more than enough of a challenge in itself.

At AJ's request, we went through the list two more times, each time looking at one or two possible variations before finally settling back on the original plan. Looking over the list one last time, he seemed satisfied, commenting

"Yeah, I think this gives us the best shot possible."

"That's all we can hope for. I feel good about Jack Sr., Pat, you and Matt with Lou's match a tossup. Anything we can steal from Ian, Milo or Swampy is a bonus."

With that, we walked over to the table where everyone had congregated, anxious to discover their opponent for their 2 ball match. I handed the list to Ian, who eagerly looked it over as Swampy and Joe each peered over a shoulder. Pointing to one of the matches, Ian gave a laugh.

"I told you about that one!"

"I knew you they'd throw Jack at you." added Joe, pointing his cigarette at the paper while holding his pint up high. "That's from the Dunes two years ago, that is." For the first time, I realized that *would* be the match Ian would want, his chance at revenge not just for the loss but even more so for all the indignity he'd suffered since then. It had been an albatross around his neck for nearly 2 years, something he dearly wanted to be rid of. As I watched him scan the page, the smirk on his face was clear to see. Jack would have his hands full.

Setting up a row of fresh pints, we toasted our opponents, eagerly talking about our matches. By this time tomorrow, the 2002 Flem Cup would be decided on another true links course, Greg Norman's recently completed Doonbeg, set amidst towering dunes on the southwest coast.

Like all links courses, Doonbeg has some truly unique holes. The 14th hole, for one, is a par 3 with a long, narrow green carved into the side of a towering dune. Its precarious location gives it the surreal appearance of an island green hovering in mid-air, perfectly manicured and suspended in a sea of long, waving fescue with the Atlantic as a backdrop. At only 140 yards, an accurate tee shot would be at a premium.

The signature, though, is the 15th, a 440-yard par 4 with its green nestled in the midst of towering dunes that form a funnel broken only by a 30 yard wide opening providing access to the left side of the green. A wide ravine splits the fairway about 240 yards from the tee, forcing a layup off the tee followed by a long approach played either through the opening or by dropping a towering shot over the dunes.

To everyone's delight, caddies were available for everyone and before long, our first group headed to the 1st tee, a hole our side would manage to win in each of the first 7 matches. Ray, still invigorated from the previous day's clutch performance, lost 2 as well but hung tough, posting a solid front nine and losing no further ground to Jack's steady play. Meanwhile, Pat stayed hot, making the turn at 2 under par net while building a 4 up lead over the game but outmanned Phil.

In group two, Sven and Swampy embarked on what would become one of the most compelling and entertaining 2 ball matches in Cup lore. Sven's level of play had been improving all week and he broke out of the gate playing inspired golf but Swampy, who had been solid all week, stayed close, closing out the front nine with a clutch birdie to halve Sven and keep his deficit at 2 down. Lou also got off to a great start, jumping to a commanding 4 up lead before Jarvo reversed the tide, winning 6, 8 and 9 to make the turn only 1 down.

Paired with Matt, I watched the youngster grab a quick 3 up lead over Greg after five holes. On 6, Matt led off with a smart play on the short par 4, perfectly drawing a mid-iron down the middle of the fairway and avoiding the intimidating gauntlet of bunkers that lay strewn about the hole to leave only a wedge to the green. Having reached a pivotal point in the match, Greg decided it was time to make a move, pulling out his driver and ripping a low draw, perfectly negotiating the moonscape before rolling up on the green to 30 feet. Two putts later, his birdie cut Matt's lead to 2 and gave Greg a newfound spring in his step.

On the next hole, the 213 yard 7th, Greg hit a towering 4 iron inside of 6 feet before draining the putt for another birdie win. Suddenly, the match had tightened and if Matt was going to crack, it would be now, in the face of Greg's sudden onslaught. But Matt was a young man we'd watch mature and season over the past few years, growing from a hot-headed youngster to a slightly less hot-headed but far more focused and experienced veteran, familiar and comfortable with pressure. Like his father, he was a fierce competitor and I saw no sign of panic in his eyes; only calm, focused determination. After all, it wasn't as if Matt was blowing up and he knew that Greg's birdie barrage couldn't last forever. Sure enough, with a pair of pars on the next two holes, one good enough to win, he turned back Greg's charge, making the turn with a 2 up lead and playing solid golf.

For my part, I'd come out playing what was, by far, my best golf of the week, firing a birdie, 3 pars and a couple of bogeys over the first 6 holes. Despite that, I couldn't shake Milo or even build a lead. Standing all square on 7, I watched as Milo stiffed a 3 iron to 4 feet for a birdie and his first lead of the day. After my first mental lapse of the day led to a bogey on 8 and a 2 up lead for Milo, things got even worse when another natural birdie on 9 allowed him to make the turn at 3 up.

I was 1 over par net, my best 9 holes of the week, yet I was being shredded by a buzz saw named Milo, who was 5 under par net, 2 over gross. Making matters worse was the fact that I'd be giving him his second, and last, handicap stroke of the day on 10 - the very next hole. Needing to stay focused, I assured myself he couldn't keep this pace up forever.

Behind us, Smokin' Joe and AJ were, surprisingly, both struggling. After AJ became the seventh consecutive Yank player to win the first, the match quickly descended into a strange malaise of mediocrity, each player struggling to find any consistency. With Joe shooting an inexplicable 12 over par net, AJ was only little better, leading only 2 up lead at the turn.

Ian, on the other hand, had no such problems. In a match he'd been waiting on for nearly 2 years, the motivational factor provided by the humiliating loss simply could not be overstated. Throughout that time, he'd been reminded time and time again of his personal guarantee and how it alone had cost us an incredible Cup victory. He was sick and tired of it and he wanted REVENGE.

Focused and confident, the England Captain came out playing inspired golf from the start, winning each of the first 6 holes. Finally, on the 7th, Jack stemmed the tide with a birdie win but Ian's attack was relentless and after a par halve on 8, another birdie win on the 9th would put him at even par *gross* at the turn, 3 under par net and 6 up over poor Jack.

At the turn, we led in 6 matches and trailed in only 2 - the two we'd expected to lose - and our match-setting strategy seemed to be working to perfection. It was an eerily similar situation to where we stood at the same point in last year's Cup, right before the wheels came off. This time, we would need to hang tough and finish the job. After all, I told myself, we were due a few breaks.

But like a movie sequel with the same predictable plot, events in the groups ahead were already taking an ominous turn. As I looked down 10, a long dogleg left par 5, the unlikeliest of heroes, Ray, was once again turning the tables for England. Wins on 10 and 11 had allowed the determined Brit to level his match and after he safely found the fairway on 12, a long par 4, the stage was set for one of the most bizarre and, for us, destructive incidents in Cup history.

It began with Jack's wayward drive into the tall grass on the right side of the fairway. As the group searched for the ball, Jack heard a shout from nearby.

"Oi've got it, sir." His caddy yelled, pointing down. "'Ere it tis."

With the ball sitting down in the long grass, Jack couldn't quite identify it. He looked quizzically at his caddy.

"Are you sure that's my ball?"

"Oi yam, yessir, oi yam. Twas the line 'Oi 'ad and 'Oi'm sure 'Oi can see your mark – dere, on the side and a bit under. See? You can see the 'Ti' in Titleist. See it dere?"

Leaning over to examine the ball, Jack could see two of the three dots he routinely used in marking his balls. Peering at the other side, he could see only the "Ti" of the ball name, Titleist. Satisfied, he took the wedge his caddy offered and, with a mighty swing, somehow managed to lift it just far enough to reach the fairway. Positioned for an approach shot no longer than Ray's, he was back in the hole.

Arriving at his ball for his third shot, Jack's heart sank as he looked down. It was a Titleist 2, not the 3 he'd been playing. His crestfallen face said it all as the caddy approached.

"This isn't my ball," he said disgustedly, realizing he'd incurred penalty for both losing his ball and hitting the wrong ball and the hole was certainly lost, giving Ray a 1 up lead. Wasn't the caddy's fault, of course, what with the ball buried deep in the thick grass and lying in a way that made it impossible to verify the number. Anyone could have made that mistake and, ultimately, he was responsible. Oh well.

"No, it tisn't, sir." the caddy whispered as he stood the bags up nearby. "'Oi dropped one down fer you, 'oi did. You just knock it up on the green. No one'll be the wiser."

At first, Jack's eyes widened as he processed what the caddy was saying but they quickly narrowed to an icy stare. The caddy, for the first time realizing he may have cheated for the wrong American, averted his eyes, nervously fidgeting as he waited for Jack's next response. His anger boiling, Jack walked over to Ray, explained what had happened and conceded the hole. Returning to the caddy, Jack's words were terse as he struggled to keep his temper in check.

"I'll take my bag"

"Oh, no sir. 'Oi didn't mean nuttin' by it. 'Oi taught 'oi was helping, so 'elp me."

Jack was having none of it.

"Give me my bag or, so help me, or I'll walk in right now and you can explain it to your boss."

Looking at Jack's steely blue eyes, the caddy relented, sheepishly standing the bag up before stepping away, only Pat's bag remaining on his shoulder.

Not surprisingly, Jack did not recover from the incident. His focus gone, anger and fatigue further conspired to destroy what little game he had left and Ray's mix of pars and bogeys were enough to close out the match, 4&3.

Far worse was the fact that Pat, who'd been sharing the same caddy, seemed affected as well and by 16, his 4 up lead had been cut in half. After halving 16, Pat was dormie 2 but Phil was pressing play.

One group behind, Swampy and Sven remained locked in their extraordinary match. Through 15 holes, not one had been won with anything other than a net birdie or eagle and after capturing 15, Swampy headed to the 16th tee where, for only the third time all day, he would be all square in the match.

In the same group, Jarvo doggedly refused to give in to Lou's erratic but solid play. After erasing Lou's early 4 up lead by winning 10, Jarvo promptly found himself in another hole when Lou came roaring back to life by winning 11 and 12. Down again, Jarvo's reply was to capture 13 and 14 to square the match yet again. With matching pars on 15, they, too, headed to 16 all square.

Meanwhile, my match was teetering on the brink as we started the back nine. Hole 10, the #2 handicap hole, is a long dogleg left par 4. There, I would be giving Milo his second and final stroke of the round. After watching Milo split another fairway with his tee shot, I duck-hooked my 1-iron into some thick rough only 100 yards or so off the tee. After hacking my way back to the fairway with a 6-iron, I faced a decision. Trailing by 3 holes, I was laying a shot, I was still short of Milo's drive and I was facing a 240 yard shot down a narrowing chute of a fairway that was only 15 yards or so wide at the throat of the green where a large hillock covered in tall fescue bordered a deep bunker on the right. All the way down the left side of the fairway and on past the green ran a small creek bordered by a stone wall marking the course boundary. The safe, smart shot was obviously to lay up but with the way Milo was playing, I needed at least a halve and with my current state of affairs, playing safe simply wasn't an option.

Throwing caution to the wind, I fired my last, best hope, ripping a 1 iron straight as an arrow, right at the pin. Perhaps my best strike of the day, I watched it bound down the fairway, heading straight through the opening in front and coming to a stop about 12-15 feet from the pin. I would have a makeable par putt.

Perhaps shaken by my unlikely approach shot, Milo finally made a mistake, fading a 5 iron onto the fescue covered hillock at the front right. Suddenly I had hope that a miraculous turning point could be in the process of happening, visions of Milo struggling in the cabbage dancing in my head. Faced with a delicate little chip shot out of an unpredictable lie atop the mound, though, Milo played it perfectly, running it up onto the green and leaving it about 8 feet. After burning the edge on the high side for a conceded bogie, though, Milo crushed whatever hope I had left by draining his par net birdie putt for the win and a 4 up lead.

Having played what were easily my best 10 holes of the week in 1 over par net, I was 4 down, the victim of Milo's astonishing 6 under par net total. Although the final match score would be 6&4, it might as well have been 10&8 because I was done, knowing that (1) there would be no collapse by my opponent, and (2) I had already thrown my best at him. The bottom line was that, today, it was not good enough. I was beaten and we both knew it.

Matt continued his solid play, unaffected by my troubles and forcing Greg to make birdies to make up any ground. When a brilliant eagle on 13 gave the youngster a 3 up lead with five holes to play, the air seemed to go out of the emotionally drained Brit for good and two holes later, Matt had a 5&3 win.

In the final group, AJ and Joe continued their puzzling exercise in joint futility, each searching for any sign of their normal ball striking abilities. Joe was at a complete loss, unable to get any of his game straightened out despite Ian's steadying influence and encouragement, while AJ was only marginally better, unable to stretch his lead past 3 up despite numerous chances.

Finally, though, Joe came alive with a par win on 14 and when another followed on 16, AJ's lead was down to 1. One last time, though, uncharacteristically poor ball striking would cost Joe dearly and AJ's bogey on 17 was enough to win the hole and end the match, 2&1.

Joe's struggles, though, had not affected Ian in the least and although Jack picked up his level of play a bit on the back, he would not make up any ground, eventually falling 6&5 to Ian's relentlessly solid play. Despite a few bogeys down the stretch, the England Captain finished with a 2 over par net and through 72 holes, his Stableford total stood at 6 over par while his lead had grown to 12 over his closest competitor, AJ.

At this point, with England's lead standing at 9-½ to 7-½, they needed a half point to retain the Cup and a full point to win it outright for the second straight year. Like 2001, though, we continued to hold out hope with three matches left undecided. Pat was dormie 2 while Lou and Sven were both all square and none of them had trailed all day. We needed to win all three but with a little luck . . . maybe?

After pars on 14, 15 and 16, Phil confidently strode up the path to the 17th tee. First up, he was now playing mistake free golf and this hole would be no different. With three well struck shots, he was in for birdie and only 1 down with all the momentum as he and Pat headed to 18, a long par 4 bordering the beach on the right.

Like Milo, Phil was brutal to play against when he was on and as he stepped up to his ball on the final tee, he was squarely in one of his grooves, splitting the fairway with his drive. Knowing the stakes, Pat rose to the challenge, blasting his drive on the same perfect line as Phil's but 25 yards further. Needing only a halve to win the match, Pat breathed a sigh of relief.

One group back, our fortunes took a significant turn for the better when Lou and Sven each won 17, making each of our boys dormie 1. Down to the last hole in all three matches, we were 1 up in all three. A halve on 18 in each of the three matches would be enough to bring the Cup back to America.

As we watched from beside the green, Phil's thinly struck approach left him in a swale about 20 yards short of the green. He would have to chip up or over a steep embankment to the raised green, a tricky little shot that had him looking at a near-certain bogey. Suddenly the advantage was Pat's, the hole his to win.

Knowing Phil was in a bit of trouble, Pat focused on making one last, good swing. Finding the green would cement the win but anything near the green would still leave him with the advantage, needing only to halve the hole. Golf is a funny game, though, and the pressure of the moment can cause even the best golfers to alter their swing in some minor yet fatal way and as Pat swung, his normally reliable draw failed him - miserably.

Playing towards the right side of the green in anticipation of his normal right to left trajectory, the ball instead went left to right, arcing majestically up and out, sailing across the beach and dropping through the gray, early afternoon sky before disappearing into the surf. With the ball went our hopes in bringing the Cup back to America. Back in control, Phil calmly chipped up to 10 feet and 2 putted for a bogey win to cap his unlikely comeback from 4 down with 5 to play. With 3 pars, a birdie and a bogey over the last five holes, Phil had somehow salvaged the half point needed to clinch retention for Team England. That was not enough, though, and we all knew it. Nothing short of an outright win would be enough to satisfy Ian and Team England.

Before long, Lou and Jarvo worked their way up 18 and as Lou walked by, he let us know he only needed to 2 putt from 15 feet to halve the hole and win the match. After knocking his first putt about a foot past the hole, Lou glanced at Jarvo, perhaps expecting to hear "*that's good*" but with the match on the line, Jarvo offered no such courtesy. Casually reaching across the hole to knock it in, Lou nearly missed it, leaving the ball only an inch or two closer, losing the hole and leaving the match a draw. The careless mistake assured the Brits would now win the Cup outright but it wouldn't matter in the end.

In the final match, Swampy pulled out one last bit of magic, playing a delicate little 30 yard chip to within 10 feet and draining the putt for one last net birdie – his ninth of the day (Sven had seven) and sixth on the back nine, and in doing so became the third consecutive Brit to level a match by winning the last hole. Despite his 37 Stableford, the day's best (topping Sven by 9 full points), Swampy trailed on 14 tees and never led against the resourceful American. When the final putt fell, though, neither player was the slightest bit disappointed in the result.

Players struggle against the course, the elements and their own minds but every once in a while, you are privileged to play in a match where both players exceed their hopes, where only birdies or better need apply towards winning a hole and where, in the end, there is nothing left to do but shake hands and say, *"that was amazing!"* In the eyes of both players, this was just such a match and as far as they were concerned, a halve was the only fair result.

With word of Ian's and Milo's wins now old news, a celebratory mood broke out alongside the 18th green as the Brits waited for the last two groups to finish up. With all matches decided, the score stood at 11 to 9, England.

As I stood near the 18th green, I contemplated the fact that I was now down 2-0 in my five year wager with Ian – and I'd *still* never won a Flem Cup, standing now at 0-5. Mustering as much dignity as possible, I congratulated each of the Brits before moving off to the side, jealous of their joy but determined to lose with as much class as I could muster. Finally, Ian and Joe finished and after congratulating them both, I began the long trek back to the clubhouse, one I was happy to make alone with my thoughts.

Before long, though, I heard someone approaching from behind and, glancing back, I saw Swampy gaining ground quickly as he trotted along. Perhaps he was hoping to expound on his great match with Sven, I thought, or even commiserate about my solid play against a tough opponent, I didn't know, but despite his cutting sense of humor, I'd come to know Swampy as a good-hearted soul, always there with a helping hand or word of encouragement. Slowing, I turned to meet him as he stuck out one hand and placed the other firmly on my shoulder. At first, he just stared at me, a frozen grin on his face. Slightly unnerved by his silence and goofy look, I spoke first.

"Congratulations on your match with Sven. Sounded like a real barnburner. You played well."

"Oh yeah, our match was amazing to be part of. Sven played great and I was really pleased with my own play. *Really* pleased. More importantly, I wanted to congratulate you! You've got yourself quite a record there. One that won't be broken, will it?"

Flummoxed by his cryptic comment, I could only stand and stare at the big dumb grin on his face. *Record? What record?* Confused, I noticed the rest of Team England approaching, loosening my grip as I tried to separate my hand from Swampy's but he had other ideas, his big bear paw tightening its grip even as I relaxed mine. As I squirmed slightly, he said not a word, just staring at me. *What's this?* I asked myself.

Then it hit me. He was waiting for the group and within moments, the tsunami arrived, his teammates gathering round in eager anticipation of . . . what? I didn't know. He continued in his most good natured voice.

"Oh c'mon! You know what I mean. Your new record! *You din't win a single point.* By my reckoning, not only 'ave you never won the Cup – that's oh for five, i'nt it? – but, you're now the first golfer to not win a single point. Not a fraction. Nothing! Zero! You're pointless!"

Desperately, I ran through my matches one by one as snickers rose from the group. Day 1 - lost. Day 2 - lost. Day 3 - lost. Today - *lost.* As the truth settled in, he continued.

"Now, we've been talking, the lads and I, and we've decided your record setting accomplishment deserves a new nickname. We've decided that nickname should be . . . Donut. Donut Dow. I like the sound of that, it 'as a nice ring to it. 'Ow 'bout you? I mean, if the shoe fits . . . "

Feeling like I had just been smacked across the head with a 2x4, there was nothing I could say or do. He was right. I hadn't even managed a halve. None of my matches had even reaching the 17th tee! Feebly, I defended myself.

"Well, yeah . . . I . . . but . . . I played well today! . . . did you hear what Milo did? . . . we should have won the other day! . . . are you sure? . . . . . *oh crap!"*

Seeing Swampy had, indeed, caught me unaware of my plight, the England players broke out in full-fledged laughter, some bent over with their hands on knees, nearly on the ground, as I struggled for words. Even my own teammates were smiling to themselves as they shuffled by, having overheard what Swampy had planned for me after I'd trudged off. Swampy, however, wasn't through.

"Since you din't know that, you also may not have realized that OUR Cap'n - you know, Ian - is not only winning the Stableford by a mile but 'e's also the first player to go undefeated! That's grand, i'nt it? Shall I congratulate 'im for you? Or would you prefer to? 'E's right 'ere . . "

Finally released from Swampy's grip, I turned back towards the clubhouse, oblivious to the laughter happening at my expense. Ian's exploits were not even something I could contemplate just yet, having only just been made aware of my own epic failure. Within a span of only 10 minutes, we'd lost the Cup, I'd discovered I was pointless and I'd been awarded a new - and unwanted - nickname to commemorate the big zero: Donut. I was a man on the edge.

By the awards dinner that night, I'd regained enough of my dignity to graciously congratulate Ian and his team as they celebrated at the hotel. He did have a tremendous Cup, winning all four of his matches, and by the next afternoon, he'd added his first Stableford championship, running away with it by 12 points over Milo and 17 over AJ. After lunchtime, we were once again saying our goodbyes as the Brits headed home while we would settle in for one last night in Ennis before our flight from Shannon in the morning.

I spent the final evening in Ennis writing the final article of the season for the website, putting on my Indie hat one last time with a long, hard and objective look at what had transpired.

The first and easiest thing to write about was the positive: the close matches and individual shots that were crucial to England's win. There is no shortage of heroes, led by Ian, Milo and, of course, Ray. For our side, though, it was a different story; one with lots of questions and no answers. Matt came out smelling like a rose; leading us in points for the second straight year. No longer the young, temperamental lad we felt the needed to shelter, Matt was as feared and respected an opponent as anyone on either side. AJ had been solid as well but aside from those two, the biggest concern wasn't the fact that we lost so much as it was *how* we lost.

Golf is a game that tests a competitor's character like no other; a game where there are two unrelenting, unwavering, unsympathetic and, in the end, unconquerable opponents: the golf course itself (including the playing conditions) and one's own mind. To the non-golfer, it is just swinging a club and 'chasing a little white ball' but the fact of the matter is that striking a ball precisely so that it goes precisely the right distance in precisely the right direction has an unimaginably small margin of error. The difference between a great shot and a disaster can be a razor thin margin, making unyielding focus and concentration a must lest the slightest stray thought throw off your effort.

In a team match, you add to that the self-inflicted pressure of wanting to be a contributing member of your team. It is a burden that every player feels, proudly when you are playing well but like an albatross around your neck when you are not. The challenge lies in channeling your energies, focusing your mind and blocking out distractions. Even a perfect ball strike can be disastrous if you've carelessly chosen the wrong club or taken a bad line or otherwise failed to manage the course intelligently. Adrenaline can be good or bad, depending on how it is handled. When all these aspects of the game are put in the pressure-packed crucible of a serious team competition like the Flem Cup, it becomes the ultimate test of self and it was a test we'd failed 2 years running when it counted most, on the back 9 of our 2 ball matches - and failures like that are not easily forgotten.

Facing questions that cut to the core of each individual, I knew those questions would remain unanswered for thirteen long months as we marinated in the *what ifs*. It wasn't a stretch to imagine the most dreaded word in the sporting world - choke - floating around, unspoken, in a few minds. Swampy's pre-Cup letter had proven prophetic and twice now, we'd had things firmly within our grasp on the back 9 of the final day only to have it fall apart as England's clutch play and our mistakes collided. Hours spent hitting balls at the driving range or playing friendly matches wouldn't erase the memories of what happened when it mattered most or calm the demon fears of future failures. In competition, failure breeds failure in a vicious cycle that only success can break; a conundrum that we would somehow have to work out for ourselves.

15

Pebble Beach

A quiet night followed by the long trip home gave me ample time to reflect on the sadness of seeing another year end, facing an even longer than usual winter of dreary nothingness thanks to the earlier Cup schedule. Rather than October being a glorious month of building excitement, it would be nothing more than a long, depressing reminder of our loss, the beautiful Fall weather empty of purpose, our competitive fires extinguished for the year. It would be mid-November with the holidays approaching before the feel of life would to return to normal.

For me, Christmas has always been a time to reflect on the unexpected twists and turns life had taken during the previous year while pondering what might be in store for the next one. In late 2002, my future seemed bleaker than ever. My business was in what would prove to be a fatal downward spiral while my marriage consisted of little more than extended periods of silence, resentment and bitterness separated by brief, uneasy truces. My children continued to drift away from me for reasons I could not fathom and, despite my best efforts, I could not entirely forget that my best friend had been diagnosed with terminal cancer.

The older I got, the harder it had become to find things that truly captured my interest. Things that did - like the Cup - more often than not ended in disappointment. This year's Cup fit into that formula precisely. It had been a truly special event, filled with great friendships and fierce competition, and I had focused on it with increasing excitement throughout the previous summer and fall, building expectations in my mind of how things *should* play out. Not surprisingly, those expectations crashed and burned in the face of the simple reality that other people have their own hopes and expectations, wants and desires. There were times I could only watch myself descend into a sullen, resentful shell if things really didn't go the way I'd like. It was an aspect of my behavior that only made me ashamed.

Why doesn't this make me feel the way I thought it would?

I'd asked that question over and over in life but the answer was only beginning to dawn on me. The problem lay not in the events or the things or the people that failed me but in the expectations *I* had created and *my* issues. This prompted a new question.

What is wrong with me?

It was a question I dared not wrestle with for long.

Ian's bi-annual body scan in early December brought good news once again: the cancer continued to lay dormant. The bleakness of the original prognosis had given way to cautious optimism among us all, a feeling bolstered by the sight of Ian being as active and seemingly healthy as ever, playing golf, traveling on his boat, skiing and continuing to live the good life the way he always had - with gusto. The annual Austria ski trip was followed by one in February after which golf season would kick off with the March Majorca trip. After that, he would spend the spring, summer and early autumn golfing, boating and travelling. Finally, in November, there would be the Flem Cup. Except for the bi-annual reports, we didn't discuss the cancer at all.

The Majorca trip had always intrigued me. While the Flem Cup trip could be described as a golf trip with some drinking, the Majorca trip could more aptly be described as a drinking trip with some golf. One Majorca story in particular always stuck in my mind as distinctly Ian-esque.

Unlike the Flem Cup, morning golf on the Majorca trip was simply not tolerated. A typical day included an afternoon round of golf followed by a nap followed by dinner followed by another nap followed by some serious nightclubbing that would likely wind up around 5 am. On one particularly wild night, Ian partied past sunrise. Despite that, still drunk and with 2-3 hours of sleep under his belt, he dragged himself to his 12:45 pm tee time.

The first hole was a 390-yard hard dogleg right; tree-lined tennis courts dangerously tucked into the corner of the dogleg. Legend had it that Seve Ballesteros once drove the green, a deceptively long carry, but attempts by mere mortals to carry the dogleg typically ended in disaster, disappointment and danger (for the tennis players).

Trying to match Ballesteros was not on Ian's mind that morning. Not much was. It would be all he could do to hit the little white ball in the middle without face planting in the process. With a pounding headache, nausea and blurred vision, Ian had it all going for him that morning, dark sunglasses his only protection against the painful light of day.

Bordering on a major walkway of the sports complex, crowds of up to 30 people or more would stop as they were passing to watch golfers teeing off, both as a courtesy and a curiosity. The people who had stopped early that afternoon were unaware that anything at all was amiss, completely oblivious to Ian's difficulties with routine activities such as standing upright without swaying and walking in a reasonably straight line.

Finally, Ian's turn on the tee arrived. He steadied himself over the ball as best he could, drawing a deep, cleansing breath in a vain attempt to steady the tee box. Finally, with no other alternative, he made his little heel-hop and unleashed as mighty a swing as he was capable of, hoping against hope that he wouldn't miss the ball entirely while half-expecting he would.

Through some extraordinary combination of muscle memory and lucky timing, the driver face caught the ball flush and the ball rocketed out, carrying out and over the corner of the tennis courts, straight as an arrow towards the green as the crowd began to 'oooh' and 'aaah' in response to its magnificently bold trajectory. Holding their collective breath as the mighty blast began to descend, all eyes peered through the chain-link fence in hope of spotting a landing. Ian, having nearly fallen over on his follow through, had no idea where the ball had gone - only that it had elicited a seemingly positive reaction from the crowd.

Then - *there it was!* - bounding along the hard fairway straight towards the green, sending up a roar from the assembled throngs that only grew as it neared the green. Finally, it came to rest only 5 feet or so short of the green, a mere 30 feet from the hole. Unaware of where the ball actually was, Ian took it all perfectly in stride, offering up his best Queen's wave and head nod from behind his dark sunglasses as he was driven away.

But as you might expect, the story didn't end there.

Facing a legitimate eagle opportunity and possible 'legend' status back home, Ian's skulled his second shot across the green and into the rough, chunked his third barely to the fringe and 3 putted for a double bogey. With the handicap stroke he got on the hole, Ian's net bogey earned him 1 Stableford point, his first - and last - of the day. Of the next 8 holes, 6 times he would finish 'in pocket' while on the other two, he would record triple bogeys. His new, nearly unbreakable 9 hole Stableford record cemented in place, Ian retired at the turn.

With winter turning to spring and life blooming once again in northwest New Jersey, I began to focus on an upcoming golf trip that, for the first time in a very long time, was not focused on the Flem Cup. Shortly after Ian's diagnosis in early 2002, I'd made him and Joe an offer they couldn't refuse for the golf trip of a lifetime: Pebble Beach. After all, what better time to plan the trip of a lifetime, I asked, than under the uncertainty of Ian's gloomy prognosis? So I arranged it, letting Ian choose the final member of our foursome for rounds at Pasatiempo, Black Horse, Spyglass Hill, Pebble Beach, Poppy Hills and Half Moon Bay. 14 months or so in the planning, it was finally coming to pass and I was stoked.

Surprisingly, Ian's choice was someone I'd never met before: Andy "Miffer" Smith. A husky fellow in his 30s, Miffer had become fast friends with Ian and Joe over the previous years, a testament to his golf game (he played off of a 4 or 5 handicap) and his social skills (an affable fellow always ready for a good laugh and a beer or three). With no changes to the Cup team between '01 and '02, he'd been unable to garner a spot but he was all in for the '03 Cup and I was eager to see him, and his game, up close and personal.

Leaving the airport, we headed to our hotel in Santa Cruz to get some food and sleep. The next day we would be starting our trip at Alister MacKenzie's home course and design gem, Pasatiempo Golf Club. We had agreed to play best ball Stableford each day while rotating partners. Ian and I started off strong, building a 5 point lead on the drizzly front 9 and stretching it to 6 points after 11 before slowly giving it all back. By the time we reached 18, I found myself needing to sink a straight 4 footer for a halve that would feel more like a loss. Striking it tentatively, it barely slipped in the side door. The highlight of the match, other than the spectacular course, came late in the match as we passed a house where a talking bird roamed the large backyard deck overlooking the hole, hurling golf-related wisecracks and insults at passing golfers.

After having some lunch, we headed off for the Monterey Peninsula, perhaps *the* ultimate golf Mecca. Next up would be Black Horse, a solid but unspectacular course where Joe and I would lose by a lopsided margin to Ian and Miffer. Heading back to the hotel, the excitement was starting to build because we had arrived at the real meat of the trip: Spyglass Hill and Pebble Beach on consecutive days.

Arriving at Spyglass Hill around 8am, we were greeted by beautiful, sunny weather framing what is truly a breathtaking golf course. After the opening par 5 led us down the hill to the ocean, we enjoyed five holes played over and through the sand hills and dunes, one stunning ocean vista morphing into another as we played. From there, we headed back up the hill as the course changed character dramatically, seaside links giving way to graceful hardwood forest, but although the character changed, the brilliance of the holes did not and as we meandered through the magnificent old growth forests of towering cypress and oaks, we became more and more amazed at the beauty and character of the course.

Paired with Miffer, I once again enjoyed jumping out to a big lead and by the turn, we were up by 7 points. Stopping to buy jumbo hamburgers at the turn, we were warned to watch out for food-pinching ravens. Perhaps a bit skeptical of a bird making off with the large burger, we took few bites as we teed off on 10 and drove to our balls. With cart path only in effect, we made sure we closed and locked the styrofoam lids on our containers before fanning out across the fairway for our second shots.

As I walked to my ball on the far side of the fairway, a shout from Miffer made me stop and turn around. Back at the carts, a huge raven was standing next to an open container on the floor of the cart - Miffer's container. The thief had simply pulled the container out of the compartment, dropping it on the ground to pop it open. As we watched, the bird opened its beak wide, grabbed the partially eaten burger, bun still clinging to the top side, and lumbered off, flying low and heavy across the fairway right in front of us, no more than 20 feet away as smaller birds dive-bombed it in hope of making it drop its prize.

Staring in stunned amazement as the events unfolded in what seemed like slow motion, we were snapped back to reality by the realization that there were still hungry birds behind us, picking over the remains of Miffer's box and eying the remaining unopened containers. Racing back to the carts, the birds scattered as we grabbed our boxes. We had become believers, keeping our food close at hand from there on out.

After extending our lead to 8 points, Ian and Joe both got hot just as our games started to disintegrate, led by mine. Like at Pasatiempo, by the time we reached 18, we were tied. There, getting my final handicap stroke of the day, I hit my tee shot out of bounds to take myself out of the hole entirely. With Miffer on his own, he played it well, leaving himself about 20 feet for birdie. From there, we could only watch as Joe chipped in from far across the green for a birdie and when Miffer slid his birdie putt by the edge, my pair had lost - again.

For our once-in-a-lifetime round at Pebble Beach the next day, we hired caddies, a crucial element in getting the absolute best experience possible on one of the most famous and picturesque golf courses in the world. As we strolled along, enjoying every second, we soaked in the incredible scenery of Carmel Bay, the cliffs of doom, the mansions bordering the course and the activity on the beach at Carmel. Finally, we reached the infamous par 3 17th hole, home to the tilted hourglass green and site of two of the most memorable U.S. Open moments ever: Jack Nicklaus' 1 iron that hit the flagstick in '72 and Tom Watson's impossible chip-in from behind the green to beat Jack ten years later. Today, the pin was on the back half of the hourglass, not far from where it had been when Watson chipped in.

Partnered back with Ian, we were 2 points down to Miffer and Joe. Playing Stableford rather than straight match play, I would be getting a stroke on 17 versus the group and I was desperate to take advantage and help get us back into the match. When Miffer and Joe found the greenside bunkers, one left and one right, we had the opening we needed but neither of us could capitalize, my weakly slapped 3-iron just making the front right corner of the green and Ian's long iron pushed far right of the narrow green.

Reaching the green, we found that Joe and Miffer were in opposing traps, each plugged in the face furthest away from the green, leaving them with severely downhill plugged lies and nearly impossible shots. Despite their considerable skills, just getting their balls out of the bunker and keeping them on the green would be an enormous challenge.

With opportunity knocking, we had our own issues. Ian faced a 30 yard pitch from the thick rough to the far right of the green that had to be hit very high enough and land very soft at a precise distance, carrying just past the bunker Miffer was in. Getting it anywhere close would be nearly impossible, leaving a bogey as probably his best outcome.

Despite being on the green, I was facing my own difficulties. Positioned on the front of the green (the bottom part of the hourglass), I had no chance of putting my ball and keeping it within 15 feet of the hole due to a steep ridge sloping steeply towards the middle of the green from the right side of the throat of the hour-glass. The slope would push a putt from my position far left of the pin and the further right I hit it, the further up the slope it would go, the further left it would be pushed, the more speed it would run out with and the more I risked leaving my ball stuck on the fringe. As I surveyed my situation, my caddy spoke up.

"Tough shot."

"Yeah. What do you think?"

"Chip it."

At first, I thought he was joking but when I looked at him, he just nodded and smiled.

"Don't worry about the divot; I'll take care of that. Keep your hands ahead of the ball, lock your wrists and don't decelerate."

Handing me my lob wedge, he stalked around the green, scanning the ridge from all angles. Finally, he used the flagstick to point to a spot on the far side of the ridge.

"Here. Land it right here."

With my chances for an elusive victory running out, I threw caution to the wind. A delicate chip shot with a lob wedge from a tight lie was not really my thing but I had to try something.

Taking a firm swing with my hands forward and wrists locked, I felt solid contact. Looking up, I saw the ball high in the air, crossing the ridge and landing only a few inches from the caddies target spot. From there, it took one short hop, checked up and began trickling down the far side of the ridge, tracking straight towards the hole.

As my three playing partners looked on in stunned disbelief, the ball finally stopped 2 inches from the pin, dead on line. After high fiving me with a big grin on his face, my caddy picked up my perfectly cut divot, covered the gash and lov-ingly replaced it, tamping it down with his foot.

"The green doesn't mind the divot when you hit a shot like that!" he laughed.

As we expected, Miffer and Joe each bogeyed the hole, allowing my par net birdie to make us even for the first time all day. With a new found spring in my step, we headed to the most famous golf hole on earth, the 18th at Pebble Beach.

Following a round or two of pictures on the tee, the four of us proceeded to hit perfect drives before setting off on the greatest walk in golf. Soaking in the scenery with every step, we breathed in the salt air, looking out over the sunbathing sea lions in Carmel Bay and scanning further out in search of dolphin fins. The vivid whites, greens and blues of the setting only intensifying the sense of perfection we each had in being there. I asked Ian if he wanted to pinch himself and he looked at me, chuckling and shaking his head.

"I 'ave been, lad. I 'ave been."

We were in no hurry for our journey through perfection to end so we took our time, snapping pictures of the incredible hole and scenery as we went. Following solid second shots, we continued our stroll, embracing the moment as our match faded to momentary insignificance.

After talking over my 200 yard third shot with Ian, we decided it would be best for me to lay up with a 7-iron, willing to take our chances with my short game and confident that Ian, another 20-30 yards closer, would find the green. With a solid strike, I positioned myself for a simple little chip shot over the left edge of the front bunker. As I stood there, confident in our momentum, my peace was shattered when Ian pulled his routine 6 iron, the ball arcing gracefully out over the seawall and across the rocks before descending into the surf, 40 yards or so into Carmel Bay. Looking back and forth in stunned disbelief, he could only shrug his shoulders. After Miffer and Joe each found the green with their approaches, leaving themselves with long birdie putts, the match pressure shifted squarely to me as I surveyed my little 40 yard chip over the front bunker.

After crisply striking my quarter-swing wedge shot, I looked up to see it arcing on a beautiful trajectory, just as I'd envisioned it, straight towards the pin with enough distance to carry the bunker and mound guarding the front right. As it neared its pinnacle, I was a happy man.

Good line . . . good distance . . . as long as it misses that stupid little dead branch up there . . .

Crack.

As the ball dropped down into the bunker, I could only stare skyward, unable to believe the dumb luck of what has just happened. The very tip of a tiny, dead branch! Had I taken 100 shots *trying* to hit it, I would have failed. What were the odds?!? Finishing with a double bogie, I had once again been on the losing side.

Sadly for me, though, the day was far from being over. In the pro shop, we discovered that since we'd played Pebble, we could now play the third of the three PB Resort courses, Spanish Bay, for the bargain price of only $100. After taking a leisurely drive along 17 Mile Drive, we reached the links-style course with plenty of time for lunch and an afternoon round. Teeing off just past 2pm, I found myself becoming obsessed by an incredibly annoying attribute of the course: the fact that it is surrounded by what was designated "environmentally sensitive areas". You were not allowed to enter any of these areas, even if your ball was in plain sight. Bordering most fairways, my mood darkened as I steamed over the stupidity of building a golf course with such restrictions.

After suffering the penalty 3 times on the first 5 holes and struggling badly with my putting, my frustration was boiling over and when I pulled my 3-iron approach on 6, I turned away in disgust, half-heartedly whacking my club on the tire of the cart - only it hit the wheel rim, not the tire, and bent the shaft, making the club both useless and illegal to carry.

Increasingly mad at the world, I drove up to the green only to sheepishly find my ball in the fairway, pin high, just left of the green. Adding insult to injury, I proceeded to knock in my little pitch shot for a birdie - the bittersweet highlight of an afternoon that would continue to unravel before coming to an embarrassing head on 8, a straight forward par 4 with a wide fairway bordered by a road on the right and a marsh down the left.

Feeling completely useless to my latest unlucky playing partner, Miffer, I proceeded to make matters worse by slicing my driver far across the road and out of bounds. Determined to calm myself, I followed that with a decent swing, finding the fairway with about 160 yards left to the green.

Feeling myself sinking into a mental quagmire, I was desperate to get my game going. With a deep breath, I tried to relax and compose myself, focusing on just making one good swing to turn things around. After all, I'd had that happen before - why not today? Knowing 36 holes were rarely kind to me, I was doing my best to focus on a shot by shot, hole by hole approach. Let's just start with one nice, smooth swing and solid strike, I told myself.

As I took the club away from the ball, everything felt good. *Relax - nice and smooth.*

The mind, however, is a terrible thing to use in golf and somewhere between the top of my nice smooth, slow backswing and impact, the swing thought of *relax – nice and smooth* morphed into to *KILL BALL!*

With an out-of-control, hatchet-like downswing, the heel of my club slammed into the ground at a steep angle well behind the ball, causing the face of the club to turn over and producing a fat, chunky pull. Going airborne for only a moment or two, the ball took two bounces before disappearing with a muted splash into the muck of the nearby marsh.

Finally, I had reached my breaking point. Flying into a full-fledged rage, I had to mete out the appropriate punishment to . . . what?

Ball? . . . gone . . . Cart? . . . better not do that again . . . Club? . . . DAMN YOU, CLUB!!!

Like an out of body experience, I futilely tried to harness my emotions as I found myself winding up for something I hadn't done in 25 years or so. Taking four or five short, running steps down the fairway as the small voice inside yelled *stop, don't do it!*, I opted against the advice, choosing instead to unleash the beast by flinging my poor club as far down the fairway as I could.

The only problem was that, like my ball, I pulled it.

Aside from the fading "wooo . . wooo . . wooo . ." helicopter noise the club made, there was only silence as the club arced up and away, out across the marsh, four pairs of eyes looking on in stunned disbelief. Finally, the silence was broken momentarily by the *splat* of the club landing atop the muck, pausing momentarily before sinking beneath the murky surface, leaving only the silence.

As the shock of the moment passed, Ian, Miffer and Joe burst out in hysterical laughter at my pathetic antics. In the space of only a few short holes, I'd bent one club and thrown another into a marsh. Three holes later, unable to pull myself out of my foul mood, I would quit as we walked past our hotel room, blaming everything except my own monumental and uncontrollable stupidity for my day's premature end.

Back on my best behavior after the embarrassment at Spanish Bay, the last two days consisted of uneventful rounds at Poppy Hills and Half Moon Bay. Predictably, I lost both days, extending what had become a truly remarkable streak

Since winning my Singles Day match against Ian in 2001, I had played in 12 meaningful matches - matches I really cared about. There was the Harkers tournament with Jack, the four losses in Ireland and six consecutive days here in California. I had lost every single one except one - and that one ended in a halve.

As I flew home, I found myself once again confronted by the question: *what's wrong with me?* Having learned nothing from Ireland, I'd once again allowed my own selfish expectations to destroy what I had set out to do - spend a week with my best friend in golf paradise. Once again, I was embarrassed and ashamed of my behavior. So what if I didn't play well or win any matches? So what if some local rules were annoying? Get over it. Get over yourself! *What is wrong with me?*

16

The Plan

By mid-August, I'd played only a handful of times since Pebble Beach, discouraged by my recent propensity for poor play under pressure. With little enthusiasm for the game, the upcoming Cup seemed like a cruel joke. The sad fact was that no one on the American side was playing much golf as the Cup approached. We were a dispirited and uninspired lot.

In England, things went on seemingly as they always had. For the first time, the England side saw some significant turnover, losing Ray, Greg and Swampy. With Miffer having taken one spot, two remained open and Ian chose a 2 handicapper named Stuart Bright and a 19 handicapper named Richard Smith. Already aware of how formidable a foe Miffer could be, Ian assured me that Brighty was just as tough a match, maybe tougher. Richard, on the other hand, was a solid 19 and Ian viewed him as England's version of Lou. Apart from golf, Ian was spending his summer time enjoying life with Caroline. With neither working, the two were nearly inseparable and with the latest body scan delivering the same good news we'd become accustomed to, life was good.

One morning in mid-August, my phone rang. Picking up, I was happy to hear Ian's familiar greeting. Just calling to chat, talk naturally turned to details of the upcoming trip. He was in fine spirits, uncharacteristically offering up some glib quotes and info about his new players for me to use on the website. I could tell he was supremely confident in his team's chances and was eagerly looking forward to collecting on our wager. He even gave me some pithy quotes to post.

"The acquisition of Miffer is a big upgrade for the team; at least in drinking ability. Miffer has an empty keg in his stomach. Literally! I saw an x-ray!"

"Although we'll miss Swampy's cutting humor, we won't miss his cutting slices. Brighty will give us yet another very solid low-handicapper who is a superior match play player."

"Richard will be our answer to Lou, a solid 19 handicap and tough as nails."

Continuing in his chipper mood, Ian proceeded to do something completely out of character issuing his Day 1 pairings . . . two months before they were due and six weeks before handicaps would even be finalized. Generally the result of careful consideration and planning, it sounded as though he were doing it entirely on the fly, making them up as he went along.

"In Match 1, I'll play with . . . Miffer. In Match 2, Smokin' Joe'll play with . . . Milo . . . no . . . Brighty. In Match 3, Milo will play with . . . a . . . Phil, and in Match 4, . . . no, wait . . . Richard. Milo will play with Richard . . . and Phil will play with . . . who's left? . . . oh, right. Jarvo. Yeah, that's it. 'Ave you got that?"

As he began, I was so unsure that he was being serious that I didn't even write anything down. Realizing he was, indeed, serious, I asked him to give me the pairings again, writing them down this time. Finally, I read them back.

"So, these are final? Once I post them, they're issued and you can't change your mind unless you lose a player and then it is a straight replacement."

"Yep, they're final."

"What about the afternoon matches? Do you want to wait on those?"

"Roight . . . the afternoon. No, no, I'll do that now. What's the format?"

"I don't know. I guess we'll do a scramble but I really haven't given it a lot of thought."

"Roight . . . OK . . . well, I'll give you those as well. I'll play with Brighty . . . Joe can play with Miffer . . . we'll put Phil and Milo back together . . . and Jarvo and Richard"

I couldn't help but be stunned. Usually the model of careful planning, the whole exercise was very un-Ian like. Reading them back one last time, I elicited only yeps and uh-huhs.

"So that's final?"

"Yeah, that's final."

I held off posting them all that day and the next, half expecting a call of regret that never came. Finally, on the second evening, they were posted with commentary focusing on contrasting the pathetic state of our side compared to England's stronger than ever team, which held an embarrassment of riches. I kept wondering what Ian was up to but couldn't come up with an angle that made sense. His squad was their best yet and his confidence, soaring since Ireland, could only be bolstered by the news of the sad state of affairs concerning his underachieving, apathetic opponent. Who could blame him? With their improvements and our disarray, this year's Cup could get ugly.

Throughout the next few weeks, I pondered what it all might mean but as the end of August approached, I finally came to the only logical conclusion: it was an act of supreme confidence, clearly crossing the line into the realm of arrogance. I found myself offended and nurtured that reaction, encouraging my anger to grow as it slowly but surely re-stoked my competitive fires.

During that time, I had my interest piqued while playing in a Pinehurst Tournament at Harkers. Pinehurst was a format I had never played but I found it both interesting and challenging, differing from a scramble (which we used in '01) in several intriguing ways. In a Pinehurst, each teammate tees off and then plays his *teammate's* ball as it lies (a scramble always allows for improved lies). After each player's second shot, one ball is chosen (again, playing it as it lies) and the player who did *not* hit it to that spot begins an alternate shot format that continues through the completion of the hole.

Perhaps I liked it because I had some success at the tournament - I don't know - but after marinating in Ian's arrogance for a few weeks, my energy became focused on developing new strategies and tactics for our admittedly uphill battle. Many pieces would fall into place over the weeks that followed but the decision that started it all was a simple one: change the afternoon match format from a scramble to the more difficult Pinehurst format. In as humble and unobtrusive a manner as possible, the news was released.

Team U.S. Changes Format; Team U.S. Reportedly Not Even Practicing

By: Datzit Indaruf, Flem Cup Correspondent

MYRTLE BEACH, Sept. 1 – In a surprise announcement, Team U.S. has announced the format for the 9-hole afternoon matches scheduled for the first two days of this year's Flem Cup will be Pinehurst. Why Team U.S. has made this change is not entirely clear at this time. Pinehurst is a far more difficult format, one that brings strategy and teamwork into play – strengths more associated with Team England than the Yanks. Only time will tell whether this format change is the latest in a string of mistakes for beleaguered American Captain (for now) Scott Dow.

In other news, there continues to be no positive life in Team U.S. except for Matt Tanis, who continues to improve in leaps and bounds as he enters his senior year starting for one of the top high school golf teams in the state. As for negative life, Dow's play continues to worsen while others are hardly playing at all.

Following a lackluster 2002 with an even worse 2003 season, Dow's most recent failure occurred during the Harkers member-member championship where his effort included a missed 2 inch putt and a litany of other unforced errors. Other than that, sighting any Team U.S. player on a golf course has been a rarity. Reportedly, Pat and Lou have played twice each all summer while Sven has played 3 or 4 times, AJ has played 9-holes twice and Jack Sr., who has been battling a variety of ailments, has only played 5 times.

Perhaps the greatest concern to Captain Dow is the fact that Jack Jr. has only played about 6 times yet has managed to post a pair of 74s that have caused his handicap index to plummet to 5. Though admirable in principle, that will be a very difficult standard to play to on the long, difficult courses of Myrtle Beach.

As for the effect of all this lethargy on the team's lone bright spot, young Matt appears unconcerned by the team's lack of playing time or the quality of their play, citing a lack of financial or emotional commitment to the Cup.

"Hey, I get out of school for 4 days and its free! If these other bozos want to go to just socialize and lose again, what do I care? I'll win my 3 or 4 points, kick some Limey butt and come home with my head up. My only regret is that 'ole Swampy wimped out this year. I was going to be on him like a cheap suit."

Another sign that should have team officials worried are the player's frequent use of phrases like "I'm really just looking forward to the socializing", or "I'm just looking forward to hanging out at BummZ again". Most sports psychologists would translate those sentences into "We're going to lose" but hopefully the Americans have some shred of competitive spirit left because they have only 2 months to get their games in shape – or face a complete debacle.

***

As expected, I got a call from Ian within a day or so about this new Pinehurst format. I carefully explained it to him, assuring him I just wanted to try something a little more challenging and fun.

"Remember, it's primarily alternate shot and that's not a format we play over here. I just thought it would be a fun change. Don't you guys play that several times a year?"

"Well, yeah, we do. It actually does sound interesting – good for a change, eh? By the way, you'll be pleased to know that I'll be coming as a 6."

"Really? Down from a 7? That means you're playing well."

"I have been. We have one more tournament before the season ends but there is no possibility I'll get a lift to 7 so you can mark me down for a 6."

"Good. The way I've been playing, I need all the help I can get. This whole year has been horrible."

"Ah, keep your chin up, lad. I'm sure you'll be fine."

After hanging up, I sat back to reflect on what was unfolding as a three-pronged strategy, thankful Ian had re-engaged me in the upcoming Cup. Whatever happened, we would not go down without a fight and I planned on using every weapon at my disposal. His hubris had inspired me to get to work on our side, a side that was, after all, an extremely competitive group of men who needed no motivation beyond the arrogance of an opponent.

The first of my three-prong strategy was focused primarily on Team England's mental state. Knowing that overconfidence had been the downfall of many a stronger side in the history of sport, I wanted to instill as much of it as possible in our opponents. By mid-September, my plan was in full swing with every article posted and conversation with Ian focused on projecting the image of an apathetic and weak Team U.S., one that stood in stark contrast to Ian's cool, relaxed, seemingly invincible squad.

In early October, Jack Jr. reported that he'd suffered a meniscus tear in his left knee and although neither he nor his doctor thought it would be a problem for the Cup, an article dutifully reporting the injury (in the most dire terms possible) soon appeared on the website. Before posting it, I spoke to Ian about all of our issues, moaning about our problems with health, enthusiasm and quality of play. As we were about to hang up, he casually mentioned that his season-ending handicap would be 7 after all. Puzzled by the about-face, I let it slide, planning instead to use Indie to make hay of it. The full article posted the next morning.

Team U.S. Chances Grow Dimmer, Jack Jr. Tears Up Knee; Captain Ian Jennings Gets Controversial Handicap Lift

By: Datzit Indaruf, Flem Cup Correspondent

MYRTLE BEACH, Sept. 15 – In quick succession, Team U.S.'s increasingly faint Cup hopes have been dealt two blows. First, Jack Tanis Jr. suffered a knee injury while playing soccer over the weekend and is now questionable for the upcoming Flem Cup.

"I hope Jack gets better quickly." Captain-For-Now Donut Dow lamented, "He's Matt's ride!"

Tanis' torn meniscus will only heal properly with rest, team physician Dr. Ima Wanker told reporters. The restrictions placed on his activities are comprehensive: all physical sports, golf and using the toes of his left foot to help him count for his accounting practice.

The second blow is that Team England Captain Ian Jennings, long-known for his titanic temper and unquenchable appetite for control and power, reneged on his recent pledge of being no more than a 6 handicap for the Flem Cup. Only 5 days ago, Jennings claimed

"I 'ave <u>no</u> chance of getting a lift to 7 from 6. None at all. I simply don't have enough matches left in the year to make that sort of move. My score would 'ave to be so 'igh as to be thrown out, so you see it's quite impossible."

By yesterday, Jennings was singing a different tune when we caught up to him at the Angel.

"'Aving only one more match . . . I am totally confident . . . that the result . . . will be an effort . . . that will re-establish me . . . at the 7 'andicap . . . I so richly deserve. Of course . . . don't think . . . that I won't be trying . . . just as 'ard as I would be . . . if I weren't playing under . . . different circumstances. There will be absolutely no . . . consideration . . . concerning my 'andicap needs . . . past or present . . . including the upcoming Flem Cup. Any thoughts in that regard . . . will fail to have no impact on the results . . . of my efforts. I mean that . . . with all sincerity . . . 'onestly . . . thanks for coming . . . and beers are on the 'ouse – thanks Singe!!!"

As Singe's jaw dropped, Ian strode down the stairs to the car park and beyond, taking no further questions.

In unrelated news, Renishaw Park professional John Oates, ex-Flem Cupper and the man who announced Jennings' initial handicap bump down to 6, prematurely returned from a family holiday in order to hold his own news conference. After ignoring a question about a rumored sighting of him detailing Jennings' BMW at 11pm Saturday night, Oates entered a trance-like state when asked about the handicap issue, robotically reciting:

"Mr. Jennings is a man beyond reproach. Recently awarded a 6 'andicap by mistake, 'oi believe 'e should actually be a 10 'andicap due to the tragic Achilles tendon injury 'e sustained while performing 'is normal super-'uman activities a few short years ago. In pursuit of that and in my official capacity as club professional, 'oi've petitioned the R&A to give this gentleman an unrestricted 10-'andicap, effective immediately. Absent that adjustment, 'oi've further petitioned the R&A to issue 'im a 10-'andicap for all golf matches 'eld within 5 days of an overseas flight due to the agony of not being able to properly stretch said Achilles tendon during said flight.

'Oi dare think that this is only fair; 'oi truly do. And 'oi also think that it's truly ironic that only a body part associated with a great 'ero loike Achilles 'imself could stop Mr. Jennings, a man 'oo reminds me, and many others, I'm sure, of the god-like Greek warrior."

Jennings, bracketed by two large construction workers nearby, gave a curt nod of approval before turning to leave. Snapping out of his trance-like state, Oates quickly followed, head down, waving off any further questions.

* * *

By early October, Ian was calling me a couple of times a week, trolling for information on the matches. It was a curiosity I happily fed with tidbits of bland, believable disinformation. The reality would be very different. The second prong of my strategy involved the tactics we would use in the form of a drastically new and improved pairing strategy. For the first time, we would be pair players with one and only one goal in mind - *winning*. Many years earlier, the trip, and even the Cup, had originated as a social event, built around an acknowledged tradition of trying to get everyone chances to play with everyone. After sticking to that approach the first two years, the team agreed it was time for change. From here on out, we would find successful pairs and ride them as long as they remained successful. The premium would be on performance and chemistry - and I had some very intriguing pairings for when the time came to announce them.

But I would let that news dribble out slowly. First, he would have to wait until the day the handicaps became official on October 10 to find out that all the same old pairings I'd been feeding him, the ones he'd been chatting about down at the Angel, were not at all the pairings he'd be facing on Day 1. I would then let him wait another two weeks, until our Day 2 deadline on October 23, to discover the full scope of the strategy change with our Day 2 pairs, leaving him just 4 days to analyze what we'd done with our Day 2 pairings before setting those matches.

As he waited, the wheels of my virtual printing press were running, prepping a new shiny object to be dangled before England's eyes with a story I hoped would be the equivalent of shoving a stick into a hornet's nest. Purely a distraction, the article contained an interview with me in which I, as Team U.S. Captain, laid out my case for the American side being retroactively awarded the 2001 Flem Cup due to a handicapping error that resulted in the American side being unfairly penalized to the tune of 12-15% off their rightful handicaps. Naturally, correcting the error would result in changing the result to a 12-1/2 to 11-1/2 Yank victory.

Of course nothing would be changed so I ended the interview with the provocatively innocent comment that *"even if the correction is never made and the right thing never done . . . just knowing that everyone knows the truth is enough for me."*

Finally, October 20 arrived and with 2 weeks to go, my propaganda machine was running at full speed, locked and loaded for the first appearance of the second prong of our strategy: our new pairing strategy.

When Ian chose Miffer as his partner on Day 1, it seemed a powerhouse pairing at first. I knew AJ would have to be part of the solution but who would be his partner? Then it hit me - Lou. I had never really paired them together before but they got along really well off the course and I could see them as having good chemistry. More importantly, Lou would be getting a stroke from *both* his opponents on every single hole – including all five of the par 3's. With AJ playing his normal consistent game, every par by Lou would be a net birdie and with Lou capable of 5-7 pars, I saw a very difficult proposition for Ian and Miffer.

With AJ and Lou as one pair, it struck me that a sound strategy would be to capitalize on the remaining Tanis' close-knit makeup by playing Jack Jr., Jack Sr., Chris and Matt together. That left Pat and me as the final pair and we'd always played well together.

For the 9-hole Pinehurst matches, I switched the pairs a bit after setting up a spreadsheet to run our complex handicap calculations and maximize any handicap strokes we'd be getting. Against Brighty and Ian, AJ and Sven would be getting a fat 3 strokes while Lou and I would be getting an even fatter 4 against Jarvo and Richard – and those were in addition to the 1 stroke each of our two other pairs would be getting. With the #1 handicap hole being the 7th, all four of our pairs would get a stroke at that crucial point, late in the match. All of these factors were considered in setting the matches.

After posting the Day 1 matches on Oct 10, I called Ian to give them to him myself. After reading them off, I gave Ian as much time as he needed to fully digest the differences, looking for some sort of strategy . . . but what, exactly? I, of course, continued to reassure him of how poorly we were all playing so what difference would it make?

"Look at the year we've all had, Ian. Even pros can't just turn things around on cue. We've been playing terribly all year. You were there in Pebble; my game has been terrible all year."

Finally, nearly two weeks later at around noon on the 23rd and in plenty of time for Singe to print it out and post it at the Angel, the article announcing the Day 2 pairs posted.

Day 2 Pairings For Team U.S. Analyzed

By: Datzit Indaruf, Flem Cup Correspondent

MYRTLE BEACH, Oct 23 – Captain-For-Now Donut Dow has announced his Day 2 pairings for Arrowhead - the longest (at 6800 yards) and arguably most difficult of the Cup venues (although TPC-Myrtle Beach – the Day 3 venue – has been called a "bear"). The 4 ball pairings are Matt and Jack Sr., AJ and Lou, Dow and Pat, Jack Jr. and Sven. The Pinehurst pairings remain unchanged from Day 1.

Surprisingly, the Yanks made only one change in 4 ball, swapping low-handicappers Matt and Jack Jr.. This signals a new strategy compared to past Cups where partners were exchanged freely. England now has until October 27th to make their own analysis of these pairings and set the matches for Day 2.

Odds makers in both London and Vegas, meanwhile, have been stunned by the volume of both dollars and pounds flooding into the American side after England peaked at 15:1 favorites right after news of Tanis' injury was made public. Milo's rib injury turned a trickle into a flood, the latest odds as low as only 5:2 in favor of England retaining the Cup.

But there is more than just Milo's rib injury. Nearly twelve months of lethargy on the American side is rumored to be over amid scattered reports of actual practice and playing time cropping up here and there. But surely it is too little too late? After all, the weather has begun to change on both sides of the Atlantic and practice schedules will be more and more unpredictable as fall settles in – and for the Americans, there remains much work and little time before having to face the powerhouse England squad.

Finally, in light of Captain (for now) Dow's recent attempt to blame his team's 2001 loss on math errors in the handicapping process, reactions have been received from two England players – Milo and Swampy. They are reprinted here in their entirety.

"In a far flung corner of England there lies a quaint pub called The Angel Hotel. In a small smoke-filled room to the right of the entrance there is the Rave Cave. This room exhibits various sporting memorabilia including cricket, football and golf. Within this room there is a coal fireplace, above it a mantel. This mantel is adorned with sporting trophies, one of which is the prestigious Flem Cup. On the plinth of the cup is a plaque on which the names of past winners are engraved deep into the metal for all eternity. For the avoidance of any doubt, I asked St John Harris, proprietor and custodian of the Cup, to inform us of the name etched upon the Cup for the year 2001. 'England', he said . . . and so it shall remain, for all time." - *Paul "Milo" Miles*

It was with just a tad more vitriol that Swampy's response came in:

To American Captain Donut Dow,

Damn you!! You go on about the 'honorable' nature of The Cup but all you think of is winning. If winning is that important, how is it your guys have played so little golf this year and your handicaps have gone up? Pathetic. As dyed in the wool Brits, we believe that you only get out what you put in. You know . . . John Lennon and all that pish posh.

If you can't stand the heat, get out of the kitchen; if you swim with the sharks, don't throw in your chum and if you don't have the figure, stop wearing the lingerie. Truth is, you might as well forget the Flem Cup as a competitive spectacle. This is exactly why we let you win your so-called "War of Independence". Can you imagine if we'd beaten you a la the Flem Cup? 200 years later, you'd still be whining! *'Yeah, but we only had buck-skin jackets, beaver pelt hats and Bowie knives! You had nice red coats and muskets. And we never bothered with target practice cuz me and bubba was busy trying to hook a cat-fish fer dinner.'*

Deal with it, Dow! You know, I know – even Lou, the great man, knows. You ain't got a burgers chance of going cold on a fat farm of getting that trophy changed.

And you goin' down bro' . . just like '01.

PS. What's it like to have set a record that can't be beat?"

Trowbridge, no stranger to outrageous comments, is known for wanting to "spank" Matt Tanis in a match after being thrashed by the teenager, 5&4, in their 2001 2 ball mismatch. Wiser heads prevailed in Ireland, however, and Swampy has now retired, reportedly hiding . . . er, living . . . at an undisclosed location near Birmingham.

Apparently unwilling to leave it at personal humiliation only, he chose to drag his entire country into a historically-challenged version of the Revolutionary War, an event universally considered to be the beginning of the end of England as a world power.

In reality, though, who can say that the ploy Swampy describes hasn't worked out well for Britain, what with America bailing them out of not one but two world wars. If done purposely, as Swampy suggests, it truly was a stroke of genius.

***

After posting the article, I gave Ian a call to personally deliver the news of our Day 2 pairings.

"Yeah, that's right. The Pinehurst pairings are the same as Day 1." I finished up, positively giggling in anticipation of hearing his initial response but there was nothing, only silence, until I finally heard

"Hmmm…"

Silence. Then, a few seconds later, I heard it again

"Hmmm…"

Mentally high-fiving myself, I knew he was flummoxed, totally unprepared for what we had done. If nothing else, it showed him that we actually had a new strategy and were, perhaps, far more engaged than he'd been led to believe. After hanging up, I smiled again as I pictured the conversations that would happen at the Angel over the next few nights as they wrestled with their own deadline, October 27, for the Day 2 matches.

With the second prong's pairing strategy deployed, I once again turned my efforts to the psychological warfare battle. Ever so slowly, I was preparing to unveil the third and most crucial prong of my strategy - our preparedness. Having relentlessly fed their overconfidence, the time to destroy it was fast approaching.

In fact, that process had already begun with the passing comment in the article about "rumors of Yanks increased playing time". Initially an innocent and little noticed reference, the rumor would be repeated in upcoming articles with increasing frequency and certainty over the next week or so, each time planting additional seeds of doubt and uncertainty in the minds of the Brits. Finally, a day or two before travel day, an article would post concerning a blockbuster interview with Captain Dow revealing every detail of our thorough preparation and the true state of our team. England would have no time to react – and they would know it. Their confidence of facing an underprepared and outmanned opponent shattered, they would fully understand they would be facing a well-prepared and angry team.

I smiled as I thought of all the questions Ian would be bombarded with over the next 10 days, questions that would keep changing as the news I was feeding them changed, questions he'd be unable to answer. In a couple days, Ian would release the matches for Day 2 and I'd get to see how he reacted to our new pairing strategy. In the meantime, various news items would continue to trickle out, each one subtly planting and nurturing a sense of doubt and uncertainty in the minds of the Brits.

Finally, on October 26, Ian called me with the matches for Day 2. I could immediately see that he had, indeed, reacted to our new strategy, his pairings now mirroring our new strategy of putting a low handicap golfer with a high one in group. He sounded confident once again, clearly over his surprise in what we had done. I smiled to myself, knowing he remained blissfully unaware of the third prong of our strategy - our preparation. Soon enough, I thought as my plan played out, day by day. Soon enough.

With travel day being Thursday, November 6 and England's golf season pretty much over, I decided that the previous Saturday afternoon, November 1, would be perfect for posting the big article on our tactics and strategies. I only wished I could have been at the Angel that night.

Insider's Look: Team U.S. Strategies & Tactics

By: Datzit Indaruf, Flem Cup Correspondent

MYRTLE BEACH, Nov 1, 2003 – In an exclusive interview with Team U.S. Captain (for now) Donut Dow, FlemCup.com has gotten an inside look at the new – and secret – strategies and tactics used this year to somehow tip the scales toward the Americans for the first time. Dow was unusually candid in providing information on this secret American training plan - a plan he cleverly nicknamed 'THE PLAN' - that was devised and implemented the past few months. For Team England, it is, to say the least, a worrisome development at this late stage.

###

FlemCup.com: *What began the process of developing what you named 'THE PLAN'.*

Captain-for-now Donut Dow: *Well, the entire team – me most of all – had been in a funk for most of 2003. I didn't care about playing and I wasn't looking forward to Myrtle Beach. When Ian surprised me by issuing his pairings in mid-August, nearly two months early, I thought he must be up to something clever but after thinking it though, I became convinced he wasn't and that meant only one thing – Mr. Perfect Ireland was overconfident to the point of arrogance . . . and that pissed me off. That was when I began to hatch THE PLAN. The first part – making sure everyone knew how badly and how little we were all playing – was easy because it was true. Then I decided to change our 9-hole match format to Pinehurst, a format you really need experience with. First, I assumed England wouldn't bother practicing it and I was right. Second, I set up several practice sessions where we did play it in inter-squad matches with the teams we'd be fielding in the Cup.*

FC.com: *You practiced the Pinehurst format?*

CFN Donut: *Absolutely. We have been practicing relentlessly as a team and as individuals for 6 weeks or so. Starting in late September, we scheduled inter-squad 4 ball matches every Saturday. We got great weather and added 9-hole Pinehurst matches afterwards whenever we could. For the first time, we have been practicing very hard as set pairs.*

We also changed our pairing strategy. When I first got the Day 1 pairings, Ian and Miffer seemed like quite a challenge but it struck me early on that Lou and AJ could be a really, really tough match for them. If AJ played his normal solid, steady golf, Lou could just grip it and rip it, playing more aggressively than normal because he'd be getting a shot every hole from each opponent. We scheduled a course with five par 3s primarily for that reason. Anything close to his normal share of 5-8 pars, all net birdies, plus the occasional natural birdie net eagle will make him very tough to keep up with for two low handicappers. Keeping the Tanis family members together also seemed a good strategy. That left Pat with me and we play well with each other.

We also dropped the whole 'social' thing. For years, we'd used the "everyone should play with everyone" mentality. No more. We set the pairs and left them; even during the practice rounds, which were quite competitive. Performance and chemistry was what we were after. NOBODY wants to lose again.

FC.com: Do you assume that you will just be able to turn things around on five rounds of golf?

CFN Donut: Of course not. That is why I, personally, have spent every single day over the past 5 weeks – 34 consecutive days and counting – at the Harkers Hollow driving range and putting green, working to improve every single facet of my game. I have hit thousands upon thousands of 1-irons in that time, grooving an effortless swing that will easily and consistently send the ball on a low line, 220 to 250 yards out. Oh, sometimes it might only go 180 to 200 yards but rarely do I get into any trouble. In fact, my plan is to use 100% irons, establishing a monotonous consistency that will slowly drive my opponents mad.

Allow me, though, to give credit where due. All of our motivation and focus grew from the arrogance of a single man, my friend and counterpart, Captain Jennings, and I can only say 'thank you, Ian, I owe you a great debt'. It was his giddy hubris that inspired this plan, reinvigorating not just my own competitive nature but the entire team's as well. This year, we will settle for nothing short of complete and total victory. Without his foolish and reckless behavior 2 months ago, I don't think any of this happens.

Finally, I want to mention that I do have one more thing up my sleeve for the Brits.

FC.com: And what would that be?

CFN Donut [looking at his watch]: Not now. This interview is over. I have an appointment with my mental weightlifting coach.

###

So the plot of the 2003 Flem Cup thickens with these new revelations. Is CFN Donut Dow making up the story, hoping against hope that England will buy it and show up all 'fraidy-scared'? Or is it true, meaning the Americans will be showing up loaded for bear, far better prepared than ever before? With less than a week to go, we won't have to wait long to find out.

***

The next day, talking to Ian on the phone, he brushed off the article with a half-hearted "I knew you were up to something" but I could tell he was shaken a bit by the news of our extensive preparations. Over the same time frame, preparations by Team England consisted mainly of bicep crunches using pints as dumbbells while dreaming of the inevitable 3-peat.

I'd done everything possible to win this year, filling the air with shiny objects while nurturing and coaxing out England's enormous level of overconfidence through website stories and casual conversations. Meanwhile, behind the scenes, a radically different pairing strategy coupled with the most seriously competitive practice we'd ever engaged in made us more prepared than ever. Finally, understanding the plan and buying into it resulted in our collective mindset going from one of apathetic hopelessness to confident, revenge-minded focus on winning. Now, with the "interview" being posted and The Plan completely unveiled, my fondest hope was that their overconfidence would be fatally compromised, turning surety into fearful uncertainty about what, exactly, they would be facing come Friday.

Finally, on Tuesday, November 4, my last shiny object was unveiled through a website article I'd been crafting revealing the mysterious 'something else' I had up my sleeve.

Investigative Report: Dow's Secret Weapon Exposed

By: Iva Tufshot, Investigative Reporter

WOLLA WOLLA BING BONG, AUSTRALIA – Many believe claims of a "secret weapon" by American Captain-for-now Donut Dow mean nothing more than his self-inflicted all-iron play – a risky strategy at best on the long Myrtle links – while others think it mere bluster from the Yank, a sadly transparent attempt to get past last year's disastrous 'donut' performance in Ireland. But this reporter's investigation has found a deeper – and far more sinister – meaning.

We began by carefully examining differences in Dow's play the past two years. Surprisingly, we found the quality of his play was not dramatically different. Although he averaged 2.5 strokes more per round in Ireland, that was a fairly average increase for the group on the tougher Irish links. His clubs were the same so why was he such a pathetic loser in 2002, unable to collect a single match point?

Stumbling across a picture of him taken during the 2001 Cup, I was immediately struck by a major difference in his appearance – a very distinctive hat. A bit of digging revealed that this was an Akubra *hat, made for the Australian Outback and so prodigious that he had to leave it home in 2002, fearful that in Ireland a wind gust might lift him clear off the ground a la The Flying Nun.*

Over the years, many people have laughed at The Hat*, especially Team England players who disdainfully refer to it as a 'daft hat'. But where, exactly, does* The Hat *come from and is there something more significant here than just a hat. It has been a mystery – until now.*

DAFT HAT INVESTIGATION:

As the Daft Hat *investigation unfolded, I was surprised to find myself sucked into a past so fascinating that it ended up leading me on a 10,000 mile odyssey to discover its origins . . . and its power. A secret no longer, the story of the* Daft Hat *is guaranteed to send chills up the spines of all but the most craven England players, hitting their psyche where it hurts most – England's sordid and brutal history of colonialism and subjugation of native peoples.*

The story began in early summer, 2001. Alone in Australia on business, Dow decided to do some sightseeing in the Outback. As often tragically happens when stupid people blithely wander into that vast, barren wilderness, he got lost. Things got so bad, in fact, that he began preparing himself to die, gathering himself into a ball as dingoes yipped in the gathering dusk and vultures circled overhead.

Mustering the last bit of his ebbing strength, Dow was in the process of scrawling one final note in the hardscrabble earth to his mother, saying "the dingoes ate your baby", when, out of nowhere, he appeared, a small, withered man who was clearly not your typical 'throw another shrimp on the barbie, Sheila' Aussie. Dow correctly assumed he was an Aborigine, one of the ancient, native peoples whose tribes had lived in harmony with the land for thousands upon thousands of years. Either way, helpless and near death, Dow found himself being carried to a nearby tribal village where, over several weeks, he was nursed back to health.

It was during a restless night, dreaming of the approaching Flem Cup, when Dow began talking in his sleep. The only word recognizable to the Aborigines was "Anglanders" – Englanders. Now the Aborigines hate the English with the white-hot intensity of slightly more than ten thousand suns due to the fact that England sent its worst convicts and prisoners to the Aboriginal homeland to rape, pillage and subjugate the indigenous peoples, a favorite hobby of the Brits back in the day. Mistakenly thinking Dow was English, the tribe decided to do what they did with all Englanders who wander into the outback – smear him with honey and stake him to an ant hill.

As fate would have it, though, a small item fell out of Dow's pocket as he was being staked down – an American flag pin given to him by his friend, Terry Neal. Recognizing the flag, they realized Dow was, in fact, American. Having heard legendary stories of a mighty race of people who had, against all odds, driven the stinking English from their own soil, the Aborigines released Dow with profound apologies. To honor him, they immediately organized a wild 3 night celebration of tribal dancing and drunken debauchery, culminating in unbridled consumption of s'mores and rum punch around the campfire. By the time Dow was teaching them American drinking games like quarters, he was an honorary member of the tribe.

After several moons, Dow knew it was time to leave because, well, the Chief told him that it was time to leave. Before that sad day, however, the tribe wanted to throw him a big going away bar-b-que with lots of food and giant Foster's wolla-wolla-billa-beer-bongs. Sitting at the table of Chief Mereelly Haitum Limeez, the two were downing Fosters like the brewery was closing when talk turned to golf, a favorite pastime of the Chief. When Dow described the Flem Cup and the upcoming match against Team "Anglaise", the Chief's eyes lit up and he immediately signaled for his warriors to bring the American a great gift - the Daft Hat.

As Dow gazed in wonder upon the Daft Hat, *Chief Mereelly Haitum Limeez explained that it was no ordinary hat. The soft, brushed covering was made from only the finest selected short hairs of Englishmen who had carelessly wandered into the outback and died or been killed in tribal uprisings over the years. Started by the great Chief Killall da Limeez many moons ago, tribal craftsmen could only work on the* Daft Hat *one night a year: the wild cele-bration commemorating a great victory called,* The Day We Took A Crapload of English Short-Hairs.

In order to invoke the most powerful magic, the Chief explained, the ceremony must co-incide with "The first full moon after the fall harvest . . . when the Dingoes run with the Koala Bears . . . and the Kangaroo watches the Crocodile eat the Brown Snake . . . the magic . . . it will come."

The evidence has shown that these conditions indeed make for powerful magic. Only the Daft Hat *could have been responsible for the miraculous recovery shots that defeated Team England Captain Jennings time and time again in 2001. Stunned by those defeats, for two years Jennings has struggled to comprehend how in heaven's name those shots were even pulled off, especially after witnessing Dow's "unaided" talent level in Ireland. With this new evidence, can there be any doubt left where those shots came from? Aboriginal magic!*

But before giving Dow The Hat, Chief Mereelly Haitum Limeez warned him that the Daft Hat *was not quite complete; that it needed a few more English shorthairs. If Dow took it with him in 2001, it would only have a portion of its potential power. Feeling he needed it anyway, Dow took it and achieved solid results individually but the Yanks lost. Following that defeat,*

Dow returned the Daft Hat *and asked Chief Mereelly Haitum Limeez to complete it for the 2003 Cup.*

Three weeks ago, Dow received a Fed Ex delivery that included a very nice note from the Chief (he's such a nice man). It was the Daft Hat, *completely finished.*

So when Dow is standing, head-down, he may well be examining his shoes and wondering how he could have let them get so dirty but it is far more likely that he is seeking spiritual connection – through the Daft Hat *– with the great Aborigine Chief Mereelly Haitum Limeez, asking for deliverance of the 'Anglaise' by the short hairs.*

In other news, it seems that despite November 6th being travel day, several TUS players reportedly are going to make the trip easier by leaving Nov 5th. That contrasts with Team England's travel schedule of leaving early Thursday morning, having an extended layover in Charlotte, NC and only arriving in Myrtle Beach 9 hours before the first tee-time. Odds in Vegas and London have dropped to even money and in some parlors the Americans are even a (very) slight favorite. Three days remain until the first ball will be struck for the 2003 Flem Cup, the weather looks fantastic and the players appear ready.

***

After posting the article, I sat back to imagine the scene at the Angel, perfectly timed for the send-off party. With all of my psychological weapons deployed and the preparation finished, the only thing left was executing on the course and on that subject, I felt as confident as I had in a very long time. Finally, Thursday morning arrived and I set off before dawn to meet up with Lou in Delaware and head south.

17

The 2003 Cup

By 5 pm, Lou and I rolled into Myrtle Beach, the last arrivals from our side. AJ and Chris had actually flown down Wednesday night and played a practice round the next day at our Day 1 venue, Thistle. The rest of the Tanis family and Pat had driven most of the way last night, staying in North Carolina and getting to Myrtle in time for their own practice round this morning. By 6, Team U.S. was assembled at BummZ, greeting each other with a grim determination, knowing we were here for one reason – to win.

After a couple of beers and a bite to eat, we still had several hours to kill with Team England due in around 11pm. After killing 4 more hours, Jack, Lou, Chris and I headed over to the airport and by 11:30 or so, our opponents dragged themselves through the arrivals door, tired and frustrated. Weary from the long trip, there was no interest in more than a single beer at BummZ.

The piercingly blue sky and warm temperatures the next morning were glorious reminders of why we continued, year after year, to return to Myrtle Beach in early November. Arriving at Thistle by 7:30, we had our game faces on, loosening up on the driving range and putting green, focused and ready. Finally, I watched as Lou, AJ, Miffer and Ian headed over to the first tee. After exchanging handshakes, Lou led the way, splitting the fairway with a long drive. I returned to my routine, smiling at the prospect of Lou doing that all day while getting a stroke a hole.

As I'd hoped, our new ace pairing jumped on the Brits with both feet, winning the first 3 holes and making the turn 5 up, having won 5 holes without a loss.

The second match, Matt and Sven against Smokin' Joe and Brighty, went off a bit better for the Brits, but not by much. All square after six straight halves, Matt's 80-yard wedge to 6 inches on 7, a 424-yard par 4, gave him a kick-in birdie and when he followed with another bird on 8, he and Sven made the turn 2 up.

In the third group out, I battled the normal butterflies by focusing on the hundreds of hours of practice and play I'd put in over the previous 6 or 7 weeks, knowing I'd grooved my swing as much as possible, focusing my mind on two simple swing thoughts: tempo and release. Taking my backswing up to 80% of parallel, I paused briefly before starting the downswing, accelerating under control. Feeling the weight of the club head, I released my hands smoothly and completely, squaring the clubface to my line at impact. Feeling the solid *click* at impact, I knew without looking up that the shot was straight and true. *So it begins*, I thought to myself as I watched the ball land and bound down the fairway before rolling to a stop, some 240 yards away.

With my ill-fated 2 ball match against Milo 13 months ago in Ireland adding fuel to my fire, the match went exactly as I'd dreamed as Pat and I dominated through a steady diet of pars supplemented by the occasional birdie. As a team, we made the turn 7 under par net, 6 up over the Brits.

In the final match, both Jacks had been advertised as "vulnerable" to England because of their various physical ailments. Unfortunately for Phil and Jarvo, it turned out to be a case of false advertising when each showed up feeling fit and playing well enough to make the turn 4 up.

With 9 holes played in each of the four matches, a total of 36 holes had been played. Of those, we'd won an astonishing 19 while the Brits had won just 2. Our leads were 5 up, 2 up, 6 up and 4 up. None of that meant anything to us, though. We were each fixated on one immediate objective: finishing the job on the back 9.

In Match 1, a brief rally by Miffer and Ian had cut the lead from 5 up to 3 up after 12 but wins on 13 by AJ and 14 by Lou ended the match in decisive fashion, 5&4. Match 2, meanwhile, had remained the closest of the day with our side's 2 up lead intact through 13. On 14, Sven suddenly came alive, reeling off a pair of net birdies and with a halve on 16, he and Matt closed out the match, 4&2. Incredibly, it would be the only match to last past the 14th hole. In fact, by the time the match ended on 16 green, Matches 3 and 4 had already ended, Pat and I winning 6&4 and the Jacks winning 5&4.

At lunch, the scorecards told a disturbing tale for England in terms of individual scores. In the two previous years and 160 rounds of Cup golf, there had been only four rounds with a Stableford score of more than 36 (even par net). There was Pat's 40 at Adare Manor in 2002 and three 37s. On this day, no fewer than five of us turned the trick with Lou, Jack Sr. and Pat carding 39s to go with my 38 and Matt's 37. Our "underachievers" were AJ at 36, Sven at 34 and slacker Jack Jr. at 30, a score that normally would put him near the Day 1 lead.

For England, Smokin' Joe led the way with a solid 35, a score that would have put him in 1st place after Day 1 in either 2001 or 2002 but only placed him 7th in 2003. The bottom line was that we were a team that was focused on revenge, playing well and playing at an unprecedented level. Shell shocked, the Brits ate quietly as they contemplated the 9-hole afternoon matches amid whispered questions of "*what's* the format".

Sitting together as a team, we'd agreed not to say a word beyond the normal cordialities following our morning matches, adding in one more piece of gamesmanship. Finished eating, we rose as a team without a word, heading out to finish the job we had started in the morning.

In the first match out, Jack Sr. and Pat jumped out to a 3 up after 5 holes, coasting in with a 2&1 win against Milo and Phil while, in the third match, AJ and Sven followed a slightly less dominating script, jumping out to a 2 up lead early before coasting home with a 2 up win.

Sandwiched between the two were Lou and I, facing off against Jarvo and Richard and getting 4 shots. Somewhat embarrassed to be getting them, we wouldn't need any of them. After winning 1 with a routine par, Lou and I simply went off. On 2, after Lou knocked his long approach shot to 40-feet and I drained the long birdie putt for a 2 up lead. On 3, we reversed the script when I knocked my approach to 25 feet and Lou sank it for another birdie to go 3 up. Feeling positively giddy at this point, I rolled in another 20 foot birdie putt on 4 only to then declare a loss of hole penalty on our side because Lou had touched my putting line with his putter while discussing the read. By then, so disheartened were Richard and Jarvo that they actually tried to dissuade us from awarding them the hole but I insisted. I could see the resignation in their eyes and wanted nothing more than to extend their suffering as long as possible. Sure enough, another win on 5 got us back to 3 up and after the Brits finally managed to halve a hole on 6, our win on 7 ended it, 4&2.

With seven matches played, we had seven easy wins and the Cup score stood at 5-½ to 0. As the first three groups gathered behind the final green, the only thing we knew about the last match out was that Jack Jr. and Matt had gone 1 up after winning the 7th in their match against Joe and Miffer. Peering back across the lake, we saw them arrive on the tee with Jack and Matt hitting first, telling us all we needed to know - the match wasn't over yet and Matt and Jack were still 1 up.

The last hole at Thistle West is a 558 yard dogleg left par-5 with a large lake bordering the entire left side of the fairway as well as in front of the tee and the green. With the tees set across the lake, players could bite off as much of the lake as they dared and if they successfully took an aggressive enough line, big hitters could go for the green in two.

With the last turn of the fairway going hard left, a long approach to the green meant a long carry across both the lake and the deep bunker guarding that side of the narrow green. The far safer and more conventional route would be to play your second shot down the fairway and get as close as possible to the hard dogleg in order to take both the water and the left bunker out of play.

As we stood in small groups on the mounds behind the last hole, the stakes had shifted from the big win we'd hoped for to the unthinkable – a complete whitewash. Watching all four tee shots find the fairway, we watched Joe hit first and play a safe shot down the right side, leaving about 80 yards in, a perfect lob wedge distance for Miffer. With Joe safely in play, Miffer took the more aggressive approach, launching a towering fairway wood from about 260 yards out that barely cleared the water, coming to rest in the bunker about 20 yards short of the green and leaving a very tough shot. There was no doubt their next shot would be Miffer playing from Joe's ball.

Jack and Matt had each hit monster drives, leaving both within striking distance of the green from about 240 yards away. Playing first, Jack decided to match Joe's safe play, hitting a so-so shot that stopped about 120 yards from the green. Up next, Matt ripped a fairway wood straight at the pin but it landed with a thud in the face of the bunker before rolling back towards the bottom, leaving Jack with a decent lie for a straight-forward, uphill bunker shot. After discussing the options, the two made their decision: Jack would play from the bunker.

After double and triple checking his distance, Miffer hit a beautiful lob wedge, landing it about 15 feet short of the pin but overspinning it and by the time it stopped, Joe was left with a 35 foot uphill putt for birdie.

Still away, the Brits surveyed their putt from every angle before Joe finally settled in and stroked his putt, firmly up the hill. Halfway to the hole the speed seemed fine but its pace quickly died over the last 10 feet or so, leaving Miffer about 3 feet for the par.

Playing for eagle out of the bunker and needing only a halve to win the match, we were in the driver's seat for moment, just long enough for Jack's well documented bunker-demons to show up. Making the cardinal sin of attempting to *lift* the ball with the club rather than hitting down into the sand and letting the sand lift it out, Jack's cautious, defensive swing left the ball exactly where it started – at bottom of the bunker laying 3.

Up next, Matt landed his sand wedge exactly where he was aiming but rather than kicking right and spinning down the hill a ways, it simply stuck where it landed, leaving his father a slippery 5 foot downhill putt for a par they now needed to halve the hole and win the match. It was a straight putt, very fast, and Jack gave the ball only a slight nudge to get it moving. Ever so slowly, it trickled towards the hole and as we held our breath, I noticed Jack madly contorting his body in a language I well understood, contortions intended to somehow bring the ball back on line. Sadly for us, they would not work and when it slid by the left edge, Team England breathed a collective sigh of relief as Joe conceded our bogey, grateful for the meager quarter-point portion they were about to receive. Thinking back, I remembered how, only 13 months earlier, they had made the most of my individual donut. How disappointing it was now to barely lose out on the opportunity to repay that with a team donut.

Looking around, I could see a little air had gone out of our team balloon and as Jack dejectedly knocked his ball away, I had to remind myself that it had still been an awesome day, one ending with us in complete control, 5-¾ to ¼, and a 5-½ point lead would be fine, I told myself, just fine. Behind me, conversations turned to the dinner plans before pausing respectfully as Miffer settled in over his straight in putt. After a moment or two, he swung, stroking it firmly. Reaching the front edge with plenty of pace, we watched the ball begin to disappear as a muted and slightly sarcastic cry of celebration began to rise from the lips of the Brits . . . but it quickly died.

Accelerating as it dropped, the ball whipped round the back half of the hole, speeding up to the point where it had just enough to sling itself back up and out of the hole, straight back at Miffer before stopping an inch below the hole.

This was no wobble as the ball burned the edge of the hole. It was the dreaded, full wrap-around, half-way down, 180° lip out - a rarity indeed. Head thrown back, Joe stared skyward as Miffer chose the opposite approach; bent over, face in his hands as his putter fell to the ground.

From the spectators, there was dead silence . . . but again, only for a moment.

As the Brits stared, mouths open in disbelief, a cry of pure joy went up from the American side followed by laughs, whoops, hollers and high fives. Only Jack Jr. and Matt were subdued, smiling sheepishly and shaking their heads in disbelief as they walked over to their distraught opponents, extending their hands in sincere commiseration of what could only be called terrible luck.

It had been a gift and though we all knew it, we didn't care. It was the perfect end to the perfect day, with eight matches played and eight matches won, but our dominance went far deeper. England had not led for a single hole in a single match all day. In my wildest dreams I hadn't imagined *THE PLAN* working out this well. In addition to near-perfect strategy, tactics and execution, we'd brought along Lady Luck, an invaluable but untrustworthy teammate. From the previous night's late arrival to Miffer's lip out, every good break was ours; every bad break theirs. It was a complete and total domination . . . and it was *awesome.*

As we drove back to the hotel, I mulled over the possible teaser headlines I would put up on the web site, eventually settling on *"ENGLAND DESTROYED, LOSES ALL 8 MATCHES".* After doing a bit of work on the main article, which I would finish and post later, I headed downstairs to the pool and hot tub area, cold beers in tow, for a little team chat on not letting up. As we settled into the wonderfully relaxing water, I proposed a new goal: closing out the Cup before the 2 ball matches. To do that, we'd need to win 6-1/4 of the next 10 points available. Everyone enthusiastically agreed, eager for some serious payback for previous two years of losses.

At the same time, Ian was holding a meeting of his own, trying to rally his dejected troops with his best inspirational speech, appealing to the prototypical, never-say-die English attitude. Unexpectedly, his cell phone rang. Answering, Singe was on the other end, demanding to know what the hell had happened and by the time the call ended, Ian's mojo was gone. His thoughts fatally interrupted, he had nothing left beyond leading the boys out for a great meal at Carolina Roadhouse. Eventually, we would meet up at BummZ and when Miffer entered threatening to steal my "magic" hat, he made my day all over again, knowing those shiny objects really do work sometimes.

The next day would be at Arrowhead, another course with three separate nines, and with another round of 9-hole Pinehurst matches scheduled, we would be playing all three. The day dawned perfect yet again and the Brits, not surprisingly, came out re-energized, lifting their level of play as ours returned to earth from the stratospheric heights of Day 1.

Their goal, I was well aware, would be to slowly eat into our lead, hoping to be 2 or 3 points down by the 2 ball matches. Ours would be to break even in the 4 ball matches and continue our domination of the Pinehurst. Not surprisingly, each of the day's 4 ball matches would turn out to be tight, three reaching the 18th hole and the other ending on the 17th green.

In the first group, Jack Sr. and Matt jumped out to a quick 2 up lead but Ian, playing with Phil, won three holes on the trot to grab a 1 up lead at the turn. All square again on the 16th tee, Ian was simply not going to be denied and on the course's toughest hole, he followed a booming drive with a 5 iron to 6 feet before dropping the birdie putt for a 1 up lead that would become the final margin of victory when Phil sank a clutch 5 foot par putt to halve 18 for England's first point.

In the second match, AJ and Lou played Smokin' Joe and Jarvo and although our side outscored the Brits by 7 Stableford points as a team, they just couldn't put them away. Sitting 2 down with only four holes left, Jarvo's win on 15 brought England back to 1 down and after halving on the next two holes, pars by both Joe and Jarvo on 18 were enough to win the hole and end the match, all square.

It was a similar story in the day's third match as Pat and I took on Miffer and Milo. Despite leading all day and controlling the match throughout, we couldn't quite close the deal for a win. Going out hot again, I was 2 under net at the turn and Pat was nearly as good but with Miffer nearly matching us shot for shot and Milo chipping in when needed, our lead was only 2 up after 10.

Despite halving six straight holes to go dormie 2, the Brits just wouldn't go away and when Miffer won 17, we needed to halve 18 for the win. On in regulation, I'd left myself 4 feet for par when Milo dropped a bomb from 20 feet for his own par and when I burned the edge, our match ended with another draw.

In the last 4 ball match, Jack Jr. and Sven were up against Brighty and Richard in a match that could have given England some real momentum - but it was not to be. Taking control early, the two brothers made the turn 3 up and although a run by the Brits narrowed the deficit to 1 down after 15, Jack's win on 16 was followed by a halve on 17 that ended the match in our favor, 2&1.

With England having set the 4 ball matches, I was happy with our 2 point split, especially considering we were the first team not to lose in that situation. I also remained hugely confident for our chances in the afternoon Pinehurst matches, a confidence that proved well-placed when we won three matches and halved the fourth. With two days in the books, the Cup score stood at 9-3/4 to 2-1/4. We needed only 2-1/2 more points to clinch the Cup.

The next morning, we awoke to possibly the worst weather we'd ever had for the Cup. Colder than Marsh Harbor in 2001 and as windy as Lahinch in 2002, temperatures beneath the thick, gray canopy of clouds would struggle to reach the mid 40s while the howling northwest wind would make it seem much colder. For the first time, we'd be playing the TPC of Myrtle Beach and the first match out would feature this year's first Captain's match with Milo and Ian facing off against Jack Jr. and me.

The previous night in BummZ, a confident Smokin' Joe had wagered $20 on Ian and Milo, predicting the match would be a bloodbath. He would be right about on the prediction, just wrong on the team. As focused as I'd ever been, I went out and played the best match of my life. On a weather-challenged day, with the rest of the group *averaging* 12 over par and only 2 other players managing scores better than 10 over, I stood 6 *under* net after 11 holes.

With the match all-square after the 5th, we went on a birdie, par, birdie, par tear to make the turn 3 up. After halving 10 with another par, I made the radical move of pulling out my driver for the first time since September, splitting the fairway as Ian shook his head in disgust. When I followed that by holing my 7 iron from 145 yards for an eagle, we had a 4 up lead with 7 to play. From there, Jack took over, winning 12 and 13 to finish off the old fashioned arse-whuppin', 6&5.

In the second match out, Sven and Pat jumped all over Joe and Phil, reaching 4 up after 10 holes before the Brits rallied to get back to only 1 down after 14. Re-focusing, wins by Pat on 15 and 16 closed out the match, 3&2, and lifted us to within half a point of the Cup.

Miffer and Richard, out next against Matt and Lou, would not be the ones to give up that half point. With England 1 up after 8, the two proceeded to win the next four on the trot to go 5 up with 6 to play, eventually coasting in with a 3&2 win.

It would be the day's final match, pitting Jack Sr. and AJ against Jarvo and Brighty, that would provide us with the Cup-clinching point. After we broke on top early (a common theme throughout the week), England twice drew to within one but made the turn still 2 down. At that point, AJ simply went off, winning 10, 14 and 15 to end the match in style, 5&3. We had finally won the Cup in what could only be described as a complete and total dismantling of the England side.

With the score standing 12-¾ to 3-¼, only the eight 2 ball matches and a couple of interesting sub-plots remained. On the negative side, Brighty had zero points and could tie my winless donut record (surpassing it, as far as I was concerned, because of the two additional half point 9-hole matches). On the positive side, Sven and Jack Jr. each had perfect records as they each tried to become the first player(s) to win 5 points in a year. On the Stableford side, my round at TPC had given me a comfortable lead of 10 points over Miffer and AJ.

At dinner that night, in order to stir things up one last time, I announced, with great fanfare, Team U.S.'s new goal: 20 points. To do that, we would need 7 wins and a halve in the next day's 2 ball matches. Following that, Ian announced the matchups he had chosen for the next day's mostly anti-climactic 2 ball matches but there were some interesting storylines remaining. Guarding his record of Irish perfection, Ian sent out Miffer, the top playing Brit, to take down Sven, and Brighty, who had actually been playing fairly well, against Jack Jr. in a match where something had to give. When I asked him for a comment to put up on the website, Ian was at his bombastic best.

"If we can win the 2 ball matches, we'll be seen as the finer golfers and Team U.S. has simply had a crap load of luck. Tomorrow, we will prove we are the better team."

The next morning, back at the familiar Heritage Club, the wind had died down but it was still chilly. During the previous night's hot tub meeting, I'd convinced the team to leave England without any hope of even a moral victory by conceding every match except Jack's and Sven's. The last thing I wanted to give Ian was a moral victory to take home. No, it was better to leave it as what it was, a crushing, ignominious defeat.

The remaining two matches of interest each ended up being interesting. When Sven, the decided underdog, nervously hooked his first tee-shot out of bounds and Miffer jumped out to a 1 up lead, no one was surprised. What we didn't see after that was Sven immediately turn things around by winning 2, 3, 5 and 6 to go 3 up. Just as quickly, though, things turned back again as Miffer won 7, 8 and 9 to make the turn all square it what could only be described as one crazy, roller-coaster ride. Heading to the back, though, Miffer carried all the momentum.

Amazingly, Jack Jr and Brighty were involved in an even more volatile match with not a single halve would be recorded through the first 12 holes, seven of which were won by Brighty. With a 2 up lead, Brighty teed off on 13, a dramatic, 200 yard par 3 requiring a tee to green water carry with a two-sided green that was, in effect, cut in half from back to front by a 3-4 foot high ridge. Coming over the ball a bit, Brighty hit it long and left, leaving himself over and facing a very tricky downhill chip over the ridge.

What happened next would settle the match.

Knowing Brighty was in trouble, Jack had an opening to get back to within 1 and grab some momentum. Focused, he drilled a long iron straight as an arrow, directly at the flagstick. As the group squinted into the autumn sun, shielding their eyes as best they could, they heard a loud *CRACK*. Staring at the pin, they could see it shaking, meaning the ball had struck it but no one could see where it ended up. With Brighty in trouble, anywhere near the pin and on the same side of the ridge would be just fine.

Arriving at the green, Jack disgustedly found his unlucky shot had not just bounced off the flagstick but it had careened all the way back, across the ridge, down the hill and almost into the water. He was left with a nearly impossible 40-50 foot putt back over the ridge for birdie. Having dodged a bullet, Brighty played a beautiful little pitch to within five feet and when Jack 3 putted, the Brit stole the hole by sinking his putt to go 3 up. Mentally and emotionally spent, Jack would eventually lose 15 and the match, 4&3.

Meanwhile, riding the momentum of his late front 9 surge, Miffer had re-claimed the lead by winning 11. He was playing the same solid, mistake-free golf I'd seen for extended periods before but golf is a funny game and just as quickly as Sven had collapsed and Miffer surged, the two reversed roles as Sven surged once again, staggering Miffer with a quick birdie, par, birdie, par combo to win 4 on the trot and take a commanding 3 up lead with only four holes to play. After losing 15, the knockout punch landed when he won 16 , ending the match, 3&2.

The last time Sven had stood on the green of the 18th hole at The Heritage Club, in 2001, he'd been forced to admit, during a memorable dust-up with Swampy that was caught on film and used in the cult classic documentary, *The 2001 Flem Cup,* that he'd managed to win a mere one half point in that year's Cup. This year, he'd led our dominating victory with a perfect 5 points from a 6-0 record. 2001 was a distant memory and the only thing missing was . . . Swampy.

That night, for the first time since handing Ian the trophy two years earlier, I held the Flem Cup, accepting it from Ian during our awards presentation. After 5 long years of Flem Cup play, including the last 2 as an international match, I finally had my first win – and it was sweet. Wonderfully, indescribably sweet.

Never again would the Brits buy any sob stories of a hopelessly unmotivated, unprepared, apathetic Team U.S. but this year the strategy worked in spades. The next day, the win was made sweeter when I managed to recover from a wobbly start to become the Stableford Champion by a slim 3 point margin over AJ. Despite needing to use my driver several times on the 7,000 yard King's North course the last day, my all-irons strategy had proved sounder and more successful than I could possibly have hoped for.

But something even more important than our win happened in 2003 – the Cup, itself, was reinvigorated. After 2 years where we seemed to wilt under pressure, the battle had been fully joined and everyone was looking forward to what would be a war in '04. We'd risen like a Phoenix from the ashes to badly bloody England's nose and there was no doubt we would face a far more focused and motivated squad next year; a challenge that I now knew we would rise to meet, rejuvenated as we'd been, our confidence renewed.

As we said our annual goodbyes, the victorious high was already receding into the past as the sadness of seeing another great week of golf and friendship end began to descend. With the all-consuming focus I'd placed on the Cup over the previous few months gone, so was the joy I'd gotten from all I'd been doing - from writing the pre-Cup articles to formulating of our strategy and our tactics to watching it unfold as I logged hour upon hour of practice and play, all done amid the growing excitement of the approaching event. Now, it was over and everything would come to a crashing halt, receding into nothing more than already fading memories. Win or lose, it was the worst day of the year and as Lou and I drove off, the depression of seeing it end was already sinking in.

18

Run-Up To 2004

It was mid-December when the phone on my desk rang.

"Mr. Dow" I heard a cheery and familiar voice ring out.

"Mr. Jennings"

"'Ow are things with you?"

"Fine, just fine. How are things in merry old England?"

"Merry as always, I suppose. But I'm not sure how merry things used to be so don't 'old me to that."

"So, how was the latest scan?" I asked optimistically.

"Fine, fine. Everything's still fine."

"Excellent. How are things at the Angel these days? Have things calmed down?"

During a call in mid-November, Ian had told me about the abuse he and other team members had endured upon their return. The Day 1 whitewash, the clinching on Day 3, the empty place on the mantle – all of it was fair game in the eyes of the unforgiving locals. Still, I knew that Ian was secretly pleased that we'd responded the way we did. If we'd lost again, we both thought interest in the Cup would begin to wane but now the stakes were higher than ever. Now he had a group of humiliated, angry golfers bent on revenge. The days of overconfident lethargy behind them, England would be loaded for bear come the '04 Cup.

"Yeah, for now, but I still get the occasional comment." He laughed. "We'll 'ave no shortage of players, that's for sure."

Having set the table, he moved on to the real reason for his call.

"What do you think of expanding the group to 12? Same size as Ryder Cup teams, eh?"

Caught off guard, my initial reaction was one of uncertainty.

"I don't know if we can do that, Ian. Maybe 10 a side but going to 12 will be tough. We're losing Matt to the Air Force Academy and it's a big jump in the logistics of everything. A big jump."

"Right, I forgot about Matt and all the work you lads put in on this thing. Well, see what kind of interest you get and we'll go from there. We've got until, what – May – to decide?"

"Yeah, that's when we reserve our tee times. I'll see what the guys think and let you know."

"Right. Merry Christmas to you, lad. You and your family."

"And you, Ian. Say hi to everyone at the Angel – and tell them I finally got all the dust and grime off the Cup. It looks fantastic here – like it was made to be here."

"I'm sure it does" he chuckled. "Just take care of it, will you please? I don't want you 'anding over damaged goods next year. Cheers."

"Talk to you soon" I said, laughing as I hung up.

Within a few days, I'd spoken to Jack about the expansion only to find out that Pat, too, would be bowing out for personal reasons. Now we would start with only 6 but we still felt confident we could get 4 new players so we decided to agree on expanding to 10 man teams.

On New Year's Eve, I picked up my office phone.

"Mr. Dow! 'Ow are you? 'Appy New Year!!"

"Mr. Jennings! I'm fine, fine. Happy New Year to you! What time is it there?"

"About 11. We've just been . . . "

His words were cut off by a loud bang.

"What was that?!" I asked, slightly concerned.

"Whoa – that was a close one!" I heard Ian say as he laughed, sounding far from his phone. A moment later, he was back. "Are you there? What'd you say?"

"What was that bang?"

"Oh, we're 'aving a roman candle war with a chalet across the valley. If you lose me, you'll know why!" His heartfelt laugh made me laugh.

"So how have you been? What's new?" I ventured.

"Everything's great . . . . sitting 'ere with Caroline. Say 'ello, Caroline"

"Allo, Scott" I heard Caroline's lilting voice call out from a distance.

Prior to Ian's diagnosis, I had barely known Caroline, mainly through brief late night pop-ins at the Angel. Since then, they had moved in together and I'd gotten to know her much better. While she matched Ian's appreciation for the finer things in life, she was also, like him, firmly rooted in the important things – friends, laughter and love. She was *real*. Having the greatest appreciation of her quick wit and verbal sparring skills, I witnessed her getting the best of Ian on more than one occasion when they crossed swords. A natural beauty whose appearance perfectly suited her personality, she'd become nearly as much of a fixture in the Angel as Ian.

More than that, she'd earned the love, respect and admiration of the locals for her selfless decision to stay with Ian, knowing what the end game probably was. The way Ian talked about her left me no doubt that he loved her deeply. Somehow, she had found within herself the inner strength to stand by him through the ordeal and in doing so made it *their* ordeal. For that and more, we all loved her.

Speaking for another fifteen minutes, I told Ian the news about Pat and that we would agree to expand but only to 10 a side. He understood, happy to have 2 new spots to fill. We spoke for a few more minutes before he hung up, ready to get back to his battle.

Being year four, it was England's choice of venues, times and formats and by mid-May, they'd been chosen. The Grande Dunes resort course would be the venue for Day 1 along with a comfortably late tee-time so the England players could sleep in the first day.

"But you'll be on England time, probably up by 4 or 5 at the latest" I'd protested, wanting to play our normal afternoon matches. It was to no avail, though - tee times would be around 11am. After making sure it was understood that we would still retain the advantage of setting the afternoon matches on Day 2, I couldn't help but think he had made a mistake. After all, with the exception of last year's Pinehurst dominance, the 9-hole matches had always gone in favor of the team setting them but who was I to stand in their self-destructive way?

As the summer began to roll by, I quickly recruited Tony Simonowicz (quickly dubbed "Tony Alphabet"), a tough match player from Harkers who reinforced my confidence that we could easily sign up 4 new players. Despite that, over the following months and despite efforts by nearly everyone at various times with various friends and acquaintances, further recruitment came to a grinding halt. I, myself, was finding other matters occupying more and more of my time and energy.

Despite my best efforts, my business had continued its death spiral, eventually leaving me no choice but to turn it over to my partner and break off with the pieces I'd been best at but it was tough. As a one man show responsible for marketing, sales, administrative tasks and actually performing the work, it was occupying more of my time than ever before.

Then there was my marriage. The seeds of resentment I had planted in my wife over the years had never stopped growing and festering and whenever she felt the need to up the ante in an argument, she would effortlessly flip through her catalog of past wrongs and simply select one as her weapon-du-jour. Her ability to hurt led me to develop an ever-thickening cocoon of indifference to her slings and arrows. I'm sure I did the same to her.

With no outlet, my response was to ignore her, retreating into a sullen silence and accepting my lot in life, escaping through pot and whatever work projects I could immerse myself in, naively assuring myself I was just waiting for the day the kids to grow up and leave. In truth, they were already gone, drifting further and further away as my marriage descended ever further into the realm of resentful tolerance and spitefulness. Sadly, the poison she had been spoon-feeding the kids all their lives had manifested itself in a way that would crush me and, in doing so, end our marriage.

Just weeks after our Cup triumph, my two daughters, aged 13 and 11, were marched into my bedroom late one night by their mother, standing behind them to provide courage and protection. They proceeded to tell me I was lazy and selfish and that it was because of me that we weren't living in the "paradise" of Holland (another byproduct of her brainwashing).

As I sat and listened, stunned into silence, I heard the poisonous and destructive words she'd been dripping into their little veins, for the first time, coming out of their mouths instead of hers. She had won a war I'd refused to engage in, teaching the children through words and deeds that their father was irrelevant to the family, unworthy of respect or love, tolerated only as a provider and laborer but apparently a failure there as well. She had turned them into outlets for her own feelings of bitterness and resentment, making my goal of staying in an unhappy marriage for the sake of the children nothing more than a cruel joke. In the end, it only gave her more time, opportunity and incentive to poison them against me.

I knew that I had failed in everything important – family relationships, love and work – but life has a way of going on, ready or not, and while I was visiting my mother a few weeks later, I finally had to spill my guts at what was happening (something I'd never done before) and was completely stunned at her response. Apparently, she had listened to my wife bad-mouth me on numerous occasions in front of friends and the kids. Raised a proper lady in pre-WWII West Orange, NJ, she never knew what to say or what to do in such an awkward situation so she kept her mouth shut, saying nothing. She then told me that she considered her the most negative spouse she'd ever known. It was an epiphany.

Encouraged to continue opening up to others, I got similar feedback and by Christmas, I'd had come to the conclusion that the only hope of ever having a healthy, loving relationship with my kids was to get out of the house. I hoped to continue to love them and be involved with them but only after removing myself from the ongoing conflict. It was an enormous gamble that would take a lot of time and effort but I hoped I could build a relationship with them as they contin-ued to grow up and mature.

Holding to that choice as my last best hope, I began to plan my exit. I was being blamed for the family not living in Holland so I began by arranging for them to spend the entire summer with her family. That would give them time to decide if that was truly where they wanted to live. My guess was that the freedoms, com-forts and conveniences of America along with the friends they had here would bring them back but it was a calculated gamble and I knew there *was* a chance they would stay there. Meanwhile, I would spend the summer making my new living arrangements in time for their return.

Over the months leading up to their departure in late June, things got pro-gressively worse as my now total apathy towards my wife and our marriage caused her vitriol and resentment to erupt time and again in front of the kids and our friends, each time only further hardening my resolve. Through it all, it was the impact of my plan on the kids that weighed most heavily on my mind.

Over many months, relations with my younger daughter had grown particularly strained despite my best efforts to love her. Finally, the night before their departure, I offered to take her to the mall and when her eyes lit up, my heart jumped as the questions concerning my plan rose once again in my mind. Gathering our things, I called out for her so we could go. Appearing from around the corner, she looked around, suddenly concerned.

"Isn't Mom coming?" She asked.

"No, I thought it would be just you and me" I said, my heart sinking as I watched tears well in her eyes. Within moments, she dissolved into a pool of tears, running to her room, unable to face the prospect of going alone with me to the mall. I walked outside, my heart breaking as I found a spot to be alone, crying to myself as I wondered again how things could have possibly gone so terribly wrong in my life and how I could have failed my children so miserably but I had no answers – only regrets.

By July of 2004, my exit plan was unfolding on schedule and I was home alone, trying to keep up with maintaining the house, running my business and finding a new place to live. In the competition for my time, attention and finances, both golf and recruiting for the upcoming Cup had taken a back seat and although we had a few interested candidates at various points throughout the late spring and summer, none signed on. By July, my visits to Harkers were few and far between and aside from occasional optimism surrounding a new candidate's initial interest, we were stuck at 7.

Ian, on the other hand, had an embarrassment of riches with which to fill his two spots, eventually choosing Mark Reid and Dave Gibson. Gibbo had a reputation as an especially tough match-play competitor and quite a character. Playing off a solid 8 handicap, he was reportedly a needler, always working to get under his opponent's skin. Reidy was the opposite, as quiet as Gibbo was loud and a good "travelling" 18 handicap (meaning he could play to his handicap anywhere). From Ian's descriptions, I knew they'd be solid additions for England.

As the dog days of August passed, we remained stuck at 7 players and when my family returned in late August, I moved into my new digs nearby. Except for Tony Alphabet, my efforts at Harkers had proved fruitless and we were quickly running out of time. Finally, in mid-September, I left on a trip to the U.K. for a training class in Chester, adding on my normal weekend visit to Spinkhill as well.

Although I'd looked forward to visiting England to run a victory lap or two, it didn't work out quite how I'd hoped. In addition to being unable to field my own 10-man team, the timing was such that I got to watch three days of Europe beating the hell out of the U.S. at the Ryder Cup in bars full of Brits.

In the true spirit of the competition, though, Ian made me an offer I couldn't refuse: to fill out my team with English players who had applied for the open spots but been denied. These fellows wanted to play in the tournament, regardless of side, and my initial skepticism turned to grateful thanks when Ian turned over Rob "Black Dog" Stevens, a gregarious mountain of a man who played off of a 4 handicap, Tony Murtagh, a solid 8 or 9 handicap, and Black Dog's good friend Neil "Casper" Havenhand, a quiet sort with an 11 handicap.

By the time I'd returned home, Cup news was already heating up as stories began arriving from all corners. Since last year's campaign of misinformation played out so brilliantly, Indie had become quite the lightning rod for information, real and otherwise, and with several articles already posted, I was amused – and a tad concerned – by an email I received on October 11 from Lou about a strange but possibly serious injury he'd sustained. Like nearly everything else that crossed my in-box, Indie quickly turned it into news.

Lou Flem Suffers 'Sprained Waist'

By: Datzit Indaruf , Flem Cup Correspondent

Myrtle Beach, S.C., October 11 - Team U.S. has been thrown into a state of near-panic as Lou Flem, half of the feared AJ-Lou pairing and esteemed producer of prodigious drives and divots, suffered a possibly serious injury, relayed in this leaked email to American Captain Dow.

I will not make any of the practice rounds as I sprained my waist yesterday. I don't want to make it any worse before the Cup. I will keep you informed. - Lou

With Lou unavailable for further comment, our reporters have been diligently checking massage parlors all over south Jersey in order to locate Lou. Needless to say, Captain Dow was not pleased with the development.

"Lou is a key member of our team, counted on to be part of our top pairing with AJ. We are extremely concerned about his recovery because this . . . strange . . . but obviously very . . . ah . . . very . . . umm . . . serious injury . . . I think . . . I mean . . . it sounds bad . . . doesn't it? . . . OK, actually I've never heard of a sprained waist but it sounds really serious."

In a curious twist to this still developing story, official Flem Cup physician and charter member of the Psychic Friends Network, Dr. Ima Wanker, has claimed to have examined Lou's waist and surrounding areas; post-accident. The good doctor filed this fascinating report:

"Dis is und extremely serious unt unusuval injury. It is very . . . ummm . . . divicult . . . to sprain vun's vaist. It requires sort of a tvisting . . . bending . . . grinding . . . writhing motion similar to . . . vel, let's not go zair. Suffice it to zay, it is nuszing most of you ever have or vil zee.

Anyvay, zis injury only happens to a small class of people – exzeptionally vaisted people – und zair is no denying zat Lou haz, at times, been in zat category. Zee pain can be excruziating but Lou has a very strong, manly vaist. Years of verk vent into making zat vaist vat it is today.

Zee gud news is zat Lou should expect a full recovery vit zee proper rest und mazzage zerapy, vich I vill be happy to administer. Having exzamined him thoroughly in zat area – tvice in front unt four times from behind, including tvice in vun day (dat vas fun, let me tell you) – I am zatisfied zat everyzing zeems to be in verking order. Alzo, Lou zeems much more relaxed und at eez after my exzaminations, a goot sign. Of course, he may not remember much about zem since zey ver pervormed unter anesthezia. Zo don't even mention it, ok?"

As the search for the missing Flem continues, Team England offered its full support, led by Milo, who suggested a truss fund be set up in support the popular American.

***

Within few days later, more news, including an update from the bewildered Lou, had arrived.

Questions Surrounding Mysterious Injury Cleared Up; England Hit By Injury Bug

By: Datzit Indaruf, Flem Cup Correspondent

Myrtle Beach, S.C., October 14 - The mystery posed by Lou's sprained waist was cleared up yesterday when American Captain Scott Dow announced that the injury was a sprained wrist, not waist. Confronted with exact text of the email, Lou responded: "I wrote waist??"

When asked about Dr. Wanker's findings, Lou shivered, saying "Ooooh, so THAT'S what that was all about. It was a shoulder massage and . . . and . . . that's all I remember. I need a shower!"

Team England has also been bitten by the injury bug not once but twice as two of its strongest players have gone down with injuries that may sideline them until Cup play starts.

Miffer was forced to withdraw during a competition this past weekend due to a back injury, reportedly <u>not</u> a sprained waist, but repeated offers by Dr. Wanker to fly to England and administer the same examinations that he performed on Lou were quickly but politely rejected by the happily married Englishman.

In other news, England Captain Ian Jennings is under doctor's orders to take the next 3 weeks off to nurse a hand injury, meaning he will not play again until Day 1 of the Cup. Exactly who Jennings was using the back of his hand on when injured is not clear but Milo has had bodyguards assigned with orders to prevent him from doing anything that might injure him again this year.

On the American side, Captain Dow received an email from Tony Murtagh, saying:

"I just wanted to point out that my parents are Irish; and even though I was born and raised in England, I consider myself an Irishman."

With that, Irish Tony wormed his way into the American's hearts. Finally, in Cup-related news, Captain Jennings announced the use of the Greensomes format for the 9-hole afternoon matches on Day 2.

***

By late October, the matches had been set for Days 1 and 2, including the 9-hole matches on Day 2 where I once again squeezed every possible stroke out of the Brit pairs. With the matches set, Indie decided to utilize the vast resources of his publishing empire to create a detailed analysis of every match, culminating in match-by-match predictions for the first two days and an allegedly computer-based projection of an overall Cup result.

Posted on the web site on October 31, the detailed predictions were my final appetizers for the fast approaching Cup. The prediction of an American lead of 6-½ to 6 after Day 2 was based on the Yanks winning the Greensomes matches on Day 2 by a slim one-half point margin. In his final analysis, I had Indie throw in one last zinger to stir up the pot one last time.

Analysis shows that the 2004 Flem Cup will likely be won by the team winning the Day 2 Greensomes matches. If this analysis proves accurate,

Captain Jennings and AGS President St. John Harris will have to answer to fans and supporters as to why the team preferred to have a "lie-in" on Day 1 rather than take advantage of the historic edge gained by teams setting the afternoon 9-hole matches.

Finally, with the rumor, gossip and innuendo all played out, my favorite day of the entire year had once again arrived. Speaking to Ian early on the morning of the 4th as he rode to Gatwick with some teammates, he giddily recounted the send-off he and the lads had received at the Angel last night.

"It was 'eaving! Simply packed! I think everyone in Spinkhill stopped in to see us off. And you should 'ave 'eard the speech I made – oh, it was a corker. Riveting, it was. I looked them in the eye, one by one, and urged them to reach down and find out if they have what it takes to win in Myrtle Beach – a valid passport, enough money and, in Jarvo's case, 3 dozen golf balls."

Hearing everyone in the car laughing, I couldn't wait to see him and all the lads again. Team England had been sent off carrying the hopes of the entire village of Spinkhill and beyond and I knew they would arrive primed to recapture the Cup. Once again, like a kid on Christmas Eve, I went to bed early so tomorrow would come faster.

19

The 2004 Cup

By 5pm Thursday, Lou and I pulled into the Breakers and, after unpacking, we headed for BummZ for a few beers as we waited for the Brits' plane to arrive. Before long, the two of us headed for the airport with Sven and Jack Jr. to pick up the thirteen Brits, leaving Tony, Lou, Jack Sr. and AJ holding down the fort. Everyone was eager to get a look at our new teammates.

Before long, Ian and Joe emerged through the terminal exit, laughing as they leaned on one another, faces aglow with the flush of the uncounted bottles of wine they'd consumed on the long trip. As we waited for the baggage conveyor to start, the rest of Team England followed, one by one. There was Phil . . . Milo . . . Jarvo . . . Miffer . . . Brighty . . . and Richard Smith, newly anointed the *Prosecutor*. Tapping me on the shoulder, Ian pointed out Gibbo – who I found not just staring me down but giving me the international sign for *"I'm watching you"* – Reidy, Casper and my partner for the Day 1, Irish Tony.

Suddenly, out of the corner of my eye, a large shadow suddenly loomed. It was Black Dog. Tipping the scales at close to 300 pounds, the big fellow towered over me a, immediately grabbing my hand and shaking it violently as he told me how much he was looking forward to the coming week. By then, Casper and Irish Tony had wandered over for introductions, joined before long by the rest as introductions were made and friendships renewed.

Within 30 minutes, we were all sitting in BummZ, drinking beers, laughing and getting to know each other as the warm-up to some serious golf. Ian, as always, was at the social center but with this team, he had lots of help. It was, without question, the best opening night we'd ever had and with a late tee time, I wouldn't be staggering back to my room until closing time, suffering from a laughter-induced headache. I had no doubt it'd be quite a week.

One of the biggest effects of the 2003 blowout was that the days of "social" pairings were gone forever, each team now focused on only one goal - winning. It was evident in every pairing, each one some sort of variation on the high handicapper / low handicapper strategy I had rolled out last year and on Day 1, no match epitomized the new norm better than Match 1: Lou and Black Dog against the Prosecutor and Brighty, each team's highest and lowest handicaps.

The storm hit England unexpectedly, just as things were looking very good with the Brits standing 3 up after 10 holes. Suddenly, without warning, Black Dog went off, sandwiching wins on 11, 12, 14, 15 and 17 around Lou's win on 13 to earn us the point, 3&1.

AJ and Jack Sr., on the other hand, controlled Match 2 throughout, coasting through the turn at 3 up before wins by AJ on 15 and 16 closed out the match, 4&2, and gave us our second point.

In Match 3, Team England got a boost from Smokin' Joe and Cup rookie Reidy against Jack Jr. and Tony Alphabet when the two Brits came out strong, quickly jumping to a 3 up lead they would not relinquish, eventually winning 2&1 for England's first point.

In Match 4, Casper and Sven seemed mesmerized at first by Gibbo, who swings right handed with a cross-handed grip (right hand on top) but putts from the left side. The Yanks were unable to muster even a net bogie on the first two holes and before they knew it, Gibbo and Jarvo had a 2 up lead they would not relinquish, eventually winning 3&2 to even the Day 1 Cup score, 2-2.

In the day's final match, Irish Tony and I took on Ian and Phil in the year's first Captain's Match, and despite their more consistent tee to green play on the front 9, we were able to match them hole for hole, recording 9 consecutive halves. On 8, Irish Tony dropped in a slick, 12-foot downhill par putt to halve and on 9, my 25-foot par putt topped Ian's 40-footer for a par to keep things level.

Having stolen the last two halves, we couldn't help but think the stage was set for a mistake or two by England and with a renewed spring in our steps, we made our turn beginning to press play. Sure enough, after another halve on 10, we won 11, 13 and 14 to go 3 up with 4 to play and coasted home to a 3&2 win, giving us a 3-2 Cup lead after Day 1.

Despite the upset loss, Ian was upbeat, comparing it favorably to last year's debacle. The fact was that, for the only the second time, the team setting the 4 ball matches had lost the day and with the previous time being Day 3 last year, that made it twice in a row for the Brits. Being entirely optimistic about the 10 matches set for Day 2, I couldn't have been more pleased.

Following another laugh-filled night at BummZ, we headed out early the next morning for the World Tour Golf Links, a 27-hole course comprised of copies of great golf holes from around the world. There were holes from Pinehurst #2, TPC Sawgrass, Pine Valley, Cypress Point, Royal Troon, Augusta, Valderamma, Royal Melbourne and many more. Some holes were reasonably authentic while others ended up with a disappointed: *"This is supposed to be . . . which hole?"* The reality was that what is a very good track fell victim to unrealistic expectations.

First out the next morning would be our two Tonys, Irish and Alphabet, facing off against Ian and Jarvo in a match that seemed to favor England. The Tony's were having none of it, though, making the turn 2 up before reeling off 4 straight wins to close out the surprisingly one-sided upset in style, 6&5.

The second match became the first match to reach the 18th hole as AJ and Sven took on Brighty and Gibbo in a battle royal. Making the turn all-square, our boys won 10 and 11 only to see the Brits struggle back, winning 14 and 16 to draw level once again but when Brighty's 6 foot putt burned the edge of the 17th for bogey, AJ's clutch 5 footer for par proved the difference in the 1 up win.

In the day's third match out, the reunited Dynamic Duo took on Lou and Casper in another tightly fought match, all square from 9 through 15 before wins by Milo on 16 and 18, sandwiched around Phil's clutch 10 footer to halve 17, clinched a hard fought 2 up win for England.

The fourth match started off innocently enough, with Smokin' Joe and the Prosecutor splitting the first four holes against Black Dog and me. At that point, not only did the wheels come off the bus for England but it flipped over, fell down an embankment, burst into flames and exploded. By the time the dust settled, Black Dog and I had won ten consecutive holes and two matches. After winning 5, 6, 7, 8 and 9 for a 5 up lead at the turn, Joe and Richard offered a $10 "press" match, meaning we would start a brand new 9 hole match from that point for $10 a man. Looking at each other with a smile and a shrug, Black Dog and I proceeded to win 10, 11 and 12 to close out the Cup match, 8&6, before tacking on 13 and 14 to close out the press match by the most lopsided 9 hole score possible, 5&4.

The final 4 ball match was one the Brits needed in a huge way and fortunately for them, they had the solid pairing of Miffer and Reidy to go up against the Jacks, Jr. and Sr. In another tight match, neither side could get beyond a 1 up lead through the front and most of the back. Finally, standing all square after 15, wins for England on 16 and 17 would end it, 2&1, turning what would have been a 4-1 disaster into a more palatable 3-2 loss for England and making the Cup score 6-4 after the morning matches.

The first afternoon 9 hole match saw Ian and Jarvo regroup, avenging their morning loss to the Tonys with a hard-fought 1 up win. Brighty and Gibbo, however, had no such luck in the second match out, watching an early 2 up lead evaporate in the face of an onslaught by AJ and Sven before eventually falling 2&1.

In the third match, the Dynamic Duo got off to great start against the Jacks, Jr. and Sr., by winning 3 of the first 6 holes to go dormie 3. Sadly, the duo seemed to confuse dor*mie* with dor*mant,* losing the final 3 holes for a disappointing halve.

In the fourth match, Black Dog and I were continuing our nearly at-will beat down of Smokin' Joe and the Prosecutor, 2 up after 4 holes, when I found myself searching for my ball in the woods on the left side of the 5th fairway. Brushing through some trees, I saw a strange looking twig hanging over the brim of my magic hat. Reaching up for it rather than removing my hat to inspect it (in hind-sight, the better choice), I was more than disappointed to find an angry looking, 3-inch wide black and yellow spider dangling mere inches from both my hand and my face. Although I remember little of the moments that followed, I'm told it in-volved shrieking like a little girl, running out of the woods in a prancing sort of way and violently shaking myself to dislodge the monster. Shaken to the core, my game immediately collapsed - a really bad thing in Greensomes play - just as the games of the two Brits suddenly came alive. While Black Dog scrambled to sal-vage what he could, Joe and Richard won 5 and 6 to level the match before three halves finished the match at all square.

In the final Greensomes match, Lou and Casper played solid, steady golf, re-peatedly holding off challenges by Miffer and Reidy for a hard-fought 1 up victory that made the Greensomes final tally 1-1/2 to 1 while extending our Cup lead to unexpectedly comfortable 2-1/2 points; 7-1/2 to 5. With 27-1/2 points making up the competition, 14 would win the Cup, a goal we were only 6-1/2 points away from with 15 matches left. England, on the other hand, would need 9 points of those 15 to carry it back to the Angel.

Although it may have seemed the only good news for Ian was that the day could have been much worse, he found a silver lining. Pairs that had lost badly in the morning played solid golf in the afternoon. Momentum can play a big role in team play and Ian now held the advantage of setting tomorrow's matches while still firmly believing he had, top to bottom, the better side. A modest 3-2 win to-morrow would mean they needed 6 points out of Monday's 2 ball play and with

England's (and our) track record in 2 ball, he would be happy to take his chances on that. Anything more than a 3-2 win tomorrow would be gravy.

Dawning bright and sunny once again, the day started off with a bang as our caravan got stopped on the drawbridge leading to Barefoot Landing while Myrtle Beach police moved in to arrest the wanted felon right in front of us. As it unfolded, I found myself being thanked and congratulated by very impressed England players, appreciative that I'd arranged such an exciting start to the day. I accepted humbly, always happy to grow my legend in their minds.

The distraction gave me a momentary respite from the nagging feeling of dread I'd had since yesterday evening. Having gotten back to the Breakers around 5pm, I conferred with the team brain trust to decide on our pairings. Foolishly, I'd allowed myself to be talked into a deviation from the simple but effective high-low pairing strategy that had led us to 4 ball victory on five straight days. Worse yet, it was my own match, paired with Jack Sr., that I was most concerned with since we did not generally play well together. Worse still, it was a mistake I was pretty sure Ian saw right off, throwing the strong pairing of Gibbo and Reidy at us.

No matter, I thought as traffic began moving again. *Day 3 is upon us and what was done was done. Mistakes or no, time to go out and play.*

Finally arriving at the Pete Dye Barefoot course, Jack and I were out first and just as I had feared, we immediately fell behind Gibbo, looking resplendent in his best Gary Player slimming black, and Reidy. Only Jack's brilliant chip-in birdie on 3 stopped us from being 4 down after 4 holes. I was struggling to put anything resembling a decent strike on the ball.

By 5, I was beginning to play better and slowly things turned around. By 9, we were the ones pressing play at only 1 down but as Jack and I secured routine pars on the next three holes, we could only watch with increasing frustration as Gibbo sank putts ranging in length from 8 to 20 feet, each time halving the hole.

Finally, on 12, we were about to level the match as Jack faced a 10 foot, uphill putt for birdie while Reidy had a fast, sloping 25 foot downhill putt for par.

Watching his race down the hill, it looked like it might run 10 feet past, at least until it slammed into the back side of the cup, popped up in the air and disappeared for an unlikely par. Now needing his birdie putt for the win, Jack was a tad over-aggressive, sliding it 3 feet past the hole and when he missed the slippery come-backer, the level match I was dreaming of had collided with the reality of a 2 down deficit. All we could do was shake our heads as we walked to the next tee.

Still reeling but determined on 13, I sank a 20 foot, big-breaking side hill par putt for what I thought was a clutch halve only to have Gibbo follow that by draining a slick 15 footer for birdie and a 3 up lead. Having made our run, we went quietly from there, 4&3.

Match 2 was the match of the day, as advertised, with Black Dog and Sven up against Ian and Miffer. Despite the big fellow's spectacular play in tying Pat's record 40 Stableford and Sven's timely contributions, the two were hard pressed to hold off the resilient Brits in a remarkably tough, well played match. All square after 10, the 11th epitomized the nature of the match when Black Dog chipped in for birdie only to be topped by Miffer chipping in for birdie from nearly the same spot. Eventually, Black Dog's birdie wins on 14 and 17 would seal the 2&1 win.

In Match 3, Ian had chosen Brighty and Smokin' Joe to take down our low handicap, long-hitting duo of Jack Jr. and Irish Tony. Another well played match saw the Brits jump to a 3 up lead after wins on 4, 5 and 6 only to see the Yanks get back to 1 down at the turn. Wins on 10 and 13, though, would extend the lead once more, proving too much for the Americans to overcome, the match ending 2&1.

With the original dynamic duo of Phil and Milo pitted against our new one of AJ and Lou in Match 4, old and new would collide with the new coming out on top – but not by much. After wins on 6, 7 and 8 gave AJ and Lou a 3 up lead, the determined Brits surged back, winning 9, 10 and 11 to even the match just as quickly but when AJ won 12 and Lou won 15, the Brits had no further answer in the third match to end with a 2&1 score.

With the day's matches even at 2-2, England needed a win in the pivotal final group – and they needed it from the unpredictable pairing of Jarvo and the Prosecutor. Unfortunately for England, the unpredictability variable would tilt towards "bad" with the *combined* Stableford score of the two only 39, 1 less than Black Dog's score of 40. Fortunately for England, the combined Stableford score of their opponents, Casper and Alphabet, would be even worse – 36 points – and the Brits somehow stumbled and bumbled their way to a 3&1 win.

So Team England had accomplished their goal of getting at least one point back. From here, the road was clear: with the Cup score 9-1/2 to 8, we would need 4-1/2 points while the Brits needed 6 points out of the next day's ten 2 ball matches at the TPC of Myrtle Beach. Having racked up 2 years of success against our 2 years of failures when it counted, history was clearly on their side. Despite 2 years success in 4 ball play, the 2 ball matches in 2003 meant nothing, meaning we still hadn't exorcised the demons of our past Singles Day collapses.

As we sipped on our beers in the late afternoon sun, Ian made sure his team knew they had something to celebrate: the end of England's winless streak in 4 ball matches. The last time England had won a 4 ball day was at Lahinch over two years ago. In the 7 days since, we had won five times and tied twice. Tomorrow was Singles Day, England's strong suit, and Ian raised his glass as he stood.

"Here's to the worm turning, boys. Their lucky streak has come to an end!"

I shook my head and smiled grimly as the England side downed their drinks, mostly because I was still kicking myself over my pairings, knowing that the door had been left open and I'd probably contributed to the momentum shift, creating a perfect environment for an England comeback. For the first time, Ian held the advantage of setting meaningful 2 ball matches. It was a prospect he was relishing and there was no mistaking his confidence.

Back at The Breakers, a brief team meeting decided our pairings and for the first time, I felt the lack of control of the leading Captain. By 6, Ian had them and we headed to BummZ for a few beers, talk swirling around the possible matchups.

20

2004 Singles Day

At 6:30, we were sitting at a long table along the wall when Team England marched into BummZ, military style, lining up at attention behind our chairs in a single line. Moments later, Ian, who had been waiting for the line to form, slowly walked it, hands clasped behind his back, inspecting his troops. Reaching the far end, he spun round and stopped, grimly scanning their faces before slowly walking back along the line of players. Upon reaching the near end again, he turned once more.

"At ease"

At his command, each player spread their feet, clasping their hands behind their backs while staring straight ahead, above our heads. Ian's words were slow and measured, playing the part of commanding officer perfectly and clearly enjoying every second of it.

"In Match 21, Captain Dow 'as chosen Jack Sr. as his first victim . . . err, player."

Pausing for the obligatory chuckle, he turned his head towards his troops.

"'Oo . . claims . . . Jack Sr.?"

Leaning forward, England players searched up and down the line, Jarvo putting one foot forward only to retreat a moment later. Milo was next, stepping out tentatively before retreating. Finally, Phil took two emphatic steps forward. Standing erect, his head snapped towards Jack as his right hand snapped to his left shoulder, Roman centurion style; loudly declaring:

"I *AM* Spartacus"

At that, the entire bar, which had been watching the drama unfold, erupted in laughter but the England players held their grim countenance as best they could; suppressing smiles and stifling chuckles as they remained erect, legs spread slightly, arms clasped behind their backs, eyes focused on the wall above our heads as they waited.

One by one, the same routine served to introduce each of our 2 ball match opponents. Reidy would play Black Dog to round out the first group. In group 2, Miffer would face Irish Tony in what promised to be a tough match while Ian would take on Sven. In group 3, Brighty would have a rematch against Jack Jr. while Gibbo would play Casper. In group 4, I would face Smokin' Joe and Milo would take on Alphabet and in the final group, in the new Roman Empire's version of feeding Christians to the lions, the Prosecutor would go up against AJ while Jarvo and Lou would have another go at deciding what was started during their big Irish adventure in 2002.

Although I agreed with Ian's choice of Richard to play AJ, I was surprised that he had chosen Reidy, who had won every match except the Pinehurst and was coming off a 34 Stableford, to take on Black Dog, who was a virtual lock the way he'd been playing. Richard had the lowest Stableford so it made sense to give him up to AJ but Jarvo, who was barely better, was playing our own worst playing golfer in Lou. I could only shake my head at the decision, knowing I would have reversed the two and gone hard after Lou.

With the matches set, Ian led us all in a toast to good luck and good golf before we careened off on one more great evening of beer, food and laughter. Too soon, the lights came on for last call as we drew ever closer to the close of another fantastic trip.

The next morning was a typically glorious Myrtle Beach day: a strikingly blue, cloudless sky, a light breeze and temperatures forecast to reach the mid to high 70s. Arriving at TPC Myrtle Beach an hour early, we scattered, each into our own routine of focusing our minds and loosening our bodies in preparation for the match at hand. At 9:50, the matches of Jack Sr. vs. Phil and Black Dog vs. Reidy were called to the tee.

Spraying the ball around on nearly the entire front 9 as he searched for any consistency, Jack Sr. somehow hung tough enough against Phil in Match 1 to make the turn only 1 down after an unlikely win on 9. In Match 2, Reidy had no such luck against Black Dog, who continued his dominating play by winning six holes and dropping only one for a commanding 5 up lead at the turn.

In Match 3, wins by Miffer on 1, 2, 8 and 9 were offset only by Irish Tony's win on 5, giving the Brit a 3 up lead at the turn. Ian, meanwhile, was being stymied by the always resourceful Sven in Match 4. Despite trailing from the start, the Yank battled back, winning 8 and 9 to level the match at the turn.

In Match 5, Jack Jr., eager for some measure of revenge for his loss to Brighty in '03, came out on fire, playing focused, flawless golf in earning a 3 up lead at the turn. Match 6 saw Gibbo, a heavy favorite, unable to shake the tenacious Casper, whose 20 foot par putt on 9 kept him within striking distance at only 1 down.

In Match 7, I also came out on fire against Smokin' Joe, standing 3 under par net after 4 and holding a 4 up lead. With his par halve on 5 slowing my momentum, my game began to return to normal as Joe began to press play, going par, birdie, par to win 3 straight and get right back to only 1 down. Struggling to regain my focus, a par win on 9 allowed me to make the turn 2 up. Match 8 was something of a mirror image to our match with Milo coming out hot against Tony

Alphabet, grabbing a quick 3 up lead before Tony fought back by winning 4 and 5 to get back to only 1 down, a score that would hold through the turn.

Already a decided underdog in Match 9, Richard started his match against AJ with some sobering news from the scorecard. While he would be getting 10 strokes, they would come in two main batches: the first and last four holes. That meant he would need to build a lead through 4 as a bulwark against the stretch of ten holes where he'd only get two strokes. *IF* he could make it past 14 still alive, he would get strokes on each of the last four holes - but that was a big if.

Sure enough, when the two reached the 5th tee all square, Richard was staring down the barrel of a loaded gun and after halving the 5th, AJ reeled off four straight wins to make the turn 4 up.

The day's final match was the rematch of Lou and Jarvo's see-saw romp in Ireland and it would not disappoint. In what seemed merely a continuation of their crazy Doonbeg match after a 25 month break, Lou twice jumped out to 1 up or 2 up leads only to see Jarvo level the match. Finally, with wins on 8 and 9, Lou took a 2 up lead to the turn.

As for our chances at the Cup, it was déjà vu all over again – in good shape at the turn as we headed to the back 9, the official graveyard for our hopes in both '01 and '02. Black Dog and AJ, as hoped, had leads large enough to mark them down for wins while Jack Jr. was 3 up and Lou and I were each 2 up. Meanwhile, of the four England leads, only Miffer's was more than 1 up.

As bits of news filtered forward and backward, it was clear we were doing well but no one needed to remind me – or anyone else – of our history on Singles Day. It was an albatross around our necks.

Before long, we had our two lopsided wins as Black Dog finished off Reidy, 6&4 and AJ closed out the Prosecutor, 7&6. With the two wins, we needed only 2-1/2 points from the last eight matches to win the Cup but just as it had in 2001 . . . and 2002 . . . the tide was turning.

Holding a 1 up lead against Jack Sr. through 12, a sudden birdie/par combo launched Phil to a 3 up lead with 4 to play and, with Jack reeling, a bogey was enough to win on 15 and abruptly end the match, 4&3.

In group 2, Miffer continued to press his advantage against the overmatched Irish Tony, holding his 3 up lead through 13 before wins on 14 and 15 would end the match decisively, 5&3. Perhaps spurred on by Miffer's relentlessly solid play, Ian also found his groove, settling into a streak of routine pars that Sven couldn't match. Par wins on 10, 11 and 13 preceded a spectacular approach shot on the 14th for a conceded birdie that made Ian dormie 4. The match would end two holes later, 4&2.

In group 3, Gibbo had similarly pulled away from Casper with a par win on the 10 and a birdie win on 11 for a 3 up lead that would hold up for a 3&2 win.

With four England wins in the bank against our two, the Brits held their first lead of the week at 12 to 11-½. With 4 matches still alive, England would need only 2 points while we still needed 2-½ to capture the Cup. Worse still, in the on-going nightmare from which we could not awaken, even those we'd been in control of were slipping from our grasp.

Having continued his superb play through the 11th hole at 2 over par gross, Jack Jr. remained 3 up. A fierce competitor who was capable of massive drives, spectacular shots and extended periods of excellent play, Jack had always lacked one thing that great golfers possess - consistency. With rare exception, it wasn't a matter of if but when he would make a mistake and against a golfer of Brighty's caliber, those mistakes could, and usually would, prove costly.

Starting with 12, a seemingly innocent string of three bogeys gave Brighty all the opening he needed and with three routine pars, the match was suddenly level. Angry at himself, Jack fought to control his emotions as Brighty teed up on 15, a tricky 428 yard par-4 loaded with trouble. Everything he had slowly, methodically built through 11 holes of solid, focused golf was gone, leaving him in a 4 hole match with his focus gone and doubt creeping in. Even great competitors can, at times, find it extremely difficult to overcome the unraveling of mind and swing that can occur in the pressure-cooker of team match play and Jack was no exception. In a potential turnaround match that could seal a Cup win for England, Jack's meltdown continued as he hacked his way down 15 to a triple-bogey.

But golf is a funny game and when you think you've got it figured out, it'll cross you up. Brighty – the monotonously consistent 2 handicapper who was holding the tee with all the momentum on his side – matched Jack shot for shot in recording a triple-bogey of his own. With the stunning turnaround, Jack's unlikely halve felt like a win, a morale boost giving him new life and renewed focus. Looking like a condemned man holding a reprieve from the governor, he walked to the 16th tee with a renewed bounce in his step.

Brighty, on the other hand, experienced the reverse effect, his face downcast after blowing a golden opportunity to deliver a body blow to his reeling opponent. A *double bogie* would have been enough to win the hole and now it was his focus that was gone, lost in a fit of self-directed frustration and anger. Bogeys on 16 and 17 (the latter from a 3-putt) continued Brighty's run of futility while Jack, rejuvenated by the unexpected gift, posted two routine pars to seal the match, 2&1, lifting our total to 12-1/2 and drawing us to within 1-1/2 points of our goal in one of the strangest turn of events we would see in this year or any other.

Meanwhile, Smokin' Joe continued to press me with solid, steady golf after his slow start. After I scrambled my way to halves on 10 and 11, he tightened the screws once more with a perfect drive down the short but tight 12th, a par 4. Desperate to rediscover the consistent ball striking I'd started with, I made several smooth practice swings with my 1-iron, focusing on releasing my hands. Finally ready, I stepped up to the ball and swung, feeling the solid click I knew meant solid contact but when looked up, I saw I'd pulled it left, straight down the edge of a steeply faced, yawning fairway bunker running down the left side.

Landing and somehow sticking on the nearly vertical face, the ball had a fairly decent lie and, despite an awkward stance, I was able to blast a pitching wedge towards the far side of the green, leaving myself with a 30 foot birdie putt.

After Joe knocked his second shot to about 18 feet, I lagged my birdie putt to about two feet. Walking to the ball, I mentally patted myself on the back for dodging another bullet, my scrambling par probably enough to hold onto my 2 up lead. As I approached the ball, I listened for Joe's voice.

"Pick it up, that's good"

I heard the words in my head - but not in my ears. It was close enough to be conceded and in a friendly match, it would have been. *C'mon, c'mon!* I told myself, beginning to take offense at the perceived slight to my putting skills. Still nothing. Reaching the ball, I continued to anticipate hearing the words *"that's good"* . . . but no sound was forthcoming.

Well, I'll just knock it in then. Bastard. I can't believe Joe didn't concede . . .

As I watched the hastily and carelessly struck ball slide past the edge, I could only stare in disbelief and by the time Joe had 2 putted for the win, cutting my lead to 1 up, my disbelief had turned to fury. Trying my best to be angry at Joe, I knew full well it was entirely my fault. I had *expected* a putt to be conceded – a cardinal sin in match play – and it was my own stupidity and carelessness that was to blame. The ripples of Joe's little stone, tossed quite deliberately into the pond of my psyche, would now expand over the next two holes as I compounded my error by fuming over it as I hacked my way to consecutive double bogies. Having started the day so well, I suddenly found myself 1 down heading to 15.

Struggling to gather myself and my emotions, I knew the match would slip away if I failed. Focusing on that thought, I pulled myself back together long enough for a par net birdie on 15 to once again level the match. Feeling focused and energized again on the 16th tee, I proceeded to hit a horrendous 1 iron, pulling it into an impossible spot in a small stand of trees on the left and handing Joe the lead right back with only 2 holes left.

Over the same stretch, Tony Alphabet had been doing his best to emulate Joe's surge, winning 10 and 11 with pars that gave him a 1 up lead and some momentum. Unfortunately, his opponent was Milo, a player I considered as mentally tough as anyone, so it was no surprise when the wiry Brit regrouped with solid wins on 12, 13 and 14 before Alphabet reeled him in a bit with a win on 15, leaving him 1 down with 3 to play. Facing a tough, side hill 3 footer on 16 for a halve, the resilient Yank's putter betrayed him and when the ball lipped out on the low side, Milo was dormie 2.

The day's final match of consequence was the epic battle: *Doonbeg - The Sequel.* The basic storyline was now plain to see - (1) Jarvo will never lead; (2) Lou almost always has a lead of 1 or 2 holes; and (3) hardly any holes will be halved. Predictably, Lou's 2 up lead at the turn had evaporated in the face of Jarvo's wins on 11 and 12 only to reappear with a par win on 13. After a rare halve on 14, Jarvo's win on 15 brought the match back to all-square with three holes left.

With three matches and precious few holes remaining (and counting the half point Milo had already clinched), the Cup stood tied at 12-½ but with Joe 1 up and Milo dormie as we teed off 17 while Jarvo was all square on 16, things were looking very bleak, indeed.

By now, the first two groups were congregating on the clubhouse veranda, watching the third group play up 18 as they sipped their post-match beers, ordered food and fired up cigars. With a cold Yuengling in one hand, Ian took a draw on his cigar, soaking in the warm, late afternoon autumn sun and the scene as teammates and opponents – friends – milled about, lifting beers, laughing and commiserating about a hard fought competition. The scene represented everything he loved; the joy of a great competition and enjoying the good life while laughing with friends. News had filtered in of the Group 3 results as well as AJ's win so he knew the situation, including the closeness of the remaining matches. As he contemplated the England comeback he'd orchestrated, he smiled, knowing that things were going exactly as planned, and for a very brief moment he tried to remember the exact details of our wager – but that would wait. After all, nickels and dimes were hardly worth wasting any time over in the midst of the glorious late afternoon sun, spectacular scenery and fellowship of the day.

With the intensity of the matches bearing down, the pace of play had slowed dramatically and as we approached the 17 tee, I gazed down across the pond to the 16th fairway where Lou and Jarvo were surveying their approach shots. Momentarily wondering how that match was going, I had no time to speculate, needing to focus on my own match and making good golf swings.

The 17th is a downhill par 3 of 170 yards to a peninsula green that juts out from the left into the pond situated between 16 and 17. Any tee shot short, long or right of the green is gone so the left side is the natural bailout spot, leaving a downhill chip across a slick green towards the water.

With the pin more or less in the center back of the green, Milo and Alphabet each struck solid shots to the center of the green, leaving Milo a 25 footer and Alphabet just outside that. Up next, Smokin' Joe was all business, tossing his cig aside before stepping up, briefly addressing the ball and firing away with his familiar, confident backswing but as the club head came through the impact zone, the *click* of solid contact I expected was replaced with a *thunk* instead. It was the sound of the club hitting the ground first.

Looking up, it was immediately clear that the ball's trajectory would not get it anywhere near the green, the splash only confirming what we already knew. In a rare display of emotion, Joe cursed, smacking his club on the ground before kicking the head in disgust.

Gathering myself, I focused on making a single smooth, solid swing. Everything else – the mistakes, missed shots and blown opportunities – fell away in the face of this one opportunity to make a good golf swing. *This is what I do*, I reassured myself, and sure enough, a well struck 6 iron safely found the middle of the green and, two putts later, our match was once again all square.

Alphabet, on the other hand, would not get his miracle comeback and after sliding his aggressive birdie try 5 feet past the hole, he could only watch as Milo lagged beautifully to less than a foot and when Tony conceded Milo's short par putt, the match was over and the Cup score stood at 13 to 12-½, England. With only two matches left, we needed 1-½ points. With both matches sitting all-square, we needed something good to happen.

Standing on 17 green waiting for others to putt, I gazed across the lake towards the 16th green. There, Jarvo's actions and movements told me he was putting. From his position, I knew he had a very slick, downhill putt. Finally, Jarvo settled over the ball and with an ever so slight movement in his shoulders, sent the ball trickling towards its target. I watched as he unconsciously took one step right, then another, perhaps trying to coax his putt that way. One second passed . . . then two . . . three . . . finally, a big fist pump for the made putt. Not knowing the match score, I only knew it couldn't be good for us.

Standing on the 18th tee, the tension was thick as I planted my tee in the ground before stepping behind the ball to survey my line as I took several swings with my 1 iron, focusing, as always, on releasing the club head through the impact zone. Fully aware of the importance of a hitting good tee shot to keep the pressure squarely on a still agitated Joe, I finally stepped up to address the ball.

The last hole at TPC is another of the course's many great holes, a 520-yard par 5 that has trouble lurking everywhere. On the tee shot, anywhere except in the fairway courts disaster. A narrow stream guarded by steep banks and heavy rough eagerly waits to swallow up any wayward shots, cutting across the front of the tee before running down the right side of the fairway for about 250 yards out before it angles back across the fairway to its final destination: the large lake bordering the left side of the hole's final 200 yards. Wrong line, wrong distance, short, right or long – the stream is in play from all angles.

To the right of the stream, large, undulating mounds rise, topped by the cart path and sprinkled with tall, stately Georgia Pines, gently swaying back and forth in even the slightest breeze. Left of the fairway, running from the tee all the way to the lake, is a stand of pine trees.

On your second shot, the border between the narrow fairway and the lake on its left is only 2 or 3 yards of very light rough while large fairway bunkers populate the swales between the high rolling mounds on the right. Finally, on your approach, you play to a large, undulating green that juts out into the lake, generally sloping towards the water, from right to left,.

With the late afternoon sun behind us, I noticed the groups gathered on the veranda in the distance, some shielding their eyes against the afternoon sun as they squinted in our direction. Setting myself in motion, I launched a weak, fading 1 iron about 140 yards and straight towards the creek, exactly where I didn't want it to go. Holding my breath, we all watched as the shot landed left of the creek, bouncing hard right off the creek bank and crossing the hazard. From there, with the slope's direction reversed, each subsequent bounce pushed it back to the left, towards the despicable hazard. My heart was in my throat as I watched, hoping that the thick rough would finally grab it and it did, the ball finally coming to rest about 4 or 5 feet right of the creek. Able to see the ball from the tee, I took that as a good sign, breathing a deep sigh of relief and knowing I had dodged a bullet.

With Joe up next, my question was whether or not he could put aside his lingering anger and frustration from the last hole. Unlike mine, Joe's misses were usually hit to the left; long, sweeping pull hooks resulting from releasing the club head early and as if on cue, there went the ball heading deep into the stand of pine trees down the left and although we would find it, he'd have no other option beyond punching it back onto the fairway, leaving him no chance of getting anywhere near the green with his third.

My lie, as I'd hoped, wasn't too bad but my stance was awkward, the ball a good foot or so above my feet. Choking down to the bottom of the grip on my 1-iron, I focused on a smooth, firm swing through the rough and the solid contact I felt at impact told me all I needed; the ball coming out on a low, hard line and reaching only 8 or 10 feet above the fairway before disappearing beyond the creek bank 100 yards or so down the fairway, straight and true. When Joe followed by pushing his fairway wood right, into a large fairway bunker about 50 yards from the green, the hole – and the match – was mine to lose.

With 140 yards to the pin and 125-yards to the front, I took dead aim at the center of the green with my 8-iron, hoping to take the lake out of play. Surveying my line, I couldn't help but notice the assembled crowd on the veranda, silently waiting for my next shot.

With a smooth swing, I caught the shot just a hair fat. Looking up, I found I had also pulled it a bit and it was gently drawing to the left, across the water and towards the front left of the green. I held my breath as cries rose from the veranda, the crowd eying the dangerous trajectory.

"That's trouble!" Gibbo growled as Ian stood by, cigar in hand, pint balanced on the railing. As we all watched, the ball cleared the water by less than a yard, checking quickly and leaving me with a 25 foot uphill birdie putt. Once again, I had dodged a bullet and breathed a huge sigh of relief.

Playing as aggressively as he dared, Joe's fourth, a fairway wood from the bunker, reached the front right edge of the green but checked quickly, leaving him with a long, curling downhill putt for par. Needing to make it, his putt ran across the top edge of the cup, leaving a 6 footer coming back. When my birdie putt lagged to 2 feet and Joe missed, the hole and the match were conceded. With the 1 up win, we were back on top, one-half point from winning the Cup with only Lou and Jarvo's match left on the course.

After exchanging the customary handshakes on the green, we headed to the veranda where players were scattered about in mixed groups, teammates and opponents, all friends, waiting for the final result, embracing a special moment in time. Emerging from the lounge with my pint, I joined Ian at the rail. I looked at him, shaking my head as I raised my glass in toast.

"This . . . is amazing. I never thought it would come down to this."

"Tis that, lad, tis that. A real testament to what this has become. Just look 'round."

As I surveyed the group, sixteen friends and competitors, I knew that, in reality, this was more testament to the power and magnetism of Ian's personality than what I'd put into it. Oh sure, there were great guys on each team, guys who were fun to compete with and against, fun to have a beer with and fun to have a laugh with. There was the website and the considerable commitment of time and money everyone made in order to make the trip an annual event but Ian was the glue, effortlessly building and holding it all together.

Magnetism, I thought. Yes – it was the perfect word; the only one that captured the scope of his role and his personality. Silently, I thanked my lucky stars that I was friends with him. Gazing down the fairway, he smiled, the late afternoon autumn sun giving him an even ruddier complexion than usual, his expression one of sublime contentment. Turning his head to look at me, he held his pint up towards the final hole.

"This is why we play, lad. *This* is why we play."

"Yes, it is" was all I could say, lifting my pint towards him. "Here's to you, my friend. Without you, none of this happens."

Staring at me in surprise for a moment, his smile broadened as he lifted his pint in return.

"Well, I'm not sure about that. You play a bit of a role as well." He laughed before continuing. " 'Ere's to a great event, whatever the outcome."

Nodding in agreement, I turned my attention back to the 18th green, watching for any sign of joy or sadness from Lou and Jarvo as they approached their balls.

"You want to go down and find out what's happened?" I offered casually.

"No. You go ahead. I'm sure you'll let me know"

Heading down the steps with Jack Jr., we waited silently at the back edge of the green as the group putted out and shook hands, still with no indication of a result. Fearing the worst, Jack and I held our breath as Lou strode our way, shaking his head.

"Ahhh. I think I blew it. Lost the last hole."

My heart sank. "You lost?" I asked apprehensively.

"Yeah . . . well, I lost the hole. We halved the match . . . but I needed to win, didn't I?"

The last Lou knew, I was one down with two to play. The last thing he expected was for me to win the last two holes and the match. Jack and I looked at each other.

"We've won"

"You're joking" Lou shot back.

"By a half point." Jack laughed, looking at Lou. "You've won it."

"You won?" Lou asked, looking at me, incredulous. "Weren't you 1 down with 2 to play?"

"Well, yeah, I was but with some help from Joe, I won both"

In a muted celebration, our high-fives prompted as much by relief as celebration, we turned back to give the crowd on the veranda a brief fist pump. The only player who didn't know was Jarvo and when he finally got the news on the veranda, his pained look was difficult to watch. He had never, in three Cup appearances, played to the level he'd expected of himself and the final margin of defeat was a crushing blow to the popular, affable Brit. Although anyone could point to a dozen matches that could have flipped one way or the other, I could see he blamed himself.

That night, at the awards dinner, the mood turned a bit more celebratory but we knew we'd escaped by the skin of our teeth. A warm bond of mutual respect had formed over the years between the teams and we knew how fortunate we had been. AJ claimed the most valuable Flem Cup player award with a perfect record in his five matches and, with the beer and wine flowing freely, tales were told of all the great shots and unlucky bounces that might have swung a match a different way. I, on the other hand, had my own take on why the Brits lost.

Earlier that afternoon, after posting the article on the day's incredible results, I'd noticed the link for the November 1 "computer analysis" of the matches. Intrigued, I clicked through to remind myself of my prognostication. As I read, my mouth dropped open. I'd forgotten . . .

Analysis shows that the 2004 Flem Cup will likely be won by the team winning the Day 2 Greensomes matches.

If this analysis proves accurate, Captain Jennings and AGS President St. John Harris will have to answer to fans and supporters as to why the team preferred to have a "lie-in" on Day 1 rather than take advantage of the historic edge gained by teams setting the afternoon 9-hole matches.

We'd won those Greensomes matches, 1-½ to 1 - the exact one-half point margin of victory we ended with. Amazing, I thought. Simply amazing.

Taking a page from Ian's book, I did my best to soak up the rest of the night; treasuring the moment; the laughter, the stories and the fellowship. Way too soon, the lights came on for last call and another trip, except for our getaway round and sad goodbyes, was over.

The next day, Black Dog captured the Stableford with another solid performance, coming in at 2 over par net for a 5 day total of 1 over par net, a new record, while AJ was once again bridesmaid, finishing 8 back.

Six days earlier, the trip had stretched out in front of me, the fulfillment of months of anticipation. Now, at 2 pm on Tuesday, it seemed more like six minutes and after dropping the Brits off at the airport, Lou and I set off on the drive home, my experience telling me the next 10 hours would flip-flop between wonderful, fresh memories of a well-earned victory and the depression of seeing another trip come to an end.

The next day, Indie sat down one last time to write the epilogue to the '04 Cup and if there was one thing I knew in my heart, it was that this thing that started four years ago, this Flem Cup, was alive and well. I believed that despite 2005 being the fifth and final year of "the wager", the Cup would continue for a long time. I knew of others, too, who simply couldn't imagine not having the Cup to look forward to. It had become a part of my life that I truly loved, regardless of who won or lost or who did or didn't play well. I could understand, perhaps as well as anyone, the frustration caused by inconsistent or sub-par play but I also knew that was a normal result for some of the players in *any* competition, even a professional one. With those thoughts in mind, Indie poured out his heart through his keyboard one last time.

2004 Epilogue

By: Datzit Indaruf; Flem Cup Correspondent

MYRTLE BEACH, S.C., November 14 – The agonizingly close 2004 Flem Cup is now in the record books, a remarkable testament to the competitive spirits of the players who make it possible on both sides of the Pond, and while it is true that some have returned home in celebratory triumph and others in disappointed defeat, the question that must be asked is simple: so what? Are not triumph and defeat, celebration and despair, success and failure part of every golf tournament that has ever been played? Did we not face those same demons in 2001, 2002 and 2003? Why should 2004 be any different? Simply because it was the closest? Ask any Ryder Cup squad and they will regale you with stories of stirring success and crushing failure – and those players are the best in the world.

Few people have swings that will hold up for 72 or more holes played over 4 consecutive days of golf. Pros can at times but even they go through difficult times, their scores sometimes varying wildly from one day to the next. Why should it any different for the likes of us? Everyone endures days when the swing is off and golf is a struggle but despite the frustration that brings, that represents the norm, not the exception. Add to that the self-inflicted pressure of a team effort and it is remarkable that we show up at all to torture ourselves.

There are two ways to look at this Flem Cup competition of ours. In the big scheme of things, this glorious competition is absolutely, 100% meaningless. Other than the short-lived enjoyment of the competition and, maybe, the result, our lives do not change one iota based on the results. We do not support our families or earn our living through our meager efforts at this wonderful yet impossibly frustrating game. To that fact, all I can say to that is: thank goodness.

Yet there are few things more important in our lives. Why? Not because of one shot, good or bad, or one match, won or lost. It is because of the friendships and laughs and heart-breaks we all share, heroics we will remember and treasure long after the bad shots and missed putts are forgotten. In that light, what is more important than this masochistic labor of love we engage in?

The beauty of sport is that there is always the next match; whether tomorrow, next week or next year, but there also must be winners and losers for that is the nature of sport. As such, we must not lose sight of what is truly important: the competition itself and the challenges we face while so engaged. Sometimes we rise to the occasion; other times we fall short but when we fail, others succeed and vice versa. So do not fear losing or failing - we've all been there. Fear instead the day when we have no more of these challenges; these magnificent competitions we embrace despite what we may face. When that day comes, whether we choose it or it chooses us, it is a sad day. Sad for the individual, his teammates, his opponents and for all those who are left playing, the competition is a little poorer.

So whether you are feeling joy or disappointment, embrace what the 2004 Flem Cup represented – fellowship and competition. Yes, Team England's spirited comeback fell just short of success in the closest Flem Cup in history. Was there one last match score that established the final score? Of course, but that was merely a matter of timing; nothing more, nothing less. Was there a single match that won or lost the Cup? Absolutely NOT. Singling out any match as winning or losing the entire Cup does a disservice to all the others. Of thirty matches, there were at least a dozen matches where a made putt here, a missed putt there, a lucky break here or an unlucky break there would have changed the outcome. The pain of defeat and the joy of victory will fade but the bond of competition and the moments spent with great friends will be with us for the rest of our days.

So let me leave you with one last thought as the holidays approach. Congratulations to all on a fantastic week and best wishes to you, your families and our extended family of Flem Cup fans.

***

As I sat back, reflecting on an article I hoped would help keep things in perspective, my mind wandered back through the memories of the last week, a week that had been as much fun as any we'd had. Every year had been different, great in its own unique way and this year's, from the nights at BummZ to the days on the courses, had been a blast from start to finish.

Closing my eyes, I let the still vivid memories carry me back to the veranda at TPC on that the gloriously warm, golden November afternoon sun. Back in the moment, I stood at the rail with Ian as we sipped our pints and puffed on our cigars, the sun getting low in the autumn sky. His face was easy to remember, the familiar profile reflecting sublime contentment on his face as he surveyed the awesome scene he was so much a part of. I let the image bake into my mind, wishing with all my heart that I could return to that spot once more. At last, I opened my eyes, returning to the present as I clicked to upload link to post the final article.

Little did I know, as I let the image slip away, that it would be a sight I would never see again.

21

England

Life soon returned to normal and before long, Thanksgiving was a memory and Christmas was bearing down. On New Year's Eve, I got my annual call from Ian at his rented ski lodge in Austria. Caroline was fine and they were having a wonderful time, as always. Next up was another ski trip in late February followed, as always, by the Majorca trip.

By the time we spoke again, it was the first week of February.

"'Mr. Dow."

"Mr. Jennings! Everything is fine. How are you and Caroline?"

"Well, not so good. We've 'ad to cancel our trip to France. There was a change on my last body scan."

My mind raced. The cancer. Had we discussed that on New Year's Eve? No, I would remember that. Had I even asked? No, things had been going so well, I hadn't even thought about it, probably by choice.

"When was this? You didn't mention anything when we last spoke."

"Well, they weren't sure about the December scan so they re-did it last week. It confirmed that there has been some change so the doctors want to start me on oral chemo. They think it will give us a good chance of stopping it in its tracks."

After speaking for another 10 minutes, I hung the phone up and sat back, reflecting on our conversation. *This was nothing unexpected*, I told myself. The specter of the cancer had been hanging over us since late 2001. From the initial diagnosis, we knew it would be an ongoing battle but four years of good news every six months had conditioned us to expect good results. Now, the cancer had awakened from its slumber, leaving the next move to the doctors as they shifted to active defense, using 21st century medical technology to block further advance.

Chemo. It was a scary word that I really didn't understand. From everything I'd heard it was a horrible ordeal but the oral chemo Ian had described didn't seem *too* bad. Every three weeks, he'd get a cocktail of pills that would target the bad cancer cells and, hopefully, destroy them. Unfortunately, the pills were not very discriminating, destroying good cells as well.

Before long, I convinced myself this would be a temporary onslaught by the cancer, one quickly beaten back by medicine and science. Ian was, after all, vibrant and healthy, his body fit and strong. Even better, he had skilled doctors and technology on his side. Scoffing at the notion of the cancer winning, this would turn out to be simply part of the ebb and flow of the battle.

The doctor had told him to maintain his lifestyle, which was fairly healthy aside from a bit too much beer and the occasional cigar so he did – just as before. In early March, my call found him in the Angel, holding court as usual, and the news was good, just as I had imagined it would be. The cancer had not spread any further and everyone hoped it might even reverse its advance. Summoning up the courage, I asked the question that had been in the back of my mind for weeks.

"So, will you be able to make it to Myrtle Beach this year?"

"Oh yes, the regimen will be long over by then. You think I'd leave the outcome of our wager in anyone else's hands? I'll be there. In fact, we've already got our team sorted. Everyone returns except for Jarvo, Reidy and, oh yeah, Milo"

"Milo? Milo's not coming?"

One of the most clutch players on either side, Milo had been on each of the first four trips, the only player to have never lost a 2 ball match.

"Yeah. Evidently 'e's going to be in Australia with 'is new lady friend. Scheduling snafu, 'e said. But 'e can't change it now as it's already bought and paid for. Anyway, we'll be adding Black Dog and Casper and you'll be pleased to know Swampy is coming back."

"Swampy! That's great. Sounds like you guys will be loaded for bear this year."

"That's what I'm 'oping for! 'Ow's your team coming?"

"Well, Pat will be back and Terry has said he wants to come."

"Terry! Terrific! 'Aven't seen him in a few years."

"Yeah, and AJ has a friend he plays with a lot. I think his name is Paul . . . something or other. AJ calls him Apple and says he gives as good as he gets in their matches so that's a pretty good recommendation. I think his handicap is 8 or 9?"

"Very good. Sounds like we won't have to lend you anyone this year."

With our conversation turning to the trip logistics, Ian asked that an extra day be added to the front end of the trip so England players could completely recover from jetlag issues and get in a practice round. I smiled to myself, knowing he had reached the point I'd reached 2 years earlier; leaving no stone unturned in the quest to win the Cup. As for the courses, we agreed to Prestwick for Day 1 and TPC for Day 2. On Day 3, we decided to mix things up by playing a 36-hole marathon of 4 ball matches followed by Greensomes matches at The Legends, a terrific 54-hole complex not too far from the Breakers. The links-style course Heathland would be the morning venue for the 4 ball matches while Moorland would host the afternoon Greensomes matches. For the 2 ball matches, we decided, once again, on Heritage. The new schedule would mean that out of 30 points, 10 would be up for grabs *each* of the last two days.

Hanging up the phone, I felt much relieved, more optimistic than ever before that the chemo would work its magic and that Ian would be there come November. Sadly, the optimism would prove short-lived and the early April scan showed the cancer spreading again, prompting the doctors to augment the oral chemo treatments with radiation treatments. Unsure of exactly what that entailed, I took solace from the fact that the doctors seemed to be staying on top of things.

By May, the news was once again encouraging as the combination of oral chemo and radiation seemed to halt the cancer's advance. The treatments, however, were starting to have a big impact on Ian, causing him to gain weight, lose much of his already thinning hair and cut way back on golf due to a propensity for blistering on his hands. Although he laughed it all off, during one call he confided that not every day was a good one. It was no secret that he had come to dread the radiation cycles, one week out of every three where all he could do was hunker down with Caroline and ride it out. As difficult as the physical discomfort was, though, it was a small price to pay for the chance of being cured. Through it all, Ian kept his upbeat, positive outlook, a crucially important part of the fight.

By June, the news from the body scan had once again turned sour, another step backward. If things didn't turn around with the next scan, they would start to administer the chemo intravenously, the most aggressive regimen. For the first time, I began to think this may not turn out the right way. Feeling helpless as early July dragged by, I finally gave in to impulse, calling Ian to find out the results of the latest scan.

"Mr. Jennings," I began, sounding as cheerful as possible. "How are you?"

"'Allo, Scott . . . Not good, I'm afraid . . . The latest scan . . . shows the cancer has continued to spread."

For the first time since he had originally told me of the cancer in 2001, I could hear Ian struggling for words, feeling my own throat tighten as he spoke. I knew what this meant both in the short run: IV treatments, nausea, vomiting, radiation, hair loss, weight gain and fatigue. Far worse was the long-term, where the prognosis was turning increasingly bleak. Finally, he continued.

"They'll be starting me on the new regimen in a few weeks. It will be inpatient. I'll be in 'ospital for several days – five or six – every three weeks while they administer treatment."

As he paused, I tried to come up with words but there was simply nothing there; only trite, meaningless comments about doctors knowing what they're doing and this thing being beatable but we both knew he was running out of options.

"They've told me I can't fly for a while. The altitude could kill me . . ."

He didn't have to finish; I had known since May's setback what was coming next.

"I won't be able to make Myrtle Beach this year."

"I know . . . you'll just have to oversee it from the Angel with Singe. I'm sure he'll enjoy having you around for once in early November."

"I'm glad to hear you say that. You know, this is something special we've built, here. I want this thing to keep going. The Flem Cup doesn't need me. We've got great people on both sides. I want it to go on. Miffer's already agreed to be acting Captain with Joe's 'elp. We'll get together to set up the matches . . . 'e'll ring me up night after the matches each day . . . it'll be fine."

Once again, tears filled my eyes as I listened to Ian, unable to speak without my voice cracking. *By November he'd be through with the chemo and we'd simply call him each day after the matches and next year, he'll be back,* I told myself.

After hanging up, I felt nothing as reality began to sink in. Although I kept telling myself he would be back for 2006, the bigger, previously unthinkable question was now unavoidable – *what if?* By the next morning, after sleeping on the discouraging news, I decided to arrange a purely social trip to England in early September. Calling Ian, I got his chemo schedule so the trip could be arranged to avoid conflict with the regimen as best as possible. Having set the dates, I sent out an email invite to the rest of the team. By the next day, we had four tickets to Manchester: Jack Sr., Lou and my fiancée, Theresa. With my divorce finalized in May, Theresa and I had gotten engaged a couple of months later. Ian and Jack Jr. had agreed to be my only non-family groomsmen and Jack Sr. would be presiding.

As September drew near, I found myself both dreading and looking forward to the trip. How did one prepare for a trip like this? Despite Theresa being in my life, I felt as empty and alone as ever. My life had continued its downward spiral as my business collapse and divorce led to a string of poor financial decisions. All the while, lurking in the back of my mind, was the growing likelihood of Ian's death, a thought I'd avoided like the plague for nearly four years. I had always pushed those thoughts aside as soon as they entered my head but now, with his condition worsening, it was no longer possible.

Finally, September 1 arrived and Theresa and I headed to Newark Liberty Airport to meet up with Lou and Jack. Flying direct to Manchester, we were picked up by a friend and neighbor of Joe's, Al Foster. For the first time ever, I would be staying at the Angel and after Singe showed us to our newly refurbished rooms, we settled in, unpacking before heading back downstairs. For Theresa, this was an introduction and, despite the occasion, I was nearly as excited for her as I was to see him again myself.

Arriving downstairs, we found a small group had already congregated. Jack and Lou were there, standing and chatting with Singe, Phil, Joe, Caroline and an overweight bald man sitting at the bar with his back to me. Hearing my approach, the man turned to look.

Despite knowing he had gained weight and lost hair, I was still shocked at the change I saw in Ian, unprepared for anyone other than the Ian Jennings I knew. Staring at me with a slight smirk on his face, he allowed me to digest his new look.

"'Ah, Mr. Dow . . . and Theresa, I presume." he said, his familiar voice unchanged. Spreading his arms, he quipped "A bit different than you remember, eh?"

And then it came – the laugh. The familiar giggling laugh I'd heard thousands of times; the one that followed nearly every single one of his jokes, stories and funny little comments, even the bad ones; the one that made me laugh at the sound. The outside may have changed but inside, it was still Ian. I smiled broadly, walking over to embrace him.

"I see you've put on some weight. Is it helping you hit the golf ball any further?"

Laughing again, he shook his head.

"Can't play at all anymore. I get blisters on my hands. I just watch now."

I cringed, remembering he'd told me. How that must kill him, I thought, but here he was, laughing and joking, doing what he truly loved. Having resolved to have nothing but a smile on my face for the trip, I knew now it wouldn't be hard.

"Ian, this is Theresa."

"Well, now. I'd heard you were a fiery redhead but didn't think you'd be so pretty. I mean, considering . . . this." With his open hand gesturing in my direction, we all cracked up. Finally, the laughter died down.

"Hello. I've heard so much about you, Ian. I'm so happy to finally meet you." Theresa said as she gave him a hug and a kiss. With a sly smile, she gave a little nod in my direction. "He is kind of cute, though. In an odd sort of way, I mean. I'm a sucker for a charity case."

Ian looked at her for a moment before busting out laughing all over again. With fresh drinks in hand, Ian began with what he had planned for us over the next week before getting down to the more serious business of the latest jokes and stories. When those ran out, he broke out the old standards for Jack, Lou and Theresa. It didn't matter that the rest of us had heard them time and time again – the master was at the helm and his stylish delivery and timing made them funny all over again. Even Jack Sr., not much of a drinker, had a second pint but by about 3 pm, we were fading and I knew it was time to move onto phase 2 of the standard jetlag recovery plan of lunch and a few beers, a nap and a normal evening.

Ian, too, was tiring. He had been greatly anticipating our arrival but his body was in a weakened state, each regimen requiring more rest and recovery time. Despite that, he took his hosting duties as seriously as he ever had, scheduling activities for all of us wrapped around a couple of rounds of golf. With Ian's unpredictable state, Joe and Phil agreed to be co-hosts for our stay and it was at Phil's urging that we spent the first full day at the Longwell Sheep Dog Trials, an exhibition of what is truly an incredible connection between sheep dog and handler. Unfortunately, Ian fell ill halfway through and left early with Caroline.

By the next day, though, Ian was well enough to join us for a few pints at the Angel before accompanying us to Renishaw Park while Caroline took Theresa shopping. Brighty, Neil and Phil joined us as Ian walked along, switching between groups as his energy and the layout allowed. At one point, as he walked along with Lou and Jack's group, he was recounting one of his favorite stories about Renishaw Park and a certain Mr. Ian Woosnam. Apparently, after playing the course, Masters Champion Woosnam described the 13th hole, a 175-yard par 3 with a very narrow, elevated green bunkered on both sides and steeply sloped from back to front, as one of the best par 3s in all England. It was high praise indeed and Ian never tired of telling the tale.

With the story timed to coincide with the group's arrival on the 13th tee, Ian immediately began pointing out the hole's numerous pitfalls before sitting back to watch the expected carnage. Jack, playing first, hit a draw with his 5 iron that landed just short of the pin, checking up nicely and coming to rest about 6 feet beyond the cup.

"Huh" quipped Lou. "That doesn't look so hard"

Ian looked at him, laughing.

"Yeah, that was good. Let's see what you can do."

Stepping up, Lou proceeded to hit the flagstick on the first bounce, stopping his ball about 4 feet away. He turned to Ian and shrugged his shoulders.

"Don't know what the big deal is. Seems pretty easy to me."

Up next, and determined to do his duty for Queen, country, course and captain, Phil proceeded to hit not one but two long, sweeping hooks into the cow pasture on the left; too far in to even bother looking for. Lou just looked at Jack.

"Huh. Must be an England thing"

Chuckling, he grabbed his hand cart and walked away, shaking his head.

A couple of days later, we headed up towards York to play Fulford where Theresa joined Ian in walking the course. Always ready to amuse the ladies and with a captive audience in Theresa, Ian decided to assign himself the role of my personal "caddy from hell", later claiming full credit for guiding me to a very respectable round through a battery of tongue-lashings and sarcastic comments that had Theresa in a constant state of amusement. Finally, the last full day of our trip arrived, meaning a day of sightseeing in the nearby village of Eyam followed by a visit to the magnificent estate of the Duke of Devonshire: Chatsworth.

A small village in Derbyshire, Eyam is famously known as the "plague village". In 1665, while the Bubonic plague was raging in London, the surrounding countryside was relatively untouched by the dread disease. That would potentially change, though, when a cloth shipment containing some infected fleas was delivered to a local tailor named George Viccars. When the unlucky man died within a week, the villagers realized what had happened and, in one of the most courageous and selfless communal acts in all history, decided to quarantine themselves rather than escape and risk spreading the disease any further.

Over the next sixteen months, 260 of the 350 residents would die, including more than 110 in July and August of 1666 alone. One woman, Elizabeth Hancock, lost her husband and six children in an eight day span. Outsiders would leave the villagers food, medicine and supplies at a 'boundary stone' in exchange for vinegar-soaked money and thanks to the noble sacrifices of its inhabitants, the plague never spread beyond Eyam. It was quite the sobering place.

Chatsworth, on the other hand, was a place of incredible opulence. The home of the Duke and Duchess of Devonshire, the stunning estate is home to priceless works of art, lavish gardens, spectacular fountains and beautiful vistas of the surrounding peak district. To our delight, we found filming had just recently finished for the upcoming release of a movie version of Jane Austen's *Pride and Prejudice*.

Back at the Angel by 4pm or so, Ian took a rest before dinner. It had been a long and tiring day for all of us and I could only imagine how he was feeling. After a quick pint, I headed upstairs to start packing for the trip home only to run into Jack heading down for a cup of tea.

"What time for dinner, Jack?"

"I'm not sure. Ian asked me to stop down around 5:30pm. I'm not sure what his plans are but if you can wait, maybe we can eat together later."

"Oh. Mind if we come with you?" I asked.

"I'm sorry but Ian asked to spend some time with me alone. I'm going down to meet with him and Caroline. In fact, now that I think about it, don't wait for me; I don't know how long I'll be."

Taken aback for a moment, I watched him turn and disappear around the corner. *Why would Ian want to see Jack alone?* Then, it hit me.

Ian was dying, a prospect that focuses the mind like no other. Although Ian was not a religious or spiritual man, I could understand him wondering about the contentment we'd all seen in Jack through his faith and his life. It was something I'd always wanted, at least in an abstract sort of way, but had no idea how to achieve. For myself, I'd never been able to slip anything spiritual past my intellect; logic and reason making me incapable of just shouting halleluiah and living my life as if something *significant* had changed simply because I'd decided to believe something for no other reason than I wanted to. Although a creator made sense to me, just because I wanted it to be true didn't make it so. As long as my intellect was unimpressed, my heart and soul remained unavailable. Believe in Jesus, believe in Mohammed, believe in Buddha, believe in Mother Earth – whatever. Without reason as the foundation for faith, I was incapable of believing.

Nevertheless, I had a tremendous amount of respect and, I had to admit, curiosity for Jack because his beliefs were lived out in his everyday life, on display for all to see in the deep-rooted contentment we all saw. His spiritual life *was* truth to him and his family, a foundational aspect of their being that I simply did not – *could* not – understand. Yes, I could easily understand how Ian, staring his own mortality in the face, would want to know what Jack believed . . . and why.

After a brief rest, Lou, Theresa and I ate dinner at The Angel. Jude and Singe had always done everything possible to make me feel at home and with Theresa, Lou and Jack along on this trip, they had really rolled out the red carpet. The Angel was, after all, more than just their livelihood or their job. It was their home and I loved them both, along with pretty much anything Jude made. Finally, around 8:30, Ian arrived, a twinkle in his eye as he beckoned us downstairs.

"Come with me"

Exchanging glances, we could only wonder what was happening as Ian led us out the back entrance and down the stairs to the car park. Exiting the building, we found ourselves surrounded by a group of 25 or 30 people sitting at picnic tables and along the low wall bordering the parking area. As I scanned the faces, I realized it was a veritable who's who of people I'd come to know through Ian over the years. Mark and Paul Nelson were there along with Mark's wife and their little baby. Mike Burrows and Mike Batty, Ian's business partners and friends, were there. All the Flem Cup regulars – Joe, Miffer, Jarvo, Milo, Phil and others – were there as well as many Angel regulars and all four of Ian's beautiful daughters.

For the next few hours, time stopped as we sat and talked, drinking and laughing about old times. Ian, naturally, was at the center of it all, laughing at his own stories and jokes as he circulated. At one point, Ian, Joe, Miffer and I huddled to iron out the last few details of the Cup, now less than two months away. Team England would be adding a 1-handicap golfer named Barry "Baz" Silvers to take Ian's spot. I shook my head as Miffer and Ian described how good a player he was.

Finally, by 11 pm or so, the crowd had thinned out to just our core group and we headed back to the Rave Cave for a final round or two. Ian was clearly done; leaning wearily against Caroline. It had been a long day – a long week – and all the energy he'd stored up for our visit was spent. He'd put out his best welcome mat for us and now it was time to head home. Rising from his familiar stool, he signaled the same. He started with Lou, giving him a big hug.

"Thanks for coming, Lou. I really enjoyed seeing you."

"Yeah, well. I needed to finally find out what this Rave Cave is all about. You take care, now."

Smiling, Lou turned away, discretely wiping his eyes. Jack was next and, holding Ian's hand firmly, he looked at him like the loving grandfather he was.

"You'll be in our thoughts and prayers. A lot of people are praying for you."

"Thank you, Jack. And thank you for tonight. It . . . it meant a lot."

Eyes moistening, Ian turned next to Theresa, giving her a big hug.

"I really enjoyed meeting you. And you keep this young fellow in line."

"I'm not going to say goodbye." Theresa began, her voice muted and cracking. "Just that I'll see you next June, at the wedding."

Turning away, she wiped away the tears that had begun flowing down her cheeks. In only a few days, she had come to love Ian as we all did, just as I knew she would. Coming to me, Ian took my hand firmly as he looked me in the eye.

"You know, I'm going to miss not being there to finish your sorry ass off in November. You can give my money to Joe after we win."

Taken off guard by his opening, I burst out laughing, the tension momentarily broken.

"I'll tell you what. We'll settle up at the wedding, OK?"

"Ok. Seriously, thanks for coming, lad, for putting this little visit together. I can't tell you how much it means to me."

I swallowed hard, trying to suppress the growing lump in my throat.

"I wouldn't have missed it" I replied, managing a weak smile as I struggled to get the words out while keeping my emotions in check. Transitioning into a farewell embrace, Ian spoke quietly into my ear, his voice cracking slightly.

"You've been a great friend. Now you go get yourself a good night's sleep and I'll see you next June."

Unable to speak, I turned to Caroline, giving her one last hug and kiss before she turned to leave, holding the front door of the Angel open as Ian shuffled past into the cool September night. The last thing I saw as the door swung shut was Ian slowly walking away, leaning on her for the walk home and so much more.

As we finished our drinks in silence, talk turned to our travel arrangements.

"Roight. What time are you lads and lady off tomorrow?" Joe asked, plunking his empty glass down onto the bar with finality.

"7:30. Will Ian be stopping up to say goodbye?"

Joe looked at me, eyes wide with surprise. His look softened when he realized I was serious.

"No, Scott, 'e won't be 'ere tomorrow. Ian doesn't like sad goodbyes."

With that, he turned to go. "I'll be over to see you off. Ta." he called out as the door banged shut and as I heard Singe latch bolt, the finality of the night's events began to sink in. The trip was over. As we finished our pints and headed upstairs, I became overwhelmed by sadness and loss, knowing in my heart that chances were I'd never see Ian again. With that thought echoing through my mind as I lay in bed, I eventually fell into a fitful asleep.

22

The Prodigal Son Returns

The next morning, Al arrived bright and early and once we had our luggage loaded, we said our farewells to Singe, Jude, Joe and Phil before heading off to Manchester Airport via a route I had taken with Ian many times – through the Peak District on the winding A628 across the Pennines, a smallish mountain range running from just south of the Midlands all the way north towards Scotland. From my first ride across I had always been mesmerized by the desolate landscape, one nearly devoid of trees, where barren hills were split by deep ravines cut by cascading streams, a region populated only by sheep and the ubiquitous low rock walls that always made me wonder who built them all and why. In the winter months, the route was treacherous, often closing as the winter rains invading the west coast of England from the Irish Sea turned to sleet, snow and ice across the Pennines. In September, though, it was a pleasant ride, winding and scenic.

Al did his best to engage us in some small talk, pointing out a couple of landmarks along the way, but except for a few brief, polite responses, we were each lost in our own thoughts as we watched the scenery slide by. Arriving at the airport by 8:30, we were on schedule for our 11am flight and by 10:15, we were boarding.

Plopping down in my aisle seat next to Theresa, I found myself sitting across the aisle from Jack. Closing my eyes, I embraced images of past trips with Ian, desperately trying to hold off the heavy sadness gnawing at the edges of my mind. By the time we'd been in the air for an hour or so, I'd run the gamut of memories, settling into a sullen silence as lunch was served – some sort of pasta dish I swallowed without notice. With our trays cleared, Theresa was dozing to an in-flight movie when Jack's visit with Ian popped into my mind – along with a curiosity to find out what had been discussed. Reaching across the aisle, I tapped Jack's arm.

"Oh, Jack? How did your visit with Ian go last night?"

"Visit?" he asked, caught off guard. "Oh, you mean at dinner time? Fine. It went fine."

"What did he want to talk about?" I asked, suddenly noticing an uncomfortable feeling creeping into my stomach as the words exited my mouth. Jack looked at me, one eyebrow raised just a bit, as he considered his response.

"Well, that was a private conversation between Ian, Caroline and me. Suffice it to say that he had some questions about my faith and what I believe."

Like a verbal runaway locomotive, I just couldn't seem to stop the words as they spilled out.

"That was it? He must have had some specific questions about God and all, didn't he?"

Pausing again, Jack considered his words carefully before replying.

"Dying is a terrifying thing to face, something we must each do someday. Anyone confronted with the end of their life has fears and questions they must face. We spoke of many things."

"Well, I don't mean to pry into private affairs or anything, but I was just wondering what sorts of things you may have talked about."

Careening completely out of control, I was fully aware how stupid my words sounded, even to me. *I don't mean to pry!?!* What the hell did I think I was doing if not prying? Idiot! Again, Jack carefully measured his response but his firm reply contained no trace of annoyance or anger.

"Everyone has their own private questions; questions that go to their very core concerning the meaning of life and what comes next – if there even is a 'next'. Ian and Caroline asked some questions last night that I did my best to answer openly, honestly and completely based on my beliefs. But it was a private conversation between the three of us. I would betray their confidence by sharing it. If Ian chooses to share it, that's fine, but you'll have to take it up with him."

I nodded, swallowing hard as I turned back in Theresa's direction. Staring out the window at the vast blue sky, I felt ashamed and embarrassed, understandable emotions considering I'd been doing my best to pry into the details of a private conversation between a minister and a dying man. As I stared out the window, I felt a tap on my forearm. Turning back, Jack was looking at me gently, his eyes expressing genuine concern.

"Ian's questions were his, Scott. Today, I'm more concerned with what your questions are."

Staring at Jack's face, I didn't know what to say but now was no time to hold back. My best friend, someone everyone loved, would probably die before he reached 50 years old. If God is real, why does he *allow* stuff like this to happen? If he is in control, does he *orchestrate* tragedies like this? Does he just not care? Who is this God Jack put so much faith in? What would he have said last night to Ian? Believe what I believe and you will be saved? Believe in what? Why? Suddenly, I felt bold and angry and the words just began to tumble out.

"I know you believe in God and all, Jack, but I've tried and it just doesn't work for me. I just don't get it. There is so much hurt and pain in the world; so much suffering. How can a God – one who supposedly loves us - put us through all this? How can Ian be dying like he is if there is a God who truly cares? I'd rather believe we're all descended from apes than created by a God who puts us through this. People kill and maim in the name of religion all the time. There is disease and sickness and hunger and poverty and evil. Where's God in all that? And everyone believes their religion is the only one that counts. I've met a lot of Christians who are so self-righteous, so holier than thou. They believe that Christianity is the only *true* religion, right? Meanwhile, there are millions of Muslims who want to kill anyone who doesn't agree with their interpretation of Islam, Jews think they are God's chosen people and all the other ones seem to be constantly fighting one another, and all for what? It's always the *other* guy who is going to hell. What about good people who live a really good life but don't follow any religion? What about good people who've never even heard of Christ, people who live in remote areas all over the world? Are they all going to hell? Isn't living a good life enough? I just don't know about all this religion stuff."

Out of things to say, I looked away, my voice trailing off as I took a breath. I already regretted some of my words but in spite of that, I also felt relief, like; *there, I've finally said it!* Looking up, I expected to see Jack turning red; apoplectic that I should so denigrate his beliefs. Whenever I'd imagined a conversation like this with Jack, or any person of strong faith, I'd seen myself in the role of Spencer Tracy in *Inherit the Wind*, administering a withering cross-examination filled with logic and reason that drove home the futility and foolishness of a belief in some all-knowing, all-powerful god. Now that I had the chance to live out my fantasy, I wanted no part of it, having nothing but respect for Jack and his sincere faith. The last thing I wanted to do was undermine or diminish the very faith he'd used to comfort Ian last night.

Yet throughout my diatribe, I hadn't seen the slightest hint of anger or judgment or offense on Jack's face. He had just sat there, expressionless, calmly waiting for me to finish, his kindly, grandfatherly look never betraying the slightest hint of upset. As I looked at him now, his gaze was unchanged, expressing only the deepest concern at my distress.

"I hear you, Scott. Let me just start by saying that anyone who claims to be a Christian yet acts self-righteous or superior is a Christian in name only and not a true follower of Jesus. And by the way, *that* is what true Christians are – followers of Jesus and not just members of some religion they believe gives them special rights and privileges with God. In fact, Jesus reserved some of his harshest criticism for self-righteous, rule following religious-types – the Pharisees and

Sadducees, as they were called in His time. Those types, sadly, will always be in the world and far too many of them today call themselves Christians.

The fact is that the Bible teaches us exactly opposite – that none of us deserves salvation and we can never earn it. It is only through the incredible grace and mercy of God that we are redeemed by what Jesus Christ did for us. God's grace is never, ever *earned*. It is given freely by God, as a gift to all of mankind. Anyone who thinks they've *earned* it is in for a rude awakening come judgment day.

But let's leave all that for a moment and start at the beginning. We've never really talked about this so I'm wondering if you would tell me your thoughts on a couple of questions. First, do you believe in a Creator? By that I mean a God who created this universe and everything in it, including you and me? Or, do you think that this universe and everything in it is just the result of random chance? Those are, after all, the only two options."

I pondered the question for a moment, forced to consider what it was that I really believed.

"Well, I suppose . . . I guess . . . I don't know. I mean, I know that science gone a long way towards proving there is no god . . . or at least probably isn't one. But I have to admit I've always thought there must have been a creator when I look at the world around me. I guess the honest answer is that I just don't know."

"Fair enough, but you must understand that no matter what anyone says, science can never prove or disprove God. As an engineer, I'm sure you know that the scientific method is a step by step process that starts with a hypothesis that is tested under controlled conditions or observed in nature for one key property – repeatability. If repeatability is found, further experiments are conducted until the phenomenon is fully understood. God, on the other hand, has revealed Himself throughout history through miracles, signs and prophets; things that simply cannot be replicated in any laboratory. Science cannot replicate or explain miracles like a burning bush that is not consumed or manna falling from heaven or a spring suddenly emerging from the top of a rock in the desert or the parting of the Red Sea so it simply declares the miracle impossible. Science also cannot replicate or explain the Bible's documented prophetic accuracy, a much bigger problem since history has confirmed so much of what has been prophesied in the Bible."

"Prophetic accuracy" I interjected. "What do you mean by that?"

"Well, the Bible has, literally, hundreds of detailed prophecies that have been proven true through science and archaeology, many only just recently and more, it seems, every day. Prophets were godly men whom God chose to speak through to deliver messages to His people. What they said was written down and if it came to pass, those writings would be added to Jewish Scripture. A single wrong prophecy was enough to label someone a false prophet. The best known are Samuel, Jeremiah, Isaiah, Ezekiel and Daniel but there were many more.

Let me give you just one amazing example. Long before it happened, Jeremiah wrote of Babylon, led by King Nebuchadnezzar, conquering the nation of Judah and carrying its best and brightest men back to Babylon to live in exile. His prophesy said the exile would last exactly 70 years and end under a great ruler named Cyrus. He went on to prophesy that Babylon, the world's greatest empire during Jeremiah's lifetime and considered unconquerable, would fall to an enemy entering through open gates. There was a great deal more than that but everything Jeremiah prophesied eventually came to pass, right down to the smallest detail. There are many, many more concerning all sorts of things that history has proven true.

Another example is the concerning minute details about the birth, life and death of Jesus, all of which proved true. We know for a fact they were written centuries before his birth. Jesus Himself prophesied the total destruction of the Jerusalem Temple in 70 A.D. some 35 or 40 years before it happened.

The prophecies and the events documented in the Bible have been corroborated in hundreds of cases by secular historical records with more being added to that list every year. Science cannot explain any of that. So put scientific *proof* of

God - for or against - out of your mind. Instead, simply allow your mind to follow the evidence wherever it leads. After all, what do real-life detectives do when they are trying to solve a crime?"

I thought for a second, caught off guard by Jack's question. "Well, they collect clues and evidence, interview people, look for eyewitnesses. Try to figure it out, I guess."

"Exactly. A big part of that, of course, is using logic and reason to reach their conclusions. Now, with that in mind, I'd like to offer a couple of scientific facts that will speak for themselves. You're an engineer. Use your reason, your logic and your understanding of statistics and probabilities to let the facts lead you where they may. The most powerful tools any detective has are intellect, logic and reason in deciding what the clues and evidence ultimately mean, agreed?"

"Sure." I replied, still unsure of where Jack was heading. "But what do you mean by clues?"

"Scientific facts that point one way or another, arguing either in favor of the existence of a Creator or against it. For instance, let's say you see a mountain that has a shape that, from a certain direction, resembles the silhouette of a person's face. We can all tell that's just a coincidence, right? In other words, that would not point to a creator."

"Yeah"

"But when you see Mount Rushmore, you immediately know there was a creator, right? It's unmistakable. Not for an instant do we consider the possibility that random forces chiseled those four famous faces in stone. It's the same thing with a magnificent building or a beautiful work of art. We instantly know these things are created works. Well, I'd like to offer you a few recently discovered scientific facts and let you decide which is more likely, the hand of a creator or random chance? Before we start, though, let me ask you my second question, a crucially important question that you may have to dig a bit deeper to answer."

Apprehensive at Jack's sudden change in tone, I answered defensively.

"O - k . . . what?"

"Do you have the courage to challenge whatever it is that you believe, deep down? In other words, are you open to being convinced of a new truth, one that doesn't agree with what you currently believe? After all, when searching for truth - which is what science is supposed to be about - preconceived notions must be put aside."

Looking at Jack for any sign that he was of joking, I saw none; he was deadly serious. I had always prided myself as someone who was willing to follow reason and logic wherever they led. In life, I looked at what people did, not just what they said. It was, in fact, the very thing that held me back from following any god or religion - lack of intellectual conviction. Without intellectual conviction, nothing *could* ever click with me. Despite that, I hesitated, reluctant to answer, perhaps fearing how, exactly, Jack would challenge me. This man, with his solid foundation of faith that I didn't understand, was suddenly making me feel a bit uncomfortable but looking at his careworn face, I knew I had to take the leap.

"Yeah, I do want to know the truth in things. If that changes my basic beliefs, so be it. The last thing I want is to be wrong about fundamental truth."

"Good. Sadly, a lot of people in this world embrace the worldview that makes them most comfortable, rejecting anything that threatens it regardless of facts or information. Mostly, I think, it's just intellectual laziness but there is also an element of rebelliousness in some. There *is* truth and enlightenment in this world but ignorance is our natural state. We have stopped teaching critical thinking in our schools and replaced it with the ridiculous belief that all opinions are equally valid. While some things are subjective, for many others there is objective truth and for those things, opinions matter for nothing. Having an opinion does not excuse intellectual laziness. We Americans live in a world of instant gratification and perpetual entertainment and our comfort is our curse, turning us away from God in the direction of comfortable self-reliance. We don't seek after God because we don't feel we need Him. We've driven Him out of our schools and our lives and we don't bother spending any time or effort looking to the mountains of evidence that He is there, that He always has been there and always will be there.

But I'm getting ahead of myself. Being open-minded and curious is the path to enlightenment but I don't want you to believe *anything* I tell you other than for the sake of this discussion. When you get home, I want you to check out everything I tell for yourself."

With that, Jack leaned forward, reaching under the seat in front of him and grabbing his carry-on bag. As I sat back in my seat, I was stunned by what he was proposing. He was going to attempt to convince me of the existence of a Creator through . . . *science*? The irony was clear. I wouldn't be playing Spencer Tracy, offering up the withering cross examination I'd imagined. Jack would! After handing me a pad and a pen, he continued.

"OK. Let's start with Darwin's theory of evolution, something taught as fact by our schools and accepted by most people as fact. Evolution is common sense in some regards. No one disputes that a phenomenon known as functional advantage exists in nature."

"Isn't that when some unusual attribute allows a species to survive better and, eventually, it becomes a normal attribute, right?"

"That's exactly right. But let's consider the bigger question that forms the basis for Darwinian evolution: that life began from nothing more than some coincidental primordial soup containing all the right ingredients, something called abiogenesis. From that original single-celled organism, we are told that every species evolved on the so-called tree of life. Of course, we have never seen a new species evolve out of an old so that is just assumed. Furthermore, no one can explain how something was created out of nothing so *that* is just assumed.

Think about the things that occur in nature. All you have to do is turn on a nature documentary to see the brutality of nature, where survival of the fittest truly does apply. No matter how cute and cuddly an animal may seem, it survives by consuming some part the food chain before eventually becoming part of it.

Now consider the human species. We are unique in myriad ways, possessing intellect, language and imagination. We are creators, building things of incredible complexity. We are explorers, climbing mountains, diving into oceans and reaching for the stars simply because they are there. We have an innate understanding of right and wrong. We long to love and be loved, both personally and communally. We appreciate and stand in awe of beauty. We have always sought after God. No other animal has these attributes and an obvious question is how and why these common aspects of our being would evolve in humans alone, especially since they actually *inhibit* our ability to survive in the natural world? Through a Darwinian worldview, it simply cannot be explained."

Jack paused for a few moments to take a swig of water, allowing me to consider his point. Why would only one, single species develop a set of attributes having no practical use in the natural world. Suddenly, that seemingly obvious fact made no sense. He continued.

"It goes way, way deeper than that, though. To be fair, Darwin developed his theory long before we knew anything about the inner workings of a living cell. In just the past few decades, advances in microbiology and associated sciences have allowed us to look deep inside cells, right down to their most basic components, and what we have found is beyond incredible.

Let me just give you one example - a functional protein. Functional proteins are the machinery of living tissue. They carry out an incredibly diverse set of functions necessary for life. Now, each protein is made up of chains of amino acids, each chain comprised of between 50 and 1000 amino acids arranged in a precise sequence. Once the chain is complete, it folds up like a complex 3-dimensional puzzle. Each protein has a unique shape and functionality that dictates what, exactly, its purpose is.

But assembling a functional protein is no simple feat. Amino acids come in all sorts of sizes, shapes and chemical properties and there are all sorts of different chemical bonds that hold them together. The problem is, functional proteins are incredibly picky.

For instance, only one type of chemical bond will work – a peptide bond – and the odds of having only peptide bonds in a 100 amino acid chain is about 1 in 10 to the 30th power. You're an engineer so you know that's a 1 followed by 30 zeroes but think about that number. A billion has 9 zeroes. What are the chances of something with a one in a billion chance of happening? How about winning three straight lotteries where you have a one in a billion chance? Like those odds? This is even less likely than that.

But that's only the start. Out of over a hundred naturally occurring amino acids, only 20 or so will work in any functional protein. They have left and right orientations - like mirror images - but *only* left handed ones will work. The odds of having only left handed amino acids is also about 1 in 10^{30}. They also have to be put together in a specific, precise order. Given those probabilities and more, it has been mathematically estimated that the chances of randomly assembling a single functional protein made up of 100 amino acids is around 1 in 10^{125}. That is an incomprehensible number but to give you a frame of reference, the total number of atoms that exist in the entire universe is estimated to be about 10^{80}."

I tried to get my head around the number – a 1 followed by 125 zeroes. I couldn't even picture a million or a billion – and this number had no name. I thought back to my childhood, when I first heard the term "google" defined as a 1 followed by 100 zeroes. At that time the term would even trump "infinity" in a childhood argument. It was the very definition of impossible – and this number had 25 more zeroes than a google.

"The 125th power?" I asked, incredulous.

"Yes, 125 zeroes. For what it's worth, I've heard it compared to the likelihood of being dropped, blindfolded, into the Sahara desert and randomly picking up one specific grain of sand marked with an "X" four or five consecutive times. The real kicker is that a living cell doesn't just have one of these functional proteins – it has hundreds and they would all have to develop at the same time in the same place to create that first living cell. It is absolutely impossible yet Darwinists tell us with a straight face that the incredible complexity of this world and the universe just simply happened by pure, random chance. If it weren't so tragic that our kids are being fed this junk, it would be laughable.

DNA is an even better example of nature's unfathomable complexity – a complexity we've barely begun to comprehend at its most basic levels. DNA makes a functional protein look like a tinker toy. A single strand contains every bit of information necessary to create a human from hair to toenails. It is both the blueprint and the assembly instructions for every living thing. Ask an evolutionist where DNA or functional proteins come from and they'll quickly change the subject.

Another recent discovery in microbiology is the molecular machine. They are amazing little mechanisms, tiny little machines that exist inside living cells to perform specific tasks. These tasks include moving things around, copying things like DNA, capturing and storing energy, feeding the cell and even building more molecular machines. Technically, they are protein complexes but the name molecular machine is much more descriptive. They perform tasks with incredible efficiency – far greater efficiency, in fact, than any machine ever made by man. Their energy efficiency, in fact, approaches 100%, which is unthinkable for a manmade machine. One recent research project discovered over 250 new molecular machines in yeast alone. Every living cell has hundreds of them and each one has what is called irreducible complexity, which simply means it is made up of individual parts that have no purpose outside of being an essential part of the entire assembly. That means they could not have been created through gradual, incremental modifications. It would be like an internal combustion engine making its own parts and then assembling itself out of thin air."

"Get out!" I blurted out with a smile, firmly believing Jack had descended into the realm of science fiction and was simply messing with me. He was not.

"It's true, Scott. *Please* write this down and check it out when you get home. These things are incredibly fascinating but, quite frankly, not terribly surprising, at least to me. After all, I believe in a God who created the universe and everything in it. I see the evidence of God all around, in what I see and what I can't see. You said earlier that science has gone a long way towards proving there is no God but I see it as the exact opposite, that science has successfully proven life is far *too* complex to be explained by random chance. It doesn't surprise me at all, when we delve deep inside God's creation, that we are dumbstruck by its complexity and perfection.

The evidence goes far beyond biology. There are a multitude of other conditions existing in incredibly finely-tuned relationships that allow the universe and life on earth to exist. The four forces of the universe – gravity, electromagnetism and the small and large nuclear forces – are fine-tuned to an unimaginably perfect degree, once again defying the randomness of a Darwinian universe. If they were altered in the slightest way, the universe would simply cease to exist, either collapsing in upon itself or atoms drifting apart into oblivion. The big bang itself is an argument for a Creator since it was a moment of *creation*.

We are also located in a remarkably fortuitous position in a highly unusual galaxy in a highly unusual solar system centered by a highly unusual sun while living on a highly unusual planet with a highly unusual, if not unique, moon - all of which is not just helpful to life but *necessary*.

The dirty little secret is that it takes far more faith - *blind* faith, at that - to believe in random chance putting us here than to believe a Creator did the job. On the other hand, when you actually take the time and make the effort to *study* the Bible with an open mind, examining it on its multiple layers, study its historicity, its historical details and archaeological proofs along with its prophetic accuracy, you come to realize that faith in it as God's word actually *is* based on reason. In fact, God *wants* us to probe, question and study His word because it *will* stand up to such scrutiny and has for thousands of years. It is not uncommon at all for a serious scholar who digs into the Bible with the intent of disproving it to become a devout Christian.

When you really dig into Darwinism, on the other hand, you find it is based on pure, blind faith. There are so many aspects of life it simply *cannot* explain. Of course, it is taught in schools as fact and that is tragic. It is nothing more than a theory riddled with holes and flaws yet it is never examined critically. Meanwhile, the volumes of evidence supporting Scripture and the existence of a Creator are purposely ignored by people with an agenda, the exact opposite of what science is supposedly all about. It is a disgrace with tragic consequences."

Jack sat back in his seat, stretching his shoulder and neck muscles as his comments sank in. I looked at Theresa, who was still dozing. The cabin was quiet except for the drone of the jet engines. Sitting back in my seat, I took my glasses off and rubbed my eyes. If all this was true, and I had no reason not to believe Jack, I had to admit that the odds against life starting by random chance were impossibly high. As I pondered that, the only one other logical possibility began to permeate my mind. Suddenly, I needed to know what Jack knew.

"Jack, why do you believe in Christianity?"

Jack thought for a few seconds before answering.

"Well, there are a number of reasons. First is the Bible. I have studied it in great depth and I believe it is the Word of God. Although people quibble over different translations, I also believe it is infallible in its original languages – Hebrew, Aramaic and Greek. It is without question the most authenticated ancient document in the world, one written by some 40 different authors over 1500 years or more yet being without error or contradiction in its pages. It is historically accurate with new archaeological discoveries being made all the time that confirm more of what is in its pages. The Book of Daniel, for instance, was ridiculed for centuries by skeptics since it used the name Belshazzar as the last ruler of Babylon. Secular history had no record of that name - until 1947, that is, when the Nabonidus Chronicle was excavated from the recently discovered site of ancient Babylon. There, on those ancient tablets, Belshazzar was listed as the crown prince of Babylon when it was conquered by Persia. The discovery allowed secular historians to finally catch up with Scriptures written 2500 years earlier. That is just one of many, many examples but to truly understand the Bible and its meaning to the nation of Israel, you must go back to its beginnings, some 3500 years ago.

The first five books, known as the Pentateuch, were written in the time of Moses when at least part of the generation that had been delivered from bondage in Egypt was still alive. Many scholars believe that those books, written in the ancient language of the Hebrews, were received word by word, letter by letter, directly from the mouth of God to His servant, Moses. The Jews call it the Torah, which means instruction. Those five books, and what follows, are for instruction.

At that time, the Israelites had heard of God's promises to Abraham, Isaac and Jacob and they had heard of what Joseph had done in Egypt some 400 years earlier. Even more importantly, they had *witnessed* the seven plagues, the Exodus, the parting of the Red Sea, the Ten Commandments, manna raining down from heaven and much, much more – all miracles God performed in the sight of His people. They had been taught to rely on God's provision for their very existence and He never let them down.

Those events were what made them a people and gave them an identity and you cannot overstate how the nation of Israel was wrapped up in being just that: God's chosen people. From birth to death, every aspect of their lives revolved around Scripture and although they were far from perfectly obedient, *nothing* was more important to them as individuals or as a nation, a *wandering* nation.

Exact copies of Scripture were made on scrolls back then under incredibly exacting conditions and oversight from the Levites, the tribe of priests given that role by God. Slowly, carefully, copies would be made. One mistake would be carefully corrected while two mistakes would cause the scroll to be destroyed. The Torah was the foundation of every Israelite's education and the center of their lives. From infancy, children would begin memorizing their Scriptures. Ancient Israel was a culture based on oral tradition, meaning people would hear Bible stories over and over, eventually memorizing them. These stories would reverently recount past events, miraculous blessings and strict punishments that their ancestors had experienced directly from the hand of God.

Through those centuries, the Scriptures slowly grew. Joshua took over leadership after Moses' death and led the Israelites into the Promised Land, providing the primarily historical Book of Joshua. King David and his son Solomon added large sections while prophets like Samuel, Isaiah, Jeremiah, Daniel and others each contributed significant writings. My point is that with Scripture as the very basis of their identity, there was absolutely no chance of slipping in new stories or changing old ones. Any attempt to do that would have been blasphemous and blasphemy was punishable by death. The Scriptures only grew when the writings of Godly men were found to be true and worthy, and that only happened in hindsight.

For many, prophecy is the most compelling – and scariest – aspect of the Bible because of its uncanny accuracy. If you study it with an open mind, you cannot help but consider the likelihood of supernatural inspiration. God told the prophet Isaiah that *"I am God, and there is none like Me, I make known the end from the beginning, from ancient times, what is still to come. I say, 'My purpose will stand, and I will do all that I please'."* In that passage, God is telling Isaiah that He is the author of all history, knows everything that has happened, is happening and will happen and that there is nothing anyone can do to change His plans or alter His timetable. The Bible's perfect prophetic accuracy proves God is in complete and total control.

A serious mistake that far too many people make is to believe the Bible is just a book of disjointed tall tales, perhaps some good advice for living. They couldn't be more wrong. The entire book is written around a single storyline – God's plan for the redemption of all mankind through a Savior He would provide – Jesus Christ. In Luke's gospel, he writes that when Jesus addressed the disciples after His resurrection, He said *"Everything must be fulfilled that is written about me in the Law of Moses, the Prophets and the Psalms."* Literally hundreds of prophecies are written about Jesus, minute details concerning where He would be born and under what circumstances, what His family line would be, where and how He would die and under what circumstances - and every single one was fulfilled in the person of Jesus Christ.

The Bible has hundreds upon hundreds documented to have been written decades, centuries or even millennia before they were fulfilled. It is tragic that so many people are infatuated by the quatrains of Nostradamus, which are cryptic, to say the least, yet so few take the time to actually study and become convinced by the Bible's perfect prophetic record. Of course, there remain hundreds of end time prophecies concerning the time of God's final judgment, including a horrific, terrifying period of time we have yet to enter known as the tribulation. People ignore these prophecies at their own risk.

So the Bible is historically accurate, prophetically accurate and unquestionably authentic – and those are all good reasons for believing it is God's word but there one more reason. As a follower of Christ, I believe the Bible is God's Word because Jesus says it is God's Word. Now, that that may seem self-serving at first but follow the logic. In order to be our Savior, Jesus had to be perfectly obedient to the end so He would be blameless in the sight of the Father. Otherwise, He would not and could not have been an acceptable sacrifice for our sins. Well, what could be more disobedient than lying about what is or is not God's Word? I dare say all of Christianity crumbles if it is somehow proven that the Bible is not God's true and inerrant Word.

That is a big reason why, for thousands of years, scholars and skeptics have been attacking the Bible from every angle imaginable, invariably failing but doing whatever damage they can in the court of public opinion. Many who have studied it with the intent of disproving it actually became Christians once they delved into its depths. C.S. Lewis, for instance, was originally an atheist who became a prolific Christian writer in the mid-twentieth century, penning classics like *Mere Christianity* and the *Chronicles of Narnia*. Lee Stroebel, an investigative reporter who is still with us, is another. Stroebel started off as an atheist trying to disprove Christianity to his wife but during that process, he became convinced of its truth and has now written several fascinating books from the perspective of his area of expertise, an investigative journalist. I recommend both.

So the Bible has stood the test of time. It is consistent and cohesive, without meaningful error or contradiction and flawlessly written on levels that go far beyond the simple meaning of the words on its pages. If you study it in any depth, it will quickly become apparent that it simply has to be supernaturally inspired."

Feeling a bump on my shoulder, I turned my head to see a drink cart stopped behind me, the flight attendant looking slightly annoyed that I'd made her stop.

"Oh, sorry" Sitting back, I bumped Theresa, whose head had slumped over a bit as she dozed.

"Hey" she said softly, sleep in her eyes.

"Hey, sorry, babe. How was the movie? I guess not so good or you wouldn't have fallen asleep."

"No, I'm just tired."

"Well, go back to sleep and get some rest."

Rearranging her pillows, Theresa gave me a quick kiss before curling up again. I looked back at Jack, who was opening a package of peanuts. I had never heard anything like this before. My experiences with Christianity were confined to special occasions like weddings and funerals where I observed services filled with strange rites and rituals sprinkled with cold, lifeless recitations of rote, meaningless phrases uttered in cultish monotone. As Jack had said, I'd been one of those who considered the Bible a source of wisdom full of stories about morality and some dubious history but he was telling me that wasn't the case at all. According to him, the Bible was divinely inspired and essentially unchanged from ancient times, that its legitimacy was buttressed by uncanny historical and prophetic accuracy, and that it revolved around a single storyline – mankind's Savior. My head was swimming. As I watched, Jack popped a few of peanuts into his mouth.

"Jack, this is amazing stuff. I've never heard it before."

"So . . ." he paused to swallow. "I've got you thinking?"

"Oh yeah. At this point, I don't know what to say or think."

"Well, that's great but I'd like to take it a little further. The intellect is great, and I know yours has to be convinced, but what God really wants is your heart."

"My heart? What do you mean?"

"Well, for the sake of our discussion, let's assume everything I've told you about science and Scripture are true. That leaves you with a pretty big question to answer, doesn't it? Bigger than any question you've ever had to answer. The question is simply: *What now?* What will you do if the things I am telling you turn out to be true?"

I thought for a moment, mulling over the question. I knew I had always wondered about God, recalling the times I'd afforded Him the opportunity to prove Himself by answering this or that little self-centered prayer. If everything Jack had been saying was true, maybe that was exactly what God had been doing all along, in His own way, of course. Maybe the evenings I'd been stopped in my tracks by a spectacular sunset or stared out at the endless ocean or gazed up at an endlessly starry sky were His way of getting my attention. A Creator was one thing, requiring at least some sort of acknowledgement. A Creator who had gone to the trouble of writing a detailed book revealing Himself and His plan for mankind – for me, even – was something entirely different. The answer passed my lips before I could even object.

"I guess I would want to find out more about Him and what He wants from me."

Jack looked at me, nodding. "That's exactly what I was hoping you might say and there is plenty of help on that road. He has given us His word, a way to draw closer to Him, but He wants us to pursue Him. If we do that, He will be there, answering the knock on the door. You see, He loves us more than we can imagine but He gave us free will, meaning we are rebellious at heart, often choosing to do things our way rather than being obedient. In other words, He gave us the option of turning away from Him because He wants us to *choose* to love *Him* and invite *Him* into our lives."

"I've always thought that the God of the Old Testament was mean and vengeful while the God of the New Testament was all love and peace?"

Jack smiled, his look indicating a familiarity with that view of God.

"Many people think that but it is an entirely superficial view. We chose to turn away from Him from the very beginning, from Adam and Eve, and in doing so, we turned from our loving creator and committed a great sin. The penalty for sin is death but not just in the way you might think. It means spiritual death - eternal separation from God. God is perfectly righteous and holy and He does not – *cannot* – tolerate the presence of sin. He gave His people the law through Moses so we would see His standards and eventually understand our utter hopelessness in reaching those standards. We all fall short of the glory of God and although we deserve justice for our sins, what we really need is His mercy."

"I hate that word - sin" I interjected. "I don't even know what that means."

"Well, sin simply means missing the mark God set for us. God says we must love our neighbor as ourselves but if we don't, if we act selfishly, we are missing the mark God has set. The problem is that our hearts *want* to be disobedient. We want to be our own bosses. We are God's most beloved creation and He has wonderful plans for each and every one of us but He wants us to love Him back and loving our Creator means obeying Him. After all, He knows what is best for us. Because we want to be our own boss and because Satan wants to lead us away from God, we miss the mark God sets for us - we sin. Make no mistake about it – there is a spiritual war going on all around us for our very souls. Satan wants us to worship him but short of that, he wants us to worship anything other than God. We can worship our job, money, sex, drugs - it's all fine with Satan because anything that replaces God accomplishes his purpose. Sin is our very nature. Why else would Adam and Eve, who lived and walked with God in paradise and who had everything they could possibly want, why else would they follow Satan's lies and break the one, single rule God had given them."

"So if God loves us so much, why doesn't He just get rid of Satan and forgive our sin?"

"That is a loaded question for which different people have different answers. There are certainly things concerning God that we do not understand and I certainly don't claim to know all the answers. My personal belief is that God gives us free will, including the ability to disobey Him. If God is pure good, then freedom of choice means its opposite, pure evil, must exist. Satan, who was God's greatest and most powerful angelic creation, serves that purpose by representing pure evil. He was so powerful that he challenged God, seeking to replace Him as the object of worship, and for that he and all the other angels who foolishly followed him were cast out from heaven.

Remember this, though. God's entire plan revolves around providing us the chance to be redeemed by Him out of our fallen state to dwell with Him for all eternity in heaven. If God did what you ask, simply forgiving us while allowing us to keep right on sinning in His presence, how would heaven be any different than what we have here on earth – a world filled with injustice and evil?"

"I guess it wouldn't"

"We can't pretend that we know all the details of God's plan or His mind – how could we? He is God. The trinity is another one of God's mysteries – three beings yet one God. God the Father, God the Son and God the Holy Spirit are each fully God, co-equals living in perfect harmony and love. Can we understand that? No, but it is what the Bible tells us and it is what we witness in living a Christian life so it is truth. Jesus stepped down off His heavenly throne to be the last, perfect sacrifice, taking the sins of all mankind upon His shoulders and accepting our punishments. He lowered Himself from the glory of heaven to be born in squalor, a human baby. He lived a humble life of perfect obedience to the Father God's will before becoming, by free will, a substitute, standing in our place as Father God poured out His righteous justice for all our sins. With that incredible act of love and mercy, God showed us just how much loves us. He sent His only Son to stand in for us when His judgment came down. All we have to do is sincerely claim that free gift of salvation that He has provided.

It is a gift beyond anything I could ever repay but I don't have to because it is free. Understanding the magnitude of what He has done for me, I am filled with gratitude that spills over into how I choose to live my life. Because He laid down His life for me, I choose to do the same for Him, laying down my own selfish pursuits and instead offering my life in service to Him. I seek His guidance and then follow where He leads.

I must have looked perplexed at what Jack was saying because he suddenly changed gears.

"Let me try to explain in a different way, by asking you a question. Are you a good person?"

Catching me completely off guard, I wondered for a moment whether I was about to get the religious lecture I'd been worried about. *No, this is Jack*, I thought, *let's be honest.*

"Well, I've done a lot of things I'm not proud of but I think I'm basically a good person."

Smiling, Jack sensed I was uncomfortable with the question.

"I know you are, Scott. I'm not preaching at you, just illustrating a point, ok? You're polite and nice and respectful, right? You've honored your parents for the most part, right? And you certainly don't steal or murder, do you?"

"No."

"So you're a pretty good person, certainly compared to a lot of other people, right? On the big scale of life, your good side outweighs the bad, even if only by a little bit?"

"Yeah, I guess so. I know I could do better but, yeah, I think I'm basically a good person."

"And I agree – you are a good guy. Now, what about me?"

"You?" I thought for a second, searching for the right words. It wasn't hard.

"Jack, you're one of the most honest, decent, considerate guys I've ever known. If I could be half as good as you, I'd be a lot more confident of standing in front of God."

Jack looked at me with a smirk.

"Thanks, but you've got me all wrong. I am totally unworthy of God, a hopeless sinner. My true nature is no different than yours or, for that matter, a serial killer."

"Seriously?!? C'mon, Jack – you? If you're not worthy, who is?"

"The mistake you and many others make is to measure yourself against human standards. When we stand before God, our judgment will be based on the standards of a God who is perfectly holy and righteous, standards we cannot, by our very nature, meet. God knows every action we take, every word we speak and every thought we think. The Bible tells us to hate is murder, to lust is to commit adultery and to lie is an abomination in the sight to God. Have you ever lied? I know I have. Lusted? Guilty again. Burned with anger against someone? Yup.

Now, those are just sins we commit against our fellow man – let's not forget about God. We are supposed to love him with all our heart, our mind, our soul and our strength. Well, I've fallen short again, letting other things get in my way at various times. No, our mistake is thinking that God will judge us by standards *we've* set. He uses His own standards and since He is our Creator that is all that matters."

Still not grasping what it was Jack was saying, much less the concept of atonement, I felt myself being crushed by the hopelessness of standing before a Creator who is judging every word, thought and deed in my life against perfect standards. I'd always thought – hoped would be more like it – that tipping the scales even slightly towards being a good person would be enough for whatever heaven there was out there. Jack, though, was painting a bleak reality of being judged under God's Law and I felt myself sinking into a spiritual black hole from which there seemed no escape. I thought of Ian, wondering how news like this would have helped him. Believing he was being completely truthful with me, my worldview was, indeed, being torn apart by Jack's words, only to be replaced by one of even greater hopelessness when I considered a holy God's judgment on my life but as I looked back at Jack, a broad smile was on his face.

"That's the bad news. No one – not one of us – can ever live up to God's standards. But God is more than an all-knowing God of perfect righteousness and justice. If He were only that, we'd all be doomed but He is also a God of perfect, infinite, unfathomable mercy and love. In Jesus, God gave us our perfect champion, our savior. The penalty for sin is death – both physically and spiritually – and Jesus voluntarily took our place to pay that penalty. Although He was also other things like teacher and prophet, that was His ultimate purpose in His first coming. When He, being completely innocent of sin, voluntarily paid our penalty, He broke the power of death.

Think of it in terms of our own court system. If you went into court having to meet God's standards while being judged by God, you would face fines and penalties you could never, ever afford. What we find, though, is that Jesus has already been to court and paid our fines and penalties in full – we simply have to use that as our defense. If you accept Him as your Savior in your heart, He will claim you as His at the judgment throne and you will be welcomed into heaven as His brother, making you an adopted child of Father God."

Despite Jack's passion, I remained skeptical about Jesus, having read many stories challenging who he was and, in some, his very existence.

"But, Jack, how do we know the stories about Jesus weren't made up? Didn't lots of ancient cultures have stories about messiahs?"

"Once again, we must look at the evidence. There is overwhelming evidence that Jesus not only lived but was received as the Jewish Messiah by masses of people, at least for a time, and that He was crucified. Secular historians, Jews and Romans alike, wrote of him as someone many Jews were following while claiming He was the Jewish Messiah. Three of the gospels are eyewitness accounts and the fourth was written as perhaps the first piece of investigative journalism by Luke, a highly respected physician who never met Jesus but became a companion to the Apostle Paul and other disciples.

The Gospel of Luke is presented by the author as a thoroughly researched historical account that records the eyewitness accounts of people like Jesus' relatives (His mother Mary, His half-brother James) and other disciples like Mary Magdalene and the Apostles. The book of Acts, also written by Luke, is both a historical account of the early days of the church and a first hand, eyewitness account of his own travels with the Apostle Paul. You probably don't know this but experts generally acknowledge Luke, through his flawless recitation of titles and names of the figures encountered, as the most accurate of all the ancient historians.

There is also the story of the empty tomb, a story that is the foundation Christianity. Without a risen Christ, there is no Christian church. Had it been a hoax, the story would have been quickly and easily debunked by the all-powerful Jewish and Roman authorities, both eager to see this new, fledgling sect called "The Way" snuffed out. Let's examine some of the details of this pivotal claim.

In the days and weeks following the resurrection, there came an astonishing transformation of hundreds of uneducated fishermen and laymen from forlorn, despairing fugitives hiding in fear of their own lives to a cohesive group of dedicated, articulate followers that fearlessly declared the truth of their belief in Jesus as Messiah. All were persecuted, many to the point of death. Why would any of them subject themselves to that unless they believed it to be entirely true?

Now, if you are fabricating a story, you need to make it believable. In each of four gospels, written by different men at different times, women are always the first to deliver the news of the empty tomb. This is significant because women's testimony in that time and culture was considered totally unreliable, inadmissible in court. That means the only logical reason to use that detail is that it was the truth. Other questions include who rolled the stone away, where the body was and what happened to the dozens of Roman guards who were supposed to be guarding the tomb? Those guards were there because the Jewish authorities feared mischief with the body and wanted to prevent it - yet the body disappeared anyway without a trace.

These are not minor details but major questions, questions with only one answer that consistently explains what happened and makes sense - that all those things actually *did* happen. In the weeks, months and years that followed, there was the explosive growth of the church despite its revolutionary message of radical, selfless love and peace for friends and enemies alike, a message that went against everything this fallen world held dear – and still does. Thousands converted on a single day, Pentecost, when God poured out His Holy Spirit.

There are many other undisputed details that make it virtually guaranteed that the resurrection story is true but there are also inexplicable stories of radical conversions following the resurrection. Let me tell you a couple.

The first is James, the son of Mary and Joseph and, therefore, the half-brother of Jesus. Imagine growing up with a brother who, when He is around 30 or so, declares himself Messiah and begins performing miracles. Well, throughout the gospels, prior to Jesus' crucifixion, James (and Jesus' entire family other than His mother) were skeptics, unwilling to believe His claims. James wasn't even there at Jesus' crucifixion. Only after seeing the risen Christ did James become a true believer, eventually becoming the head of the church in Jerusalem.

The second is the story of a man who lived back in the days of Jesus, a man who was brilliant, wealthy and powerful – Saul of Tarsus. Saul went to the best schools, learning at the feet of the most brilliant religious teachers of the day, and eventually was made a member of the Sanhedrin, the all-powerful ruling Jewish religious council. Remember that the Jewish world revolved around their identity as God's people so nothing was higher than religious leaders and Saul, at a young age, was an up and coming leader in the Sanhedrin. He was devout, a man zealous for God and sacred Scripture. For him, the Law of Moses – God's Law – meant *everything*.

When Jesus showed up on the scene, He continuously and vocally criticized religious types like Saul, labeling them snakes and hypocrites. Saul hated Jesus and His followers, labeling Jesus a false messiah and blasphemer for claiming to be the Son of God. Even more disgusting to Saul was the fact that Jesus' freely associated with unclean gentiles, prostitutes and tax collectors, elevating the lowest rungs of society while insulting and denigrating the elite religious rule followers like Saul. In Saul's eyes, Jesus deserved to die.

Once that was accomplished, Saul thought the cult would die out – but it didn't. A radical and growing sect of Jews still, for some confounding reason, followed Jesus, many devoted even to the point of death. It was inexplicable. Just after Jesus' death, Saul oversaw the stoning of Stephen, an early church leader, for blasphemy. Nearly dead, Stephen looked up to the sky, declaring to all he saw heaven's doors flung open with Jesus standing there. As he was being stoned, Stephen asked for forgiveness for his murderers, just as Jesus had for His. Perhaps that memory haunted Saul, gnawing at his conscience. Either way, Saul remained thirsty for vengeance on Jesus' followers, eventually asking for and receiving authorization to travel to Damascus in search of more blasphemous Christ-followers so he could return them to Jerusalem to recant - or die.

A funny thing happened on the way to Damascus, though.

Saul had an up close and personal encounter with the resurrected Jesus, an encounter that literally changed him overnight into Paul, the Apostle charged by Jesus to take the gospel to the gentiles. His name changed to Paul, this man would spend the rest of his life fearlessly preaching the Gospel from Rome to Greece to Asia Minor to Antioch to Jerusalem. Before his encounter with Jesus, Saul led a life of virtually limitless power and prestige. After his encounter, Paul led a life where, at various times, he was whipped, scourged, stoned, beaten by mobs, imprisoned, shipwrecked and lost at sea. He became reviled and hated in his previous social circles virtually overnight, exchanging his life of comfort and wealth for one of poverty, living outdoors for long periods on nothing more than the kindness of friends and strangers, exposed to extreme cold and heat, hunger, thirst, aching pain from an increasing number of serious injuries, capping it all off by spending his final years in a Roman dungeon before finally being beheaded by Nero.

Yet through all that he made some of the greatest contributions of any Apostle, writing brilliant, foundational letters on church theology and doctrine, planting original churches all across the eastern Mediterranean and proclaiming throughout his life of outward suffering his never wavering gratitude at being a bondservant to Christ. Paul fully understood the debt he owed Jesus for what He did – what we all owe Him – so he was content in all circumstances, living to serve his Lord and Savior.

The transformation of James into a true believer or Saul into Paul makes absolutely no logical sense from a worldly point of view. James would never have *chosen* to believe the boy he grew up with was God unless he had seen something to change his mind - like a risen Christ. Saul would never have *chosen* to throw everything in his life away to become a wandering servant of Christ. Again, the only logical explanation is that His encounter with the risen Christ was *real*, that it actually happened. Saul didn't choose Jesus; Jesus chose Saul. Why? Well, first, his sudden, dramatic conversion was and is an incredibly powerful witness to Christ, inexplicable in any context other than his very real encounter. Also, he was a powerful, compelling orator, fluent in several languages, thoroughly trained in Scripture and a brilliant thinker.

What changed Peter from a frightened, headstrong, uneducated fisherman into a fearless and gifted orator? What changed Stephen? What changed any of Jesus' disciples into someone who was willing to be persecuted, even to the point of death? You've probably heard of Christians being fed to the lions or being used as human torches at Nero's parties? Clearly, no one became a Christian in those days for the perks. There was absolutely no upside unless, of course, they were totally convinced in their hearts and souls that Jesus was exactly who He and His Apostles claimed He was – the Son of God and Savior of all mankind.

When you actually put yourself in the place of these people and in the context of that culture, it is impossible to believe it was some sort of fabricated story or scam. God has always been active and involved in the lives of men and Jesus was His ultimate gift to mankind, an unmistakable sign of His love and mercy for us, His fallen children."

Pausing, Jack sat back in his seat, once more stretching his neck and shoulders. As if on divine cue, the P.A. system crackled to life one last time.

We are beginning our final descent into Newark Liberty International Airport. Please bring your tray tables and seats into an upright position and stow all belongings under the seat in front of you or in an overhead compartment.

Turning to look out the window, I saw Theresa was awake, looking at me with a curious look.

"Hi babe, did you have a good nap"

"Yeah, I did. I woke up a little while ago but you seemed so engrossed in your conversation with Jack that I didn't want to interrupt. What were you talking about?"

"Well, it's a long story. I'll tell you about it on the ride home."

"Oh . . . Ok."

Her expression told me she had lots more questions but they would have to wait for now. Looking past her out the window, I could see the familiar hills and lakes of northern New Jersey as we headed east before making a final turn south into Newark.

Having had my entire worldview turned upside down, I felt overwhelmed by the volume of information Jack had provided. Thinking back to the night before, to Ian and his cancer, I resolved to investigate the things Jack had spoken of, to do my own research into the scientific and Biblical information Jack had related.

After passing customs and reaching the main concourse, we started down the long ramp to the pickup area. Although I knew I'd be seeing Jack and Lou again in a couple of months, there was none of the usual excitement. As Theresa walked ahead with Lou, I strolled slowly with Jack, at least one question weighing heavily on my mind. Unsure how to ask, Jack broke the ice, stopping on the ramp to face me as Theresa and Lou continued.

"Scott, I just want to stress again to not believe what I've told you. Do your own research, maybe find a church that is Bible-centered – one that doesn't try to add or remove anything from the message of the Bible or the necessity of Christ's atoning death. If you want to dig deeper still, join a Bible study group and go from there. We draw closer to God by studying His Word. It takes time and there are no short cuts but it is worth it. You have nothing to lose and everything to gain. I promise you won't be disappointed."

"Thanks, Jack. What you've told me is, well, it's pretty overwhelming but you've really got me thinking. Thanks so much. Have a safe trip home, now."

"You too" Jack said as we turned to walk on down the ramp. Pausing, he turned back, looking slightly uncomfortable.

"About last night"

I had forgotten all about the question I'd asked that prompted our amazing discussion over the past couple of hours. Jack's comment brought up my embarrassment once again but as I started to apologize, he cut me off.

"I brought Ian and Caroline a Bible from my church; one with over 50 personal messages from members of my congregation. We've been praying for him as a church for a while now. We read some Bible passages together and I prayed with them. I can tell you that he and Caroline seemed riveted to what I was saying, hearing for perhaps the first time of the wonderful salvation that Christ offers. There were lots of tears and prayers and hugs. It is not for me to judge what is truly in a man's heart but I left last night hopeful that Ian had, indeed, accepted Jesus as his savior. I hope, as time goes by, that he will continue to draw upon the Bible for encouragement and comfort. One thing I know with all my heart is that God is sovereign. His purposes will be accomplished, even through a tragedy and even when we don't fully understand of His plan."

Feeling the tears well up in my eyes, I asked the question I feared.

"So it wasn't too late for him . . . or . . .?" my voice trailed off, leaving the rest unasked, hoping Jack would answer it anyway. Putting his hand on my shoulder, he didn't let me down.

"As long as a person is breathing, it's not too late to accept Christ. God offers us the gift of salvation through faith in His Son. It is available to us no matter what sins we've committed until the moment we die. At that moment, if it remains unclaimed, the gift is forfeit. God gives us this world and this life in which to make our choice and then He judges us. Our choice is facing God on the basis of our own merits or on the righteousness of Christ. I choose Christ.

I'm sure you've heard of Jesus' parable of the prodigal son? In it, the younger son demands his inheritance from his father, an incredibly offensive act akin to saying 'I wish you were dead so I could have what will be mine anyway'. Nevertheless, the father gives it to him and the son goes off, squandering his inheritance while living the wild life. Finally, when he finds himself living in squalor with the pigs, he has a change of heart and wants to go home; back to the father he had basically spit on.

Now, any typical father – me, for instance – would have scolded and lectured and punished his wayward son but the father in this story represents God the Father. Even though the son's motives are far from pure, the lad is sincere in his repentance and the father reacts with unrestrained joy, running to meet him and showering him with kisses and affection without regard for his own dignity. There is no bitterness or resentment in the father for what the son has done, just love and joy at his return, and the father orders a massive celebration, something the Bible tells us heaven does every single time a sinner repents and accepts Christ. You could be that prodigal son, Scott. You've lived apart from God for all these years yet here He is, beckoning you to come home. You can hear it in the small, still voice within you; I know you do.

But there is another son in the story who represents someone I suspect you've had some exposure to – the older son. The older son follows all the rules, never disobeying the father. In doing so, he builds up a sense of entitlement in his heart. The older son represents Pharisees like Saul, religious rule-followers who feel God owes them salvation for their supposed obedience, that they have *earned* God's grace. Their 'goodness' is empty and self-centered, done with the *expectation* of being rewarded. It is all about them rather than God's boundless love and the unearned grace He showers us with. The older son is jealous of the reception the younger son gets upon his return, angrily and defiantly remaining outside as the celebration begins, his father begging him to come join the festivities. There the story ends, the younger son being welcomed home with a joyous celebration while the older, self-righteous son remains outside, bitter and angry.

Frankly, younger sons are easier to bring to salvation than older sons. They embrace the undeserved forgiveness God offers through Christ, fully aware of their sinfulness. Older sons don't realize their need; their pride and arrogance substituting for Christ's call to humbly love and forgive. It is no surprise that a major problem in Jesus' day still thrives today; religious types who look down their noses at sinners. Your previous impressions make my point perfectly.

Laying down your life for Christ and letting Him live through you begins with understanding the depth of your own sinfulness and your inescapable need for a savior – for Jesus Christ. True holiness begins with the comprehension of the immensity of God's sacrificial love and when that finally happens, you'll turn to Jesus with awe, gratitude and love, understanding in the depth of your soul how much He loves you to have done what He did. To claim this gift, you simply acknowledge in your heart, with silent words if that's what you choose, that you are a sinner. You ask Him to come into your life, to guide you and keep you. Then, you follow Him where He leads. You study God's Word, meditate on it and learn to listen for and to the Holy Spirit, that still, small voice within. If done right, it is a journey that will only end with your last breath."

When Jack paused once more, I jumped at the chance to ask a question that was eating at me.

"For every good thing I've done, I've done 10 bad ones. How can God overlook all of that?"

Patiently, Jack smiled.

"Scott, I know it this hard to grasp because we cannot conceive of such love but God loved us first, before we ever loved Him. Your debt for all the sin you ever have or ever will commit *has already been paid* by Jesus on the cross – and He did it willingly . . . for *you*.

When you sincerely accept Christ in your heart, you are saved for all eternity from the penalty of sin but that certainly doesn't make you sinless or perfect. You need to grow as a Christian. God has good works planned for you. He wants your life to shine with the light of Christ, being filled with love and forgiveness and mercy and humility and generosity and a heart for serving others. If good works do *not* spring from your love and gratitude towards Christ, something is wrong. Ultimately, when you die, you will be saved from the very presence of sin when you go to live in heaven, where sin does not exist and there are no more tears and no more pain.

When I truly accepted Christ, I was filled with indescribable gratitude for his sacrifice and love for me. What sprang from that gratitude was an overwhelming desire to humbly live by His example and serve Him by serving my fellow man; just as He came to serve us. You won't be perfect – none of us ever will be on this earth – but through that wellspring of gratitude you will follow Christ and your life will begin to change, bit by bit, one thing at a time as you learn to listen to the Holy Spirit. Your heart will be remade into a new heart, one like Christ's.

But you must realize that God's gift has a shelf life – your lifetime, whatever that may be – and there is no middle ground. Your last opportunity to claim that gift could come in 30 years or 30 seconds. Right now, today, God is reaching out to you, Scott. I know He wants to come into your life. All you have to do is take His hand."

With that, Jack draped his arm around my shoulder as we turned to walk down the ramp to join Lou and Theresa, who was now looking at me as if I'd joined some secret society. Cocking her head, I could see from her expression that I'd be doing a lot of talking on the ride home. Saying one last goodbye, we boarded our shuttle and headed off to the remote parking lot.

As we headed off, I conjured an image of the scene last night at Ian's, trying to imagine the emotional and spiritual impact of Jack's words on Ian and Caroline. He'd been given hope of a last minute reprieve and I found myself silently praying that he really had sincerely accepted Christ in his heart, just as Jack had hoped. It didn't take long, though, for my thoughts to turn to my own broken and battered life. I wondered why I hadn't had this conversation with Jack years ago.

No matter, I thought as the van pulled into the remote parking lot. I'd had it today.

23

Saying Goodbye

Over the next few weeks I thought a lot about my conversation with Jack, blown away by his knowledge, passion and commitment. I purchased a study bible but, despite my initial burst of interest, soon put it aside as I became increasingly tied up with work and the upcoming Cup, where my thoughts were consumed with what Ian was going through and how I could provide him with some amusement. In my mind, I saw him taking the occasional trip to the Angel with Caroline, meeting up with the lads for a pint or two as they read the latest articles Singe would post. Sometimes, as I wrote, I would picture his familiar smile and hear his contagious giggle, thoughts that always made me smile.

By early October, Indie had finished a big news story on how Captain Dow had settled on the final Team U.S. player with Richard Hanson, a 2 handicapper I'd played with once or twice in England over the years. Throughout my late summer search to fill our last spot with an American, Richard had been relentless in his efforts to join the trip and thanks to some confusion on my part and an "overheard" telephone conversation in the Angel, the first full length article of the year concerning Cup news was published.

Team U.S. Adds Final Player

By: Datzit Indaruf, Flem Cup Correspondent

SPINKHILL, ENGLAND, October 9 - Team U.S. Captain Scott Dow announced today that the U.S. side has been finalized with the addition of an English player. Dow commented "We are very, very excited to add Richard. I've played golf with him and he's a solid 2 handicapper with a competitive streak a mile wide. Although we made some mistakes while checking him out, that is all in the past now and we're excited to have him."

When asked what he meant by "mistakes while checking him out", Dow abruptly ended the interview with the excuse of a pending driving range appointment. This piqued our interest since no driving range requires appointments. At first, we'd assumed the American Captain simply enjoyed the view while walking behind Richard, perhaps partial to his stylish flamboyancy. But other questions soon arose, eventually leading us to put our crack investigative reporter, Iva Tufshot, on the case in pursuit of the truth in Dow's decision making process and what these 'mistakes' actually were. This is what she found in a report we simply call: The Twisted Mind of Dow.

By: Iva Tufshot, Investigative Reporter

After receiving numerous veiled warnings from England players and fans concerning a certain England golfer who'd been lobbying for a spot on the American team, American Captain Scott Dow got home from a September trip to Spinkhill and pulled out a crumbled up piece of paper on which a single name was scrawled – Richard Manson.

With warnings about adding the 2 handicapper to Team U.S. swirling in his mind, Dow decided some high-level investigating was what was needed. When the Google search returned some rather thought-provoking family connections, Dow became even more concerned, eventually plugging a cell phone picture he'd had taken of Manson into a hacked FBI database and finding a "likely-possible-father" match to be a certain Charles Manson - the very same one of Manson Family and "Helter Skelter" fame. When further research on Ancestry.com turned up the possibility that Richard could actually be the offspring resulting from a *tryst between Charles Manson and one Lynette 'Squeaky' Fromme, Dow began to really ob-*

sess over his findings.

Meeting in 1967, Manson immediately added Squeaky to his bevy of loony-birds residing

at his desert compound in Southern California. With the help of some official birth records and

a fertile imagination, Dow soon deduced that sometime in the late '60s, the pair produced a

son named Meryl Lynette Manson.

For a child with a father who was leader of a mass murdering cult and a mother who

would eventually try to assassinate the President of the United States, Meryl led a fairly nor-

mal early life that included extended periods of running around naked and dirty while

everyone marveled at how cute he was. Unfortunately, things took a turn for the worse when

both parents ended up in prison for life before he reached puberty.

During his teenage years, Meryl lived a very unstable lifestyle, constantly moving be-

tween boy's homes. Through unimpeachable rumor and innuendo, along with a healthy dose

of speculation, Dow soon surmised that Meryl had disappeared from the radar screen right

around his 18th birthday in 1985, never to be heard from again. Digging further while allowing

his fertile imagination to run amuck, Dow visited whosyourdaddy.com to find the true reason

that "Meryl Lynette Manson" disappeared.

There, it quickly became apparent that, desperate to evade the infamy his parents had

thrust upon him while escaping the pain of his childhood, the lad had simply changed his

name at the first opportunity. By combining his first and middle names while dropping the

feminine "ette" at the end, a new persona soon emerged . . . Meryl-lyn Manson.

Now firmly ensconced in a 1st class cabin on the crazy train, Dow went on to surmise

that Meryl-lyn did far more than just change his name. He established a whole new persona

and appearance to go with that name – and learned to play the guitar.

Around 1989, a satanic cult band named Marilyn Manson and the Spooky Kids (the

"Marilyn Manson" part a combination of Marilyn Monroe and . . . wait for it . . . Charles Man-

son) showed up on the scene named with a lead singer named Marilyn – or was it 'Meryl-

lyn'?!? Known for wild costumes and makeup that made him unrecognizable, a little known

fact that Dow claims to have uncovered is that Meryl-lyn Manson was an avid golfer who earned a scratch handicap despite being banned at all reputable golf clubs due to disreputable fashion sense.

But Meryl-lyn soon grew tired of that life, longing to get back to his first love, golf, an elitist, rich man's sport that simply didn't fit in with the teenage angst, despair and Satan worship that his fanbase really wanted. After all, with the bizarre getups and makeup, who would know? Meryl-lyn could pass the baton and move on, free to fade into the woodwork . . . which, according to Dow, was exactly what he did.

About that time, a certain Richard Manson appeared in Spinkhill. Noting remarkable similarities in swing plane and fashion sense, Dow believed that this was no coincidence, his keen investigative senses having pieced together the complex puzzle. Problem was, he'd put himself into a quandary as to what to do. Should he allow an obviously unstable man – son of psychotic parents – become part of the American team or should he continue searching, possibly even playing a man down for the Cup? On the one hand, Richard was an outstanding golfer who could show real killer instincts on the links. On the other hand, he could be a psycho man-child who could show a real killer's instincts on the links. What to do? What to do?

It was then that Dow decided to turn to his long time friend, Smokin' Joe, for advice during the now-famous conversation that was "overheard" in the Angel (attributable in no way to someone picking up a different extension and listening in).

"Joe, Joe", Dow started in an unusually animated yet hushed tone. "I thought those warnings from everyone in England were simply because Richard was such a fine golfer and strong competitor. I thought everyone was just trying to stop us from acquiring another Black Dog-type golfer. But now I understand. I know who he really is. He's . . . a . . . Manson!"

Silent for several moments, Dow listened as Joe took a drag on his cigarette followed by a sip from his pint . . . followed by another drag on his cigarette . . . and another sip from his pint. Finally, following a long, slow exhale, Joe replied:

"What's that?"

"Richard. I checked it out and found that Richard Manson is Charles Manson's son, Merylyn Manson, who became Marilyn Manson, the scratch golfer who became Richard Man-

son. Oh, I should have listened! Oh, you tried to warn me . . . but did I listen? Noooooo! What should I do, Joe? TELL ME WHAT TO DO?!?"

Listening expectantly, Dow heard it again - inhale . . . sip . . . exhale . . . inhale . . . sip . . . . inhale . . . sip . . . swallow . . . exhale. Finally, after what seemed an eternity, Joe replied once more:

"How's that?"

"Richard Manson is Charles Manson's son Merylyn Manson who was Marilyn Manson before he was Richard Manson!!!"

"Who?"

"Richard! Richard from The Angel! Richard Manson! I'm on to it, Joe! He's a Manson! Like Charles! Squeaky Fromme is his mom! I put it all together! I figured it all out!! I KNOW WHO HE REALLY IS!!!"

"Richard?"

"YES, RICHARD!!!"

"His name is Hanson, you twit."

"Hanson?"

"Hanson. With an H."

"With an 'H'?"

"With an 'H'."

"Oh . . . Well, never mind then. When you see Richard tonight, tell him he's in. Thanks, bye!"

So the Americans have added Richard <u>H</u>anson, a fine 2 handicapper who is absolutely no relation to Charles Manson, Squeaky Fromme or Marilyn Manson, as their final player.

***

Like a dam bursting, emails began flooding in faster than I could handle them, allowing me to pick and choose the ones I want to run with, staging them for daily release. After sifting through my ever growing collection, I decided my next major story would focus on an email good 'ole Swampy had sent leveling some rather explosive charges at Captain Dow. As always, Indie went with the flow, doing some research to check Swampy's numbers and within a few days, the year's first good controversy was off and running.

Swampy Levels Serious Charges; American Captain Responds

By: Datzit Indaruf, Flem Cup Correspondent

MYRTLE BEACH, S.C., October 17 – In an email containing explosive allegations, Stuart Trowbridge has resurfaced just in time for the upcoming Flem Cup. Never a stranger to controversy, Swampy was an unwitting victim in two of the most controversial incidents in Flem Cup history – the drink-buying scandal and the hot-sauce incident, both of which nearly killed him. On the flip side, he has enjoyed playing the antagonist in two of the most well timed and well documented 'in-your-face' put downs in Cup history – his confrontation with Sven at the end of the '01 cup and his confrontation with American Captain Dow following the Yank's '02 Cup debacle during which he coined the nickname "Donut Dow". His letter is printed here in its entirety with analysis to follow.

Indaruf,

It has been a while since we have spoken, mainly due to my relocation to remotest Devon. Cut off from the civilised world, I have little to do but garden and manufacture small ornate charms for my children to sell from the road side to passing tourists from "up country" for tuppence.

However, Devon was recently allowed Internet connectivity by the Government and I have again gained access to your fantastic website. As you know, I am a keen follower of this competition and return as a player after a two year hiatus due to a hotline phone call I received from our leader, golfing legend Captain Ian Jennings. Our conversation, which I recorded for posterity sake, went like this:

Jennings [authoritatively]: *Trowbridge?*

Trowbridge [surprised]: *Cap'n? Is that you?*

Jennings [disgustedly]: *Course it tis!*

Trowbridge [respectfully]: *Yessir, Cap'n, sir.*

Jennings [reluctantly]: *Can you play in this year's Flem Cup?*

Trowbridge [suspiciously]: *You want me to play in The Cup again, Cap'n?*

Jennings [sternly]: *I do!*

Trowbridge [more suspiciously]: *But you know I'm rubbish. I don't win many matches, usually drink too much and get into lots of trouble? I don't need to remind you of the Hot-Sauce incident...*

Jennings [more disgustedly]: *I know, Trowbridge, you're a liability in the best of times. I'll never forget when you 'it me in me 'ead with that wild shot at Wheatley – the one that got me banned. And then there was the drinking . . . and the hot sauce incident . . . and so much more. But I don't blame you. Well . . . for hitting me in me 'ead and getting me banned at Wheatley, I blame you . . . but not the drinking or the hot sauce. For those I don't blame you. That was Donut up to his old tricks.*

Trowbridge [innocently]: *But why would the U.S. Captain want to injure me, oh Great One?*

Jennings [exasperatedly]: *Probably the same reason I want you to play again. You see, 'e's a clever bloke but so am I, and us clever blokes are always trying to out-clever one another. Well, I'm the cleverest bloke and I've come up with a plan to stop the Yanks winning three on the trot, retaining the Cup and winning our wager.*

Trowbridge [admiringly]: *You are the cleverest, Cap'n, you are!*

Jennings [more exasperatedly]: *Shut up and listen for a change.*

Trowbridge [sheepishly]: *Yes Cap'n*

Jennings [sadly]: *You see, there aren't many players left 'oo've never played on a losing side in the Flem Cup for Team England*

Trowbridge [enthusiastically]: *Really? 'Oo are they, Cap'n?*

Jennings [more sadly]: *Well there's ole' 'Ring 'o Kerry' Ray and Stud Muffin . . . and . . . and . . . and . . .*

Trowbridge [more enthusiastically]: *'Ooo's that, Cap'n? . . . . c'mon . . . . 'oooo is it? . . . . . . 'Oooooo's the 3rd one?!?*

Jennings [grudgingly]: *YOU . . . . you are! So . . . I'm thinking . . . hoping might be a better word . . . that you might be something of . . . a . . . a lucky charm for us.*

Trowbridge [with wildly child-like enthusiasm]: *So you want ME to bring the Cup back for England and stop the Yanks don't you, what with this being the final year of your bet and all? That's it, in't it? In't it Cap'n?!? Is that it . . . ?!?!*

Jennings [resignedly]: *Yes, well, Ray and Stud-Muffin can't make it and . . . well . . . we're desperate. You're clever, Trowbridge, nearly as clever as me, and I like that in a man. In you, too. You're not bright, though; just clever. So I'd like you to try and work out what clever thing Donut's been doing the last two years to win. I know he's up to something but I can't quite work it out.*

Trowbridge [admiringly]: *He is a clever bloke, in't 'e Cap'n?*

Jennings [succinctly]: *Goodbye, Trowbridge.*

So, at my Captain's request, I started analyzing past matches through a simple spread-sheet I'd developed using the reverse Keppler vortex-inclined neural inverse statistical methodology I'd been dabbling with in my spare time. Soon, a strange handicap trend emerged: ours had consistently declined over the past two years while America's had in-creased.

In 2001 & 2002 there was but a small difference in the handicaps of the two sides, less than 1 shot per day, and we won both years. In 2003, American handicaps started their rise. Now, in 2005, the average handicap of Team US is 14.14, a rise from 2001 of 36%. England handicaps, on the other hand, declined 24% in that same span.

In a single year, 2003, the difference went from less than 1 shot to 4+ shots per player, despite the U.S. team having the same 8 core players. Now, in 2005, it's 6 shots per player. Is it a coincidence that every Team U.S. handicap has gone up over the last 4 years, some as much as 60%? I think not.

While officials here work hard to lower the overall team handicap by introducing impres-sive new blood and training methods while encouraging established Flemmers to work hard to

improve their play in all valid CONGU supported medal play events, Team U.S. has essential-
ly the same bunch of guys from 2001 and yet, except for AJ, their handicaps only go up.

In summary, I couldn't put my finger on the difference between the two sides but this is
something clever Dow has done that I found. However, I'm looking for more so I'm hoping you
can help. I've sent over all my charts and statistics for you to take a look at. If you notice any-
thing strange, please let me know.

Warm regards,

Swampy

###

The "Wheatley" incident referred to by Jennings provides a singularly fascinating window
into the complex relationship between Swampy and his Captain. Years ago, the Angel Golf
Society was playing an outing at Wheatley Golf Course in Doncaster. Ian was on the 17th tee,
nearing the end of a very good round that he was confident would put him in contention for
the day's best Stableford.

Standing as it does only a few yards to the right of the 16th green, the tee box on 17 is in
a dangerous spot, to say the least. To mitigate that danger, the course placed a prominent
sign on 16 prohibiting players from hitting their approaches to the green before the tee was
clear. Swampy, in the group behind, ignored the sign, teeing off as Jennings' group was still
teeing off on 17, pushing his tee shot to the right – directly at the group on 17 tee.

Hearing a loud "fore" and being fully aware of their precarious location, Ian's three play-
ing partners dove in various directions, covering up and protecting vital parts as best they
could. Ian, however, turned towards 16 tee, brashly searching the sky for the ball like a cap-
tain at sea scanning the horizon, confident he would nimbly avoid the projectile as needed.
Unfortunately, Swampy's shot arrived more quickly than Ian had anticipated, whacking him
straight on his considerable forehead and leaving him dazed and bleeding but still more con-
cerned with maintaining his outstanding Stableford score than the rising lump or blood running
down his face, pressing on despite advice to be taken to hospital.

A few weeks later, Ian filed a lawsuit against Wheatley alleging lack of adequate safety
precautions, arguing that there should have been a net up besides the tee. After forcing the

club to spend some £10,000 in legal fees, Ian unceremoniously dropped the suit. The next spring, Wheatley received a request from the Angel Golf Society for another outing, responding to President Singe that the club was welcome with one non-negotiable stipulation: "if, and only if, a certain Mr. Ian Jennings is not a member of the group". Ian had officially become persona non grata at Wheatley.

Now, once again, Ian had called on the inimical, irrepressible, effervescent Swampy to be his foil against Captain Donut Dow and to no one's surprise, Swampy has come out on fire, charging that Donut has been fiddling the handicaps, a serious charge that reflects directly on the character of the accused. Therefore, before proceeding with any investigation, we must thoroughly examine the character of the accused.

Over the years, Captain Donut has shown himself to be capable of spontaneously ingenious yet highly unethical tactics such as the drink-buying scandal of 2001 – a scandal he initially lied about, a testament to his veracity.

Despite repeated denials, Donut remains forever linked to the even more heinous hot sauce incident the very next day – an incident in which Ian and Swampy were nearly killed by ingesting straight DA' BOMB, a concentrated habanero pepper-based hot sauce used in tiny portions to spice up sauces. True or false, the fact that he is even suspected of such a dastardly act is testament to Donut's ruthlessness.

Suspicious England supporters still whisper about rumors that it was Donut who slipped a "mickey" into Ray's drink the night he passed out, drunk, on the bog in a bar in Ennis, Ireland, becoming vacuum-sealed to the toilet seat in the process, testament to Donut's cheekiness.

So, with these past incidents as foundational evidence of a character who, at times, has run amuck, a full investigation into Swampy's allegations was launched.

Curiously, review of the past 2 years revealed a complete absence of Dow-related suspicious incidents. Had he run out of ideas? Turned over a new leaf? Was he simply biding his time, keeping his powder dry, so to speak? Or was Swampy onto something; that Donut simply shifted strategy and tactics to a more effective area – handicaps?

The timing of each of the previous 'events' had a theme – the Americans were losing. In 2003, when Team U.S. handicaps first began to rise, the Yanks administered an old-fashioned arse-whupping of epic proportions, leading decisively from the start, so there was no need for any shenanigans. In 2004, the Yanks once again led from the start before holding on to win by the narrowest of margins. By Singles Day – when the Yanks nearly crashed and burned – it was too late for Donut to pull off any of his stunts.

So we looked at the handicap numbers; up, down, left and right – from every angle. Unable to find a "smoking gun", the investigation on to the next step, cross-examining the American Captain directly under a swinging 60 watt, energy-efficient UV curly-q bulb to get his response to the allegations.

###

FlemCup.com: *Captain Dow; now that you've seen Swampy's letter, would you like to comment?*

Donut: *Yes, I would. First, I'd prefer you call him "1-3/4 points" - a testament to his ability to play under pressure.*

FC.com: *Yes, fine, but can you comment ….*

Donut (interrupting): *No, really. He's a hacker and a slacker. He'll be losin and a' boozin, drinkin and a' stinkin, chunkin and a' dunkin. He's a malcontent, a boozer, a pathetic match loser. He's got no talent, he's nothing great; against young Matt he'd lose 10&8.*

FC.com: *Despite the excellent rhyming, that seems quite . . . mean-spirited. Are you aware he is down to a 10 handicap?*

Donut: *Really? Wow. That's awesome. I didn't think he had it in him. Tell him congrats!*

FC.com: *Now then, what about 1-¾'s "handicap-fixing" accusations?*

Donut: *Oh yes, well, about that . . . he's right. Clever lad, that 1-¾. Very clever.*

FC.com: *Are you saying his suspicions are true?*

Donut: *Of course. I now have a proven method that maximizes our chances. But I wouldn't call it handicap "fixing". More like handicap . . . umm . . . management. That's the word. Management. Nothing is more important than being able to manage your handicap. But ole' 1-¾ has certainly gotten a whiff of my strategy. Clever, yes. Very, very clever.*

FC.com: *What about the integrity of the gentleman's game ??*

Donut [after a good belly laugh]: *Yes, yes, integrity. Integrity is beating England and I'll do it by any means necessary. I admit I went a little overboard in 2003 when I first started it but how would I know my plan would work so outrageously well. Anyhow, the handicaps are "real" handicaps. You know, USGA documented and all that official crap. I simply encourage our team members to control them. That requires two components. First, they must play infrequently, at least during the spring and summer, and second, whenever playing they should play . . . well . . . as poorly as possible whenever possible. So we stink and our handicaps eventually reflect that.*

FC.com: *But how does that . . .*

Donut (interrupting): *Shut up, Indaruf, and maybe you'll learn something. There's more. So we suck as much as possible during the summer. Naturally, our handicaps go up - that's the easy part. I've encouraged the wives to make their husbands quit their golf clubs. I quit, Pat quit, Jack Jr. quit, Sven quit - everybody quit so nobody feels obligated to go play. Except Jack Sr., but he's, well, old. Anyway, spring arrives and no one plays until at least late May, preferably late June. July and August go by and we all play rarely, if at all. Finally, by the time September is nearly over, we've each played like three times – four max. Of course, scrambles and other tournaments where your scores don't count towards your handicap are encouraged and you can play as well as you like in those.*

What people don't realize, though, is that it takes tremendous discipline to play like crap through all those months but most of us have that special intangible that allows us to underperform effortlessly. Finally, in late September, I roust the team. We start practicing, get in a round or two and BAM - the handicap season is over. From there on out, scores cannot be submitted for handicap purposes. That's when I really start to crack the whip. We practice day and night, often sleeping at the driving range (we build a campfire and make s'mores) in order to groove our swings before heading out in early November to kick some Limey butt. It really is quite simple and the handicaps are all quite legit - perfectly legal. I think of it like a great veteran team peaking for the playoffs, so to speak. But I must say that I noticed, despite

Swampy's whining, that several England handicaps went up at the last minute. Coincidence? I think not.

FC.com: *So Swampy IS correct?*

Donut: *Yes. He is clever. Perhaps the cleverest Englander I know, except Ian, of course. Not bright, though. You see, Ian's also bright. Ian would come as an 8, even though he was playing to a 6. If Swampy were bright, he wouldn't be coming as a 10 right now – he'd be a 12 or 13. Clever lad, yes, but not very bright.*

FC.com: *Well, what is your plan for this year?*

Donut: *This interview is over. I have a tee-time and a fitting appointment for custom clubs . . . now get out.*

###

So our investigation concluded with Dow's cleverness - however ungentlemanly and un-ethical – seeming to be perfectly legal and openly admitted to. It doesn't help England that the Yanks are loaded with players that love getting strokes. All are capable of making par on any hole on the course – it is their consistency that betrays them, not their ability to play very well on any single hole or series of holes.

The final question is one that won't be answered today. By opening up this can of worms, has Swampy played right into Dow's hands, perhaps even ending up with that very same can of worms dumped on his head? Has he once again given the American Captain the bright, shiny object he loves to dangle in front of the Brits, distracting them from the important business at hand – namely playing solid golf. Time will tell but it seems that Captain Dow and Swampy Trowbridge may well be on a collision course this year, to what end we can only imagine.

***

When I next spoke to Ian on October 16, he was waiting for the results of the latest body scan, knowing if it came back with poor results, the doctors might stop the chemo treatments. For the first time, his voice sounded like hope was ebbing.

The chemo treatments had become an increasingly dreadful ordeal, his worst nightmare come true. Despite having private insurance through much of his life, he had now been cast into the abysmal national healthcare system of England, assigned to a common ward room with a dozen or more patients in various states of pain, discomfort and misery for 7-10 days every 3 weeks. Excruciatingly painful, the treatments sickened him to the point of making rest impossible aside from sleep-inducing drugs. He'd come to dread and hate it with every fiber of his being.

Early on October 18, I called again. Ian sounded quiet and weak.

"Hello, Ian."

"Allo, lad."

"Did you get the results?"

"The chemo's not working. They've stopped the treatments."

The finality of his words struck me like a thunderbolt. I had never really allowed myself to think that things would end this way and now my mind had nowhere to run, forced to face the reality of his imminent passing, perhaps within a few short months, and the loss of my best friend. Once more, like so many times in my life, I felt crushed by the painful weight of life's reality, powerless against the tides that swept me along in whatever direction they flowed.

From my childhood, my life had been consumed by chasing useless, superficial things, seeking to find in them some meaning or importance for myself. Deep within that self-centered focus, however, was a longing in my heart and my soul for an unconditional love and acceptance, a longing that was never satisfied. Oh sure, I justified my choices as individual freedom, willingly buying into the popular me-first narrative of my generation. The fact was that I had corrupted every meaningful relationship I'd ever had, inflicting more hurt and disappointment than I'd ever absorbed while convincing myself it was exactly the opposite - except for one friend.

And he was about to die.

As my throat choked with emotion I struggled to get out the only words I could.

"I love you . . . . like a brother."

"And you, lad" was all Ian could manage, his barely audible whisper cracking with emotion.

For a full minute or more the call went silent as we tried to gather ourselves. Finally, I reached the point where I thought I could get a sentence out without losing it again.

"Well, you better hang on for the Cup. Your team needs your guidance, eh?"

"I'll do my best, lad. I'll do my best."

Hanging the phone up, I put my head down on my desk as the tears flowed. By the next day, after relaying the news to Jack Jr. and Jack Sr., we agreed we would rename the award for most Cup points the *Jennings Award*. I ordered a trophy of a stylish golfer, powerfully posed at impact and within a week or so it was ready. With that, I began work on a tribute article announcing the change. On the front of the stand was a plate reading "Jennings Award" in large letters. On each side, additional plates had the names of each past winner: Milo in 2001, Ian in 2002, Sven in 2003 and AJ in 2004. As insufficient as it was, it was something we could do.

With travel day being Thursday the 3rd, I decided to publish the article on the night of October 31st, the perfect time to lift Ian's spirits on the eve of the trip. Everyone would see the article and pictures as they gathered one last time prior to heading down to London on the 2nd. I also received a response from Sven concerning Swampy's email. The article posted the next morning.

Sven Responds To Swampy's Accusations, Vows Revenge Over Letters

By: Datzit Indaruf, Flem Cup Correspondent

MYRTLE BEACH, S.C., October 21 - Sven Tanis has responded to Swampy Trowbridge's explosive charges concerning possible handicap fixing by the Americans - a charge that has been subsequently confirmed by US Captain Scott Dow. Sven, clearly stung by the initial allegations, appears undeterred by Dow's subsequent admission of the clever handicapping strategy. Sven's blistering reply, addressed directly to Swampy, is posted here in its entirety.

Dear Swampy,

At first word of your return to competition my heart leapt for joy as I remembered our times together during past Flem Cups, both on and off of the course. It was you that so affectionately dubbed me 'Sven'. It was you who pushed me to my competitive limits with our dramatic halve at the moonscape-like battleground of Doonbeg. It was you that filled my evenings with conversation and friendship that warmed the very cockles of my heart, causing me to remember you not as an adversary, not even as a friend, but as a brother.

As I considered your most recent accusations and your insistence on returning to Myrtle Beach carrying a torch of resentment and bitterness, I began to reflect on these things and found myself searching the true nature of our friendship. I felt betrayed as I remembered shaking your hand on the 18th green at Doonbeg, with tears in my eyes as if it was the last time our paths would cross. All the while, you may have been thinking:

"I would have beaten this jerk if it weren't for a bogus handicap! And what's up with the bleached hair, you freakin' flamer."

One can only imagine the pain of such betrayal. As I look back now, I see things in a new light. I realize it was you who cracked open the beers on a backwoods South Carolina highway, costing me a frightening interrogation by a State Trooper, a pricey traffic summons and near incarceration with some huge gap-toothed inmate named Bubba or Tiny.

It was you that immortalized on video my ineptitude during the 2001 Cup. It was you who so painfully exposed the Ennis shenanigans of Sven and an unknown Irish lad and it was you who, after helping lead your team to victory in Ireland, took your ball and went home, refusing to return in 2003 or 2004. You abandoned our competition, our friendship and our brotherhood.

Now, you have called into question our very sportsmanship and manhood, tainting the integrity of our beloved Flem Cup forever. I can only hope – nay, pray to the Lord God Almighty – that we will see each other on the first tee on Singles Day. That day, I will mercilessly destroy you to your very soul, avenging what you yourself have destroyed.

Oh, and I am coming down as a 17.

Very truly yours,

Sven (although I prefer being called "Sven the mighty one who once won 5 Flem Cup points in a single year")

Recognizing the raw nerve Swampy's letter had struck with Sven, we here at Flem-Cup.com realize that both letters are really clarion calls for mental health-related help. As an organization dedicated to helping its fellow man, FlemCup.com has turned, at our own considerable expense, to the eminent Flem Cup neuro-psycho-analyticologist, Dr. Ima Wanker, for help, receiving the following response.

The Analysis of Dr. Ima Wanker:

Zee letter vrom Sven clearly zeems to alternate betveen zee anger unt zee melancholy sadness uf a jilted lover (not zat zer is anyzing vrong vit zat). Zee anger zeems to be boileenk over unto a vow uv revench.

Alzo, Sven accuses Svampy uv carrying unt "torch of rezentment unt bitterness" yet Sven vaxes on unt on about zee pain of zee betrayal at Doonbeg as vell as his previous "outings" by Svampy over zee years. Vor vatever reason uf personal unadeqvezees, Sven clearly lonks fur zee love unt affection of his little Svamp-monster; his need ver Svampy's aczeptance unt love palpable. Let me alzo zay zat Svampy clearly has zee major issues uf his own but zat is unudder analzis vor anudder day. My counsel is zat Sven und Svampy get a room unt verk it out.

I'll zend you zee bill.

***

The next afternoon I gave the Angel a call to chat and make sure they'd seen the latest article. Surprisingly, I got no answer. Knowing it was a busy Saturday night, at first I chalked it up to an unusually loud crowd but despite several later tries, I kept coming up empty. Finally giving up, it would be Tuesday when I finally tracked down Phil and got the full story.

When Ian got the bad news on the morning of 18th, he already had a plan, phoning Phil to ask him to organize a party. A wake. His wake. Phil recounted the conversation.

"Ian, 'ow are you, pal?"

"Hi'ya, Phil. I'm all right, I suppose. Listen, I want to 'ave a bash in back of the Angel. Now, I've 'ad a word with Singe . . . I don't want 'im or Jude to do it out of the pub. I want them to be there as guests. I want a marquee, a barkeep – but not Singe – and a fully stocked bar. And I want a load of food put on . . . and I don't want Jude doing a thing."

"Right. That's a lot of work but I'm sure we can pull it off. When do you want to do this, then?"

"Saturday."

"SATURDAY? Ian, it's Tuesday."

"I know. I want it Saturday."

"Well, I can try. 'Ow many people do you think will come?"

"Well, I've started a list. Maybe two 'undred."

"TWO 'UNDRED?!?!?"

"Give or take."

Well, Phil hung the phone up and, knowing the urgency, got together with Joe, Singe, Caroline and others to frantically organize Ian's wake. After inviting the guests and calling in whatever favors they needed, everything was finally set for Saturday night. By Saturday morning, the marquee was going up, portable toilets were being added and collages were being filled with pictures of Ian's life going on display.

Ian's body, though, was not cooperating. Finally, feeling very poorly by late afternoon, he told Caroline he just couldn't go, that he simply wasn't up to it. Knowing what had been done to pull it together, she was having none of it and, after threatening to drag him there, he relented.

Arriving friends and family had spontaneously joined in the collage building, adding pictures of their own as reminders of great times past. As the wake began, story after story after story was told and retold as the drinks and memories flowed like water. Despite no official count, Phil's estimate was that some 300 people showed up to pay tribute that evening and Ian greeted each and every one of them with a smile, a thank you and at least a bit of pleasant conversation. Running on pure adrenaline, he held up the entire evening, entertaining guests, as always, through wit, laughter and good cheer. It was a remarkable evening, providing a fitting tribute and a touching farewell as tears of laughter and sorrow punctuated the long evening.

After spending Sunday at home recovering, Ian was feeling pretty good for a change on Monday. Around 8 pm, he and Caroline made the short, familiar trek up the hill to the Angel. That night, the Ian of old showed up once again, perched on his favorite bar stool as he held court, leafing through his remarkable repertoire of memories as effortlessly as browsing through a library filled with books that he knew by heart, selecting the exact stories and passages he wanted. Possessing the rare gift of being a storyteller extraordinaire, it had always been Ian's unique style that made them even funnier; the small details, the perfect timing and the contagious, boyish giggle that conspired to make them far better.

So there he sat Monday night, holding court for his closest friends, sweat pouring down his face. When Singe gave him a bar towel to help mop it up, Ian merely draped the towel over his head, giving himself the appearance of an Arabian sheik and keeping everyone in stitches for hours along with his *"remember when"* stories.

Listening to Phil, I could tell he was still on a high from gathering. It had been, as Ian liked to say, magic. With Caroline standing on one side and Joe sitting on the other, a dozen or so friends stood and sat, scattered about the Rave Cave, Singe leaning forward with his elbows on the hatch, serving drinks and soaking in every moment. Everyone knew, barring some miracle, that on some unannounced night Ian would make one final appearance on his favorite stage – the barstool at the Angel. The thought surely crossed more than a few minds that this might be that night, Ian's grand finale, so when Caroline helped Ian out the door to go home at half past midnight, everyone was still there, sadly watching as the two disappeared into the night. It truly had been *magic*.

Two days later, on Thursday, October 27th, we were but one week from travel day. The emails and news items had continued to pile up and I'd kept the flow of stories going as best I could, knowing full well that the efforts were less for him than for me and everyone else; something we hoped would provide him a smile or chuckle while helping with our own pain. I continued to imagine Caroline keeping him abreast of the news, perhaps reading him the articles as they were posted. It was all I had left.

Swampy and Sven Back Together!

By: Datzit Indaruf, Flem Cup Correspondent

MYRTLE BEACH, SC; October 27 – The following is the response from Swampy to the response from Sven to the email from Swampy. It is published unedited and in full.

Dearest Sven,

Friend, brother, fellow Flemmer. I too have missed you. Please do not judge me so harshly as this may be the poison of Cap'n Dow at work. He is encouraging a divide between the U.S. and England purely as a motivational vehicle in hopes of getting his thoroughbreds stoked for 5 November opening matches. He needs to know our friendship runs deeper than he can imagine.

Some say that if Dow's brain were a swimming pool, it would be appropriate for all ages, shallow and tepid with no diving allowed. But not me. He has a job to do and history indicates he does it very well. But ask yourself this question, who wouldn't with the resources he has available? What a great all-round team US has, so well handicapped. I hear rumors of Jack Jr. taking over the reins but see nothing has materialized. We all know that the power crazy despot dictator Dow would never allow that to happen.

Now, the Day 1 pairings have been decided and I see that we'll get to tee it up at least once during the Cup. Fantastic!!!! Looking beyond that, I see on Day 2 you are teamed with your Captain. Bring your wheel barrow, brother, for he will be heavy load to carry.

I too remember the look in your eye as we shook hands after my favorite Flem match ever at Doonbeg. I hope we have a chance to repeat that this year. Quite honestly, as long as England wins and we all have a great time I don't care what my personal achievements are. You can see from past results that this is the approach I have always taken in Flem Cup play.

Few days now remain before we meet yet again and I know, in my heart of hearts, that it will be just like old times, no matter what poison, sour grapes or hot sauce Dow wants to introduce. We'll be laughing, joking and drinking a beer........because that's what we do in the Flem Cup.

Best wishes for a warm reunion, Swampy

***

With days to go, the writing, staging and scheduling of articles consumed my world. Jack Jr. submitted an email portraying me as a power-monger unwilling to share decision making power to which I responded, in an interview with Indie, by promoting him to Major and announcing that hereafter he would only be referred to as 'The Major' or 'Major Junior'.

Finally, the evening of October 31st arrived. The tribute article, now perfected down to the last word and phrase, was done, portraying him as the great competitor and friend he'd been to so many people. I had poured my heart and soul out and as I sat at my computer, I was excited to finally post it, even more so since no one in England knew of the honor. Remembering my conversation on the plane with Jack, I felt the urge to say a small prayer for Ian, asking for him, in his heart of hearts, to receive the hope Jack had given him and asking God to watch over him. As I finished, I felt the need to ask the same for myself.

Later that night, as I was trying to fall asleep, I imagined the look on Ian's face when he learned of the tribute; how everyone at the Angel would be offering a toast to "his" trophy next time they saw him. I would call him in the morning to give him the news personally. Finally, after tossing and turning for what seemed hours, I drifted off into an uneasy, dream-filled sleep. During one dream, I heard a disturbing noise, out of place and loud. Slowly, I came out of it, waking groggily as my mind was dragged back to reality. Then, there it was again, like a strange sounding alarm clock. Finally, I realized it was my cell phone ringing.

It was Joe.

At just past midnight on November 1, Ian had died.

24

The 2005 Cup

After beating myself up for delaying the announcement of the Jennings Award, I posted a message of condolence for his family and loved ones before reluctantly turning my attention to another matter that had to be addressed: the looming trip. With both teams scheduled to depart in two days, I knew no one on the England side would miss the funeral for the Cup. Torn as I was, it became moot when Joe called to tell me that Caroline had once again shown her selfless love for Ian – and us – by putting off the funeral until November 11th, the day after the team was scheduled to return. With that decision behind us, I set about doing what I could to make the trip itself our own tribute to the remarkable life of Ian.

That night, as I tossed and turned during a fitful night of sleep, I found myself somewhere I didn't recognize with a group of people I didn't know – save one. Walking through the crowd, I came upon Ian, healthy and vibrant as he held court, entertaining the crowd as effortlessly as he always had. As he regaled the crowd with stories and jokes, I could only stand there, laughing and enjoying his company. It was wonderful.

At some point, though, he got up and started walking away. Somewhere in my subconscious the reality of his passing penetrated, turning my joy to despair. Wherever he was headed, I intuitively understood he was going away forever, that he had, in fact, died. I followed him as he passed silently through the crowd, distraught. Finally, he stopped and turned to look at me, smiling sadly as he put his hand on my shoulder.

"Don't worry, lad, it's ok. It's ok."

Then he turned away, disappearing into the sea of people as the dream faded as I awoke, sobbing. It was a dream I would not forget.

Arriving in Myrtle Beach on the evening of the 3rd, the mood was somber yet joyful. We renewed old friendships at BummZ with handshakes and hugs. Remembrances and toasts to Ian went on deep into the evening over more than a few pitchers of beer. The next night, after playing a friendly practice round at Tigers Eye, we held our welcome ceremony in my suite rather than at BummZ. After managing to get through my speech without a total meltdown, Jack Sr. offered a prayer and a few players offered personal remembrances of Ian. Those, in turn, brought back still more memories. Finally, our emotions spent, we headed back to BummZ.

As the night progressed, the general sense I got from the whole group was that we needed to take this all the way across the finish line, for our own sakes as well as in tribute to Ian. With the initial outpouring of emotions and memories behind us, I vowed to myself this week would be – *had to be* – a celebration of Ian's life and a testament to how we all loved him. Having lived with style and gusto, we were gathered here because of him and, under these remarkable circumstances, we needed to make it something special. How could we not?

At sunrise the next morning, we assembled as a group on the narrow strip of grass that separated BummZ from the beach. Being long enough for 4 golfers to simultaneously tee it up, the first group out that day solemnly lined up, setting ball on tee before readying themselves. On cue, four balls rocketed out across the beach and early morning surf, silhouetted for a few moments against the early morning sky before descending into the grey Atlantic. The scene then repeated itself for each of the day's groups in one final tribute to our friend. As the last of the twenty balls descended into the surf, we observed a moment of silence before heading back to the hotel to ready ourselves for the day's matches.

Heading out to the Day 1 venue Prestwick, no one knew what toll the emotions of the recent events would take on each individual player. Brighty and Gibbo, two of the more stoic Brits, handled it as might be expected, dominating Jack Sr. and Apple, 5&3, in the first match out.

The second match had been considered the match of the day going in but turned into a complete fizzle when Black Dog shot an astonishing 18 over par net; 17 shots worse than his 90 hole score last year. Paired with Casper, they were overwhelmed by AJ and Lou, 7&6.

In the third match, Major Jr. proved himself worthy of his recent promotion by tying AJ for the day's best score, a 1 over par net that included a 158-yard 7-iron for an eagle 3 on the 6th hole, a shot that left observers wondering if a certain someone wasn't bucking for General. Paired with Fred, the match against Baz and Phil ended with a 3&2 win for our lads.

The fourth match ended in another blowout for us, 7&6, as Sven, scrambling like a madman, teamed up with Pat for a lopsided win over Smokin' Joe and Swampy. In their personal showdown, Sven routed Swampy by a whopping 14 Stableford points.

In the final match, Manson Hanson and I faced off in a Captain's match against Miffer and the Prosecutor. Battling my emotions, I struggled throughout the front 9 as Manson Hanson valiantly kept us in the match with several mid-range putts. Against all odds, we somehow reached 12 only 1 down. There, needing a 15 foot par putt to halve Miffer, I found myself once again thinking of Ian as I surveyed the putt, remembering past matches where I would drive him absolutely nuts with unlikely shots. Having played poorly all day, my emotions were overtaking me as I went through my routine; my eyes moist with tears. Standing over the ball, my mind swirled with thoughts and emotions that I struggled to block out.

Closing my eyes for a moment, I saw Ian as he had been in the dream, healthy and robust, looking at me with kindness in his eyes.

"I miss you, my friend."

I heard his voice come back, loud and clear.

"You'll be all right, lad. Just relax; it's ok."

Drawing comfort from his words, I relaxed, letting it all go as I smoothly swung the putter. The putt dropped, keeping us only 1 down. Following that with a win on 14 to draw level, we began to press the play with solid, consistent golf, winning 3 of the final 5 holes to take the day's final point, 2 up.

Sitting on the veranda later with some lunch and a beer, I couldn't stop thinking about the encounter I'd had with Ian. It had seemed so real yet I knew it was simply my mind's way of dealing with the loss of my friend. I decided to keep it to myself.

With 20 points available on Days 3 and 4, Miffer wasn't overly concerned with the 4-1 deficit he faced after Day 1 so long as the Brits didn't lose any more ground on Day 2. His more immediate concern was that karaoke night was coming up – and that was never good for England.

After dinner, we all settled in for the entertainment. After getting off to a slow start, Gibbo and Phil livened things up by performing a head-splitting rendition of "*Paradise City*" by Guns n' Roses (literally - one person's head split open). After that, Sven continued his bromance with Swampy by belting out a surprisingly soulful and on-key rendition of Elvis' *Steamroller Blues*. With his piercingly blues eyes unabashedly focused on his Day 1 opponent, Sven crooned:

"I'm your steamroller, baby . . . and I'm going to steamroll all over you."

Swampy, however, proved up to the task, replying in kind with an inspired rendition of *Tainted Love*.

"Touch me baby . . . tainted love. Touch me baby . . . tainted love."

In a stunning and touching final act destined to become the stuff of legend, the pair brought down the house with a heartfelt rendition of *Islands in the Stream*, Sven taking on the masculine Kenny Rogers role while Swampy strutted his considerable stuff as Dolly Parton, belting out his (her?) lines with gusto and bravado if not quite the same pipes.

"Islands in the stream, that is what we are. No one in-between, how can we be wrong? Sail away with me to another world, and we rely on each other, from one lover to another."

After receiving a rousing ovation, the two left the crowd like all great entertainers: wanting more.

Knowing they needed a big day at TPC, the Brits came out smoking the next morning, determined to gain a point or more on us and eat into our lead. In the first match out, Baz and Casper topped Jack Sr. and Pat 2&1, giving them the start they needed. That win was backed up in the third match where Brighty and Richard knocked off Manson Hanson and Fred by an identical score.

In the fourth match out, we got one back as Major Jr. continued his strong play while Lou was even better, shooting a 34 Stableford. With Swampy turning in a second straight poor day, the two wore down a game but outmanned Miffer, eventually becoming the third group to win 2&1.

The fifth match out was one that Smokin' Joe had requested – demanded, actually – weeks ago, confidently predicting he and Gibbo would take down the alleged power pairing of AJ and Apple. True to his word, the two Brits came out focused and fired up, dominating the most lopsided match of the day in a surprisingly easy 5&3 win.

But the competitive corker of the day was once again mine as Sven and I faced off against Black Dog and Phil. In their pre-Cup email exchange, Swampy warned Sven to bring his wheelbarrow for this match, a prediction that proved nothing short of prophetic as I hacked my way through the first 14 holes in a pathetic 14 over par, net.

With Sven carrying the load on nearly the entire front 9, England jumped on top with wins on 2 and 3. The par 4 2nd hole proved quite the seminal moment for our side as Sven and I combined to hit no fewer than *eight* trees. After both hitting a tree to the right with our tee shots, Sven ricocheted one even further in with his second before hitting two more with his next two shots. Not to be outdone, I clipped one with my second shot before my third drilled a tree about 15 yards in front of me, ricocheted straight back over my head, bounced off another tree about 10 yards behind me and rolled to a stop just about exactly where it had started. At that point, with both Brits waiting on birdie putts, I picked up, declaring a 4&3 victory over Sven (4 trees in 3 shots whereas he took 4 shots to achieve the same result).

Somehow, though, we hung around, bouncing between 1 and 2 down deep into the match as wins on 8, 10 and 12 were offset by England wins on 9, 11 and 13. After settling for a halve on 14, Black Dog struck two flawless shots on the trouble-filled 15th, a 430-yard par-4, leaving himself 20 feet below the hole for birdie. With Sven and Phil already out of the hole, my third would, by necessity, be played through the center of a V-shaped tree about 50 yards short and right of the green. From there, I would need to drop it just over the bunker guarding the right side of the green with some backspin. Staring at dormie 3, I not only pulled off the unlikely shot but followed it by draining the 25 foot par putt for a net birdie win that brought us back to only 1 down.

With the huge momentum shift fueling my revival, I played 16 flawlessly, forcing Black Dog to make a treacherous 8-foot sidehill putt with a huge break to halve my conceded par. Rising to the moment, the big fellow drained the unlikely putt, keeping his side 1 up and reclaiming the all-important momentum as we headed to 17 tee, the peninsula par 3 that had proved so critical in last year's 2 ball matches.

Unlike last year, when the pin had been in the middle towards the back of the green, this year it was in perhaps the toughest spot on the green: situated in the back right corner about 10 feet from the water and right on top of a small ridge running from the front center to the back right. Squinting into the late afternoon November sun, I couldn't imagine a less inviting pin placement.

As the 6 handicap hole, everyone – including Phil – would get a stroke from Black Dog but when Sven plopped his tee shot in the drink, the pressure was squarely on me. Overcompensating against the possibility of a fade, I pulled my 6-iron left, missing the green entirely and leaving my ball perched on the back of a mound just past the bunker on the left. I was pin high but would be facing a long, downhill chip to the pin.

Up next, Phil knocked a typically solid shot to the center of the green, leaving himself a 20 foot birdie putt. Things got worse when Black Dog hit perhaps the shot of the day, stiffing his 8-iron to about 2 feet and setting himself up for a near-certain birdie.

Reaching the green, I looked over my 60 foot downhill chip shot knowing that I needed an up and down – a tall order, to say the least – to keep the match alive. I took at least six or seven little practice swings with my trusty 8-iron, trying my best to visualize and gauge the shot. I needed to get it close but if the ball reached the hole with any speed it would keep right on going, down the ridge and probably 10-15 feet past. Finally, I settled in over the ball.

Keeping my head down, my hands pressed forward and my wrists locked, the chip came out crisply, landing on the fringe before taking one bounce, checking and releasing. Aimed a good 6 feet left of the pin, the shot was pretty much what I'd envisioned. Standing on the back fringe, Phil and Black Dog casually watched the steady progress of the slowly decelerating ball, their faces expressionless as their heads slowly turned. As the ball continued to roll out, it started to slowly break right, steadily slowing as it crossed the smooth green.

4 seconds . . . 5 seconds . . . 6 seconds . . . the ball continued to roll . . . slower and slower . . . breaking gradually right as it slowed. 7 seconds pass . . . 8 seconds . . . tracking towards the hole. As it continued to track, I heard Sven urging it to slow down before the ridge. 9 seconds . . . 10 seconds . . . the ball slowed

to a crawl 5 feet from the hole as it broke more sharply right, coming hard off the back slope on a track straight towards the hole. Finally reaching the cup, the ball's final rotation dropped it over the front edge as Phil and Black Dog looked at each other, their faces still expressionless. Sven shook his head, smiling and chuckling.

Turning away as the ball dropped in, emotions overwhelmed me as I considered what I'd experienced prior to the shot. Caught between the pressure of the match, which was slipping away, and my emotions over the far weightier loss of Ian, I'd been squatting behind the ball to judge my line when my emotions overtook me once again. As my eyes, hidden beneath the brim of my hat, had filled with tears, I was once more filled with an overwhelming feeling of sadness, memories of my dream following close behind. Again, Ian stood in front of me, sadly looking at me, his eyes filled with compassion. And once again, his words had been clear as a bell.

"You'll be all right, lad. Just relax; it's ok. It's ok."

Wondering for a few seconds what, exactly, was going on, I rose and walked across the green to retrieve my ball, sheepishly shrugging my shoulders, relieved that my tinted glasses were shielding my still damp eyes. After Phil missed his birdie putt, Black Dog drained his 2 footer for a birdie but my birdie net ace would take us to 18 all square and when all four of us matched pars on the anticlimactic final hole, the match ended all square.

The unexpected and undeserved half point – won despite being outscored as a team by 9 Stableford points – would prevent England from completely reversing the previous day's score. Instead, the result allowed us to head to Day 3 with a 1 point lead, 5-½ to 4-½ but with 20 more points to play for, the lead was insignificant.

"Under the circumstances, that was one of the greatest shots I've seen." Phil said afterwards as we sat on the veranda, sipping our beers.

"Twas that," was all Black Dog bothered to add as he nodded slowly, puffing on his cigar. Feeling that whatever was happening was somehow beyond my understanding or control, I could only shake my head and shrug my shoulders in response to the compliments.

Early the next morning, a short trek took us to the sprawling Legends complex. There, we would embark on the Cup's first 36-hole day with the 4 ball matches being followed by afternoon Greensomes matches worth a full point each. Trailing after Day 2, England had set the matches and once again, things started well for the Brits when Gibbo and Black Dog knocked off Jack Sr and Manson Hanson, 2&1, in the first match out.

In the second match, the Major and I braced for a tough match with Miffer and Phil. Major Jr. continued his stellar play with an even par net and my play, which was far better than the previous day, was highlighted by another long chip-in birdie, this one from 40 yards for a birdie net eagle on 9 that gave us a 5 up lead, effectively ending a match we would eventually win, 5&4.

In the third and fourth matches, we picked up 2 more points when AJ and Sven defeated Brighty and Casper, 4&3 and Lou and Pat (who tied Major Jr. for the day's best score) nipped Smokin' Joe and the Prosecutor in the day's closest match, 1 up.

With the Brits losing three of the first four matches, the day's final match was huge. A win would keep them only 2 down while a loss would drop them to 4 down, a tenuous position with only 15 match points remaining. The good news was that they had the always solid Baz teamed up with Swampy against our suicide pairing of Apple and Fred.

The "suicide pair" had become a time-honored tradition for whichever side was leading heading into Day 3. By pairing their two worst performing golfers – who honored the tradition by volunteering (a dubious yet highly respected badge of honor) – the leading team was freed up to put out four very solid pairs in the other matches. The problem presented to the trailing side by the suicide pair was simple: it was a must-win match demanding as little firepower as possible, a delicate balancing act, to be sure. To add fuel to the fire, the suicide pair had two indispensable elements working in their favor – low expectations and competitive pride.

Upon arriving at the course that morning, I'd pulled our two volunteers aside for an inspirational speech, exhorting them in time honored fashion to *"try not to play crap today"*. So, with nothing to lose and everything to gain, Fred and Apple went out with one, single goal in mind: make the lives of their opponents as miserable as possible – and that is exactly what they did. Standing all square on 9, Apple won the next two holes for a 2 up lead. Desperately battling back, Swampy's birdie on 14 cut the deficit to 1 but Fred's win on 15 gave us our final margin of victory in the hard-fought 2&1 win.

Against the odds, we'd expanded our lead, assuming a commanding 9-½ to 5-½ lead in the Cup and forcing England to rally in the afternoon Greensomes matches after lunch. If they could manage a 3-2 win, they'd still need 6-½ points in 10 Singles Day matches to tie the Cup – a difficult but doable task, especially with their dominating track record in 2 ball play.

Once again, things went off well for the Brits as they won the first two afternoon matches handily; Black Dog and Gibbo taking out Manson Hanson and Jack Sr., 5&4, and Miffer and Phil knocking off Apple and Fred, 6&4.

In the third match out, Major Jr. and I broke on top early, continuing our stellar morning play in taking a 4 up lead through 10. Never the models for consistent play, though, we started making mistakes just as Casper and Brighty came alive and when the Brits won 4 of the next 5 holes, the match was all square as we headed to 16. There, just when it looked like England might pull off the big comeback win, we righted the ship, capturing 16 and 17 to win the match, 2&1.

In the fourth match, Sven and AJ also jumped on top early, carving out a 3 up lead after 4 holes before Smokin' Joe and the Prosecutor rallied to make the turn all-square but wins by our lads on 11 and 16 were enough to take the hard fought match, 2&1.

With one match left on the course, news from behind was good for England, the last report being that Swampy and Baz were 3 up on Lou and Pat with only 4 holes to play. That would bring the Cup score to 11-½ to 8-½ and as we sipped on beers, we speculated on how Miffer might match up to try to secure the 6-½ points England needed to tie the Cup.

Finally, after 20 minutes, the last group showed up and the pained look on the Brit's faces told us everything we needed to know. Perched on the edge of defeat, Lou and Pat had caught fire on the last four holes, recording 3 pars and a birdie and winning all four to take the match outright, 1 up. As bad as a halve would have been for England, the loss was virtually fatal to any hopes Miffer and the Brits had of catching us. The deficit stood at 5 points, 12-½ to 7-½ and the Brits would need 7-½ points just to tie. It was a shocking result.

Later on at BummZ, the Brits were undaunted, fully recovered from the shock of the final match result and determined to keep the focus on what this event was really about – fellowship, competition and honoring Ian. With the team result virtually decided, the drama revolved around the now coveted Jennings Award in a competition fiercer than any before it. Only once, in 2003, had even two players entered Singles Day without a loss but this year there five and, for the first time, players from each team were still in the running.

Major Jr., Lou and Gibbo were each perfect, 4 wins in 4 matches, and a win by any of them would guarantee their name would be engraved on the Jennings Award. Sven and I were also unbeaten, suffering only our unlikely halve on Day 2, and if the breaks went our way, either or both of us could get our name on the trophy. This was something I wanted more than anything I'd ever played for but I was not alone.

The Stableford was also the closest ever with Major Jr. leading by only 3 points over perennial bridesmaid AJ and 5 clear of Brighty. Combined with his perfect match record, the Major was also threatening to match Ian's unique Ireland accomplishment: to be perfect in match play and win the Stableford competition. Well aware of the stakes and hoping to get some consolation for England should they lose the Cup, Miffer brought out his biggest gun to take down Jack and defend Ian's unique record – Black Dog. It looked to be the match of the day.

I, on the other hand, fully expected to face off against Gibbo after the verbally animated, bitch-slappin' fight we'd had in BummZ the previous night, each claiming to want the other *"bad"* in Singles play. Miffer, however, chose differently, assigning Swampy to take me on while pitting Gibbo against the struggling Apple.

In Group 2, Phil and Jack Sr. would reprise their ongoing rivalry while the Prosecutor would play Fred. In Group 3, Manson Hanson and Baz would face off in one match with Apple and Gibbo in the other and in Group 4, Brighty would face AJ in another clash of low handicappers while Miffer took it upon himself to end Lou's hopes of adding his name to the trophy. Finally, Group 5 would see Smokin' Joe take on Sven while Casper and Pat would play the final match of the Cup.

That evening at BummZ was like every other night had been, extraordinary in its spirit of camaraderie and fellowship, a true celebration of the event, the friend we'd known and loved and the great friendships it – and he – had inspired. Never had we been more sincere as we toasted to great matches and great friendships. We all wanted matches that would honor the game of golf and, in doing so, honor Ian's memory. In that, we were of one mind.

Reaching the Barefoot Fazio course bright and early, our group teed off at 9am sharp. With Major Jr. and Black Dog having teed off and the entire group congregated around the first tee, the collision course predicted by master prognosticator Datzit Indaruf came to pass. With considerable help from Theresa, I was in the process of unleashing a psychological attack against Swampy unmatched in the annals of Flem Cup history. The previous night, when the matches had been announced, I quickly retreated to my room and returned with a gift for Swampy: 2 jars of hot sauce (Anal Angst and One F**ing Drop At A Time) and a hand-scrawled note suggesting he sleep with one eye open.

Now, standing on the tee, I continued the assault by donning a Cyclops mask and a wild Scotsman hair hat as Swampy teed off. As he turned, I stood there, hand extended to again wish him luck. Whether he was focused like a laser or simply oblivious, he didn't seem to notice, brushing by with nothing more than a quick shake.

Now fuming at the snub, I decided to up the ante by teeing off in the getup, forgetting all about the fact that, with few exceptions, history tells us that teeing off while wearing a Cyclops mask has been a risky gambit in serious matches. When my tee shot went all of 10 feet – sideways – I was reminded of that simple rule of thumb. My initial attack rebuffed, Swampy quickly went 1 up in our match.

But the hot sauce, the mask and the hat were mere warm-ups to my main weapon – a *"Stewie in Pocket"* voice player based on Stewie of *Family Guy* fame. On the 2nd hole, I launched my next salvo when Swampy left his 12 foot par putt short, pressing a random button on the still hidden player.

"Damn You, Vile Woman"

As Swampy looked at me in amazement, I played dumb, keeping a straight face as I chuckled to myself at my own version of shock and awe. Shaking off any effects from the disturbing weapon, Swampy ripped another good tee shot on the 3rd, just as I pressed button #2.

"Who the hell do you think you are?"

This time, he broke up laughing as I casually stepped past him to tee off, still pretending nothing was out of sorts. Finally, when he sliced his next shot into the trees, I sensed my efforts were starting to bear fruit and as he looked my way, I pressed button #3.

"Stop Mocking Me"

With my win on the 3rd hole leveling the match, I waited until 5 to allow Stewie to check in again, this time just as Swampy was lining up his tee shot. Button #4 – *go*.

"I come bearing a gift . . . it's in my diaper and it's not a toaster!"

Once the laughter stopped, I sensed Swampy was starting to feel the effects as I captured the hole to go 1 up but the final blow, totally unplanned, came on the very next hole. Lying behind the green, perhaps 8 feet from the fringe and with the green sloping away, I lofted a little flop shot that landed just past the fringe, released beautifully downhill and tracked straight into the cup for my third chip-in birdie in 3 days. After a brief celebration, I reached into my pocket and pressed button #5.

"Get me the Pentagon!"

With that, the rout was on, eventually ending with my 6&5 win.

Unlike my comedic match, though, the Major Jr. and Black Dog match was, from the start, every bit the hard fought, back and forth battle we'd expected. Making the turn 1 down, wins by the Major on 11 and 13 briefly made him 1 up before a Black Dog birdie on 14 brought it back to all square and, after the two traded pressure-packed wins on 16 and 17, the match went to the final hole, all square.

A 430-yard par 4 that gradually arcs around a lake separating it from the clubhouse, the 18th would provide Jack with his fifth and final stroke of the round and after watching Black Dog rip a monster drive down the left center of the fairway, Major Jr. launched his drive a bit right, finishing just in the rough, about 10 yards ahead of his opponent and 170 yards from the pin. Up next, Black Dog struck his approach shot just a tad fat, finishing just short with a 25-foot uphill chip followed by the Major catching a flyer that ran well past the pin, leaving a slick 40 foot downhill putt from the back of the green.

The greens had been lightning fast all day, a condition the Major was well aware of, and he struck his long, downhill putt tentatively, leaving it about 7-8 feet short of the hole. Up next, Black Dog hit a beautiful little punch and run, lagging it up to within a foot or so for a conceded par. Knowing Jack needed his putt for a guaranteed spot on the Jennings Trophy, I couldn't help but hope he would miss, bogeying the hole, halving his match and leaving the door open for me to share the honor. The Major, however, had other ideas.

Having been deadly all day with his mid-range putts, the Major settled in, concentration etched on his face. Hitting it firmly, my first thought was *whoa, that's way past* but as I held my breath, the putt dove over the front edge and rattled off the back of the cup before dropping, triggering a rare display of emotion from Jack, his exuberant fist pump and shout saying it all. His pressure putt assured his name would be etched on the trophy.

In addition to his perfect Cup record, his solid 33 Stableford would make it tough for AJ or Brighty to catch him for the championship, strengthening his even greater hope of becoming the only player besides Ian to pull off the double.

After shaking hands and exiting the green, my disappointment quickly faded as I came to appreciate the fact that it was Jack, my best friend as well as Ian's longtime friend and nemesis, who would be not only the first recipient of Ian's award but also the first to match his crowning achievement. Other than myself, there was no one I would rather achieve such an accomplishment.

In the next group, Phil was busy earning the same result he earned last year – a win over Jack Sr., who this time played quite well. Dominating from the 6th hole forward, an outstanding 34 carried Phil to the 3&2 win. Meanwhile, the Prosecutor continued his breakout year by knocking off the Fred, 2 up, in the second match of the day to reach the last hole. By winning both matches, England had staved off the inevitable.

In the third group, Gibbo, who had been expected to take a big bite out of Apple, was finding more worms than he had reckoned for. Continuing his Day 3 resurrection, Apple's was a performance for the ages, standing 2 up through 15. Gibbo's reputation as a tough as nails match player was well earned, though, and when he carded a par on 16, he was only 1 down. Pars on 17 and 18 gave Apple everything he could handle but the resurgent Yank was up to the task, matching

Gibbo shot for shot until his 12 foot par putt on 18 sealed the deal, 1 up, also delivering the Cup-clinching point in the process.

In the same group, Manson Hanson was barely holding off Baz's furious late rally for another Yank win. Seemingly in control at 2 up with 3 to play, a birdie-par rally by Baz brought the match back to level going to 18. There, both players bit off too much water on the tee shot and it took Manson Hanson's pressure-packed 10 foot bogey putt to win the hole and the match, 1 up.

In the fourth group, the highly anticipated match between Brighty and AJ was as tight as predicted through 10 holes, at which point Brighty simply went off, firing 3 pars and 3 birdies over the next 6 holes to win going away, 4&3.

In the same group, Lou's face off with Captain Miffer was the last match impacting the Jennings Award and although both players came out playing well, it was the surprising Lou who led at the turn, 2 up. With five holes left, though, Miffer got himself untracked, settling into one of his ball striking grooves, a groove that made the game appear effortless.

Like all of us, Lou wanted his name on the Jennings Trophy badly and when he reached 14 tee 2 up, he was focused on only one thing – playing solid, steady golf over the last 5 holes. In Miffer, however, he faced a player who was applying consistent, relentless pressure.

After the England Captain's solid, routine par won 14, two more pars were gamely parried by a scrambling Lou. Still clinging to a 1 up lead on 17, Miffer's fourth straight par was too much and the two headed to 18 all square. There, Lou made one final mistake – a fatal one – when he pulled his tee shot into the lake and one more routine, effortless par by Miffer captured the match, 1 up.

With four groups in, perfect symmetry reigned. We had won both matches in groups 1 and 3 while the Brits had won both matches in groups 2 and 4. Incredibly, five of the eight matches had gone to the last hole with four ending 1 up. It seemed clear to me that a split of the final two matches would be fitting – but that would be too easy. Fate had other ideas.

Sven was once again engaged in an epic battle on Singles Day – this time against Smokin' Joe. Squaring off in what would be the highest scoring Stableford match of the day, there was only one 2 up lead and it only lasted one hole. In the ultimate seesaw match, each player took the lead not once, not twice but three separate times. All square at the turn, Joe led 1 up after 10 only to see Sven win 11 and 12 followed by Joe winning 13 and 14 followed by Sven winning 15 and 16. Finally, after the back nine's lone halve on 17, Joe's solid par win on 18 brought the match to its only fair conclusion, all square.

That left only one possible outcome for the final match of the week and Pat and Casper would be only too willing to oblige. When Pat, who had led most of the day and never trailed, reached the last tee only 1 up, there was only one thing for Casper to do; win the hole and end the match all square – and that's exactly what he did. On this most remarkable of all Singles days, it was the only just outcome.

Although the final score of the Cup didn't seem close at 17-½ to 12-½, we all knew how false that impression was. The day – the entire week – had been simply extraordinary and we all knew how little it would have taken to tip the scales England's way. As we sat on the veranda, sipping our beers, puffing our cigars and soaking in the sun's warm late afternoon rays; we basked in the joyful celebration of friendship and competition we had come to love so much, knowing in our hearts that this year's Cup had set new standards in those areas.

In four years of Flem Cup play, only six out of thirty-four 2 ball matches had reached the final hole. On this day, seven of the ten went the distance, a total that included all three of the matches impacting the Jennings Trophy. In those same four years, only four players had reached the final day without a match loss. This year there were five, three of whom remained unbeaten.

Finally, Major Jr. became the first player to match Ian's Ireland accomplishment: a perfect match record and the Stableford crown. Knowing the fierce yet gracious competitor Major Jr. was, I knew Ian would have been honored to welcome him to the exclusive club.

On the flip side, Jack Sr. and Swampy, who had been called out of retirement for England, managed to carve their names in history with 0 points in 5 matches, a standard of futility I was more than happy to share.

Once again I found myself standing at the rail of the veranda in the late afternoon sun, reflecting on the events of the previous week as I stared out over the immaculate golf course. Exactly one week ago we'd been hit with the news of Ian's tragic death at the age of 49. Spurred on by Caroline's selfless act of delaying the funeral, we had journeyed to this place, hearts heavy but determined to come together in remembrance and celebration of his life. Following our sunrise tribute on Day 1, a competition filled with incredible matches had played out, punctuated unforgettably for me by the inexplicably remarkable shots I'd made, shots that were invariably preceded by precious moments of feeling Ian close by, comforting me as my mind struggled with the grief of his loss. Finally, there was Singles Day, a magical day filled with the most amazingly competitive 2 ball matches we'd ever witnessed in Cup play.

As I stood there, soaking in the moment, I couldn't help but be reminded of a similar scene only one year ago, Ian's ruddy face reflecting the sun as he surveyed the final hole at TPC. It was the last Flem Cup moment I would ever share with him, a moment I would always cherish. My thoughts once more turned to the spiritual side of life, recalling my conversation with Jack and the emotional dream I'd had the night after Ian died. For the first time in my life, I felt how fragile life really was and how quickly it could be taken, wondering again if this was truly all there was . . . or was there really something wondrous and mysterious awaiting us after our time here was spent. Scanning the majestic beauty that stretched out before me, feeling the love and fellowship I'd always longed for, my heart cried out: there must be something more; there simply has to be.

As I pondered life's questions, I was struck for the first time by the truly remarkable timing of Ian's passing. A remarkable man in life, his death was perhaps even more so, perfectly timed and memorable in every way. Passing on November 1, we were given an easy day to remember. Far more remarkable was the fact that

November 1st was arguably the one single day on the *entire* calendar year that would allow us to play the Cup *between* his death and his funeral. His impeccable timing gave us our own, personal opportunity to say goodbye to him while being here together, playing an event he'd been instrumental in building and dearly loved. Now, as if all that wasn't enough, his funeral would be on November 11 – Remembrance Day in England.

As I considered all these aspects of his passing, I found myself wondering if Ian *was* somehow here, his spirit joining us as our raw, fresh memories and emotions summoned him. Perhaps it was the only way he could have been here, by God granting him – and us – this one final blessing as an exclamation point to his remarkable life.

If he was here, I knew he had to feel incredibly proud of everything that had transpired; proud of how we battled to earn our way onto his namesake trophy; proud to see us embracing the competition he so loved; proud of our loving remembrances of him. The week had been about joy in competition, played by amateur golfers as though it actually were the Ryder Cup. How could it have been anything else? After all, it was the Flem Cup, *our* Ryder Cup, and it had become a competition worthy of the time, the effort, the expense and the angst we each paid it each and every year.

The week had been about love – love of fellowship, love of friends old and new, love of shared memories and stories, experiences and competition, jokes and laughter. It had been our one divinely orchestrated chance to properly memorialize Ian, our great friend. Despite the backdrop of sadness and the dark, empty feelings of depression and loneliness that were lurking, this week had, indeed, been a moment of bright light – and love was here in abundance.

25

Epilogue

Determined to continue with the Flem Cup, we played again in 2006 and England, led by Miffer and Smokin' Joe, evened the series at 3 wins apiece. Organizing it, however, proved far more of a struggle than ever before. My business trips to England were done and Ian's magnetic personality was no longer there. Miffer and Joe did their best to fill the void but Miffer had his own family and other priorities understandably began to creep in. Sadly, the motivation and commitment Ian had provided already seemed to be slipping away.

As for me, despite my vows to follow up on what Jack had told me, I did nothing in 2006 to follow up on what Jack had told me and nurture the fledgling faith I'd felt. When I was being honest with myself I had to admit that I might not *want* to recapture those feelings because if there *was* a God, I was angry at Him. The uncertainty gnawed at me, though, since I remained unsure if there even *was* a God to be mad at. For a while, I couldn't get past my anger to consider the real prize: the hope Jack had spoken in Jesus.

Through it all, though, deep down, I really did want to know the truth and eventually arrived at the point, with some gentle nudges from Theresa, where I found myself *needing* to know the truth. My natural skepticism remained, however, and I knew full well that my only route to conviction was the intellectual one. I needed to be convinced from every angle and after finally reaching the tipping point of action, I vowed to examine Jack's claims through the lens of logic and reason with a totally open mind, resolving to follow the clues and facts wherever they led.

Married now to Theresa, she'd been asking me to start going to church and it was an idea I was finally receptive to *with* a few conditions. Primarily, I wanted to find a church that taught with the Bible wide open, offering me the opportunity to learn not just from Sunday morning sermons but also through small group bible study. Finally, one Saturday, exasperated with my procrastinating, she simply pulled out the phone book and opened the yellow pages. There, she found Covenant Church in Buckingham, PA. Its ad said all the right things and the next morning we packed ourselves into the congregation at the small church. I immediately felt at home for one simple reason: Covenant's pastors and leaders didn't seem interested in teaching me a *religion*; they were interested in teaching me about the Bible and its leading character - Jesus Christ.

While this was happening incrementally, I was also busy satisfying my curiosity about the scientific evidence Jack had presented. It was a simple matter to find a wealth of scientific information on the Internet and in books, rekindling the amazement I'd felt with what Jack had told me about the secrets that science has recently unlocked. Taken individually, each fact pointed to an incredibly unlikely existence of life on this amazing planet. Taken collectively, they shredded the idea of being here simply by accident, pointing undeniably to not just the probability but the *necessity* of a master designer, a Creator God. At first, the shrillness of non-believers bothered me but over time I started to understand why they lash out so viciously at anyone offering facts or information contrary to their beliefs rather than engage in a reasoned discussion. Science itself had become their religion and its proponents had declared themselves all-knowing and all powerful, even though they could explain virtually nothing concerning the deeper mysteries of life. It became clear that their only defense was to disparage anyone who even raised possibility of a Creator.

One of my favorite examples of evolution's folly became the human eye. Looking at its incredible complexity through the lens of "functional advantage", simple, unanswered questions lay everywhere. Consisting of 40 or so inter-related yet independent sub-systems, each one of these sub-systems would have had to develop *independently* from one another *before* combining to create a working eye. For instance, what use is a lens without a retina, which consists of 137 million cells that receive light impressions and translate those impressions into electrical impulses? What use is a retina without an optic nerve to transmit those 1.5 billion electrical impulses *per second* to the brain? What use is an optic nerve without the cerebral cortex, the specific part of the brain that translates those impulses into color, contrast, depth and other visual characteristics that allow us to see? Which system(s) or part(s) developed first? Why did *any* of them develop when none had any useful function prior to all the others developing *and* combining into a working eye? Finally, how did this ridiculously unlikely sequence of developments occur in nearly every single animal species on earth? What made it one of my favorites, though, was the identity of one of the earliest critics of the concept.

"To suppose that the eye with all its inimitable contrivances for adjusting the focus for different distances, for admitting different amounts of light, and for the correction of spherical and chromatic aberration, could have been formed by natural selection seems, I freely confess, absurd in the highest degree." Charles Darwin, Chapter 6, On the Origin of Species

Far more important than the knowledge, though, was the fact that the scientific facts and information I was devouring were serving a much more important purpose by bringing me face to face with the question Jack had asked, a question I remembered vividly:

WHAT NOW?

As I became intellectually convinced of a Creator God's existence, I could not get away from the simple choice before me. I could simply choose to chalk it up to getting a little smarter and move on, living my life as I always had, but the question posed was of eternal importance. How could I turn my back on God? A

332 • THE FLEM CUP

God who cared about me personally? It was a question I could no longer ignore, leaving me only one way forward: keep digging in an effort to take God up on His biblical promise to reveal Himself if I were to seek Him. *What does God want of my life* was a question I could not ignore.

So I kept working my way through the Bible, reading it myself, studying it with a small group of men and listening to ministers preach on various scriptures. Just as Jack had promised, I found the Bible to be a book of history, poetry, wisdom, music, prophecy and much more, all revolving around the single, compelling storyline of God's promised Messiah. It took only a few short months studying its intricacies and depth before I came to the inescapable conclusion that the Bible *is* God's inspired word, unable to find any other explanation for the depths of its teachings, its inerrancy, consistency, cohesiveness and richness. The fact that it was written by 40 or so different authors over 1500 years or more made its perfection all the more supernatural.

I supplemented my own studies and weekly visits to church by listening to great radio ministries as I traveled for work. I was taken through the amazing Gospel of Luke with Alistair Begg, the incredible Book of Daniel with David Jeremiah and the stunning, uncanny parallels between the lives of Jesus and Israel's first deliverer, Moses, with Tim Keller. R.C. Sproul, Adrian Rogers, Chuck Missler, Michael Yussef and, of course, my own wonderful pastor, Bob Myers each not only taught me but also inspired and challenged me to apply those biblical lessons to my own life in a real and meaningful way.

Then, of course, there were the prophecies, one of the unmistakable and inexplicable signs of a God in total, active control. For centuries, doubters claimed many prophecies, including those concerning Jesus, were simply *too* accurate to be real, arguing they were written with the benefit of hindsight during the days of the early church as part of a giant scam. Those claims were shredded in the late 1940s with the discovery of the Dead Sea Scrolls, remarkably well-preserved copies of Scripture carbon dated to decades or even centuries before the birth of Jesus. That incredible discovery provided scholars with every book in Jewish Scripture (Christianity's Old Testament) except one, Ruth, and confirmed the fact that Scripture had, in fact, remained unchanged for thousands of years. In those truly remarkable scrolls, prophecies pinpointed the birthplace of the Messiah (the tiny, otherwise insignificant village of Bethlehem), his lineage (straight from King David), his tribe (Judah), his virgin birth, the exact *day* on which he would proclaim his kingship (the day he rode into Jerusalem), his mode of transportation on that day (a donkey) and dozens of minute, incredibly specific details about how he would die, all true. With the discovery of the scrolls, the prophecies there remained no question that they were written 400 hundred years or more before His life, much less His ministry, even began. The odds of any one man fulfilling all that was prophesied was far too high to even calculate yet Jesus fulfilled each and every one.

One of the most amazing prophecies concerned the fact that the nation of Israel would somehow, in some unimaginable way, cease to exist for thousands of years yet somehow be reconstituted. No other nation had ever returned to existence after being destroyed yet on May 14, 1948, in the wake of the horrors of the holocaust and at exactly the same time that the Dead Sea Scrolls were being unearthed, that unprecedented and seemingly impossible event occurred when David Ben-Gurion proclaimed: *"We hereby proclaim the establishment of the Jewish state in Palestine, to be called Israel."* These prophecies and many, many more like them are simply mind blowing, completely inexplicable other than by the supernatural, and the more I learned, the more I was brought to the inescapable conclusion that God is, indeed, in control.

As I studied and learned, God's Word was slowly but surely penetrating my heart, just as Jack had promised it would. The further along I went, the more amazed I was and the more I wanted to learn. Despite that, I still struggled with the idea of why a holy, righteous God, knowing everything about my sinful heart, would care at all about me, much less go to such lengths to redeem me. Despite my belief, desire and best efforts, I remained incapable of approaching God's standards on my best day. Struggling with my own inner demons, I remained focused on just how undeserving of God's love I really was. I was intellectually convinced that Jesus Christ not only came to earth but that He was exactly who He claimed to be, the Son of God. I stood in awe of what the apostles had experienced with Jesus but even more so what they became and accomplished after Jesus' resurrection, of how they willingly suffered and died while spreading the gospel, mankind's only salvation. It all registered in my mind but I couldn't fully embrace it, unable to get past my own unworthiness. I believed, yet felt wholly inadequate. I did not, *could* not, understand.

The first time I read through the Gospel of Mark, one verse in particular jumped off the page at me, hitting me right between the eyes. In Mark 9:24, a father, desperate to save his son from demons, has just been told by Jesus that anything is possible for he who believes.

Immediately the boy's father exclaimed, "I do believe; help me overcome my unbelief!"

The verse struck a powerful chord. Jesus saved the man's son anyway, despite the father's admittedly imperfect faith. It was a lifeline, giving me hope as my heart struggled with unearned grace. I was stuck on one little three-letter word: *why?*

That would finally change late one Sunday night in the fall of 2007. Waking up, I rolled over to look at the clock. 3:30 am. Before long, as my hope of falling quickly back to sleep faded, my mind began to roam. Pastor Myers had delivered a particularly powerful sermon that morning, one that, like many he delivered, seemed personally written for me. His words had touched my heart and as I lay there, I thought of all I had learned and all the things God was doing in my life. I thought of the tragedy that had led to my journey of discovery – Ian's excruciating battle with cancer. I prayed once again he had accepted Christ before his life ebbed away.

Thinking of Ian's suffering, my mind shifted to Jesus and the unfathomable suffering He experienced during His final days, culminating in His trial and crucifixion. Like Ian, Jesus knew His time was fast approaching but there was one immeasurably large difference. Jesus, who was perfectly healthy and vibrant, was a completely innocent man *choosing* to lay down His life to save all of mankind, many of whom despised Him during His life, millions more who someday would.

That night, lying in the dark, I was able to vividly picture His ordeal, the horrifying scourging He suffered at the hands of the Romans, glass and metal impregnated leather straps ripping open His flesh time and time again. I felt the humiliation and torment He received at the hands of Romans and Jews alike as He took the long, agonizing walk to Golgotha, forced to drag His own instrument of death – the cross. I saw the nails being driven through his hands and feet, the weight of His body hanging there, life slowly ebbing away. Finally, I thought of the moment on the cross when He looked up, crying out, "My God, my God, why have you forsaken me?"

I'd always struggled with that verse, unable to understand why Jesus, who knew what was happening and why, would consider Himself forsaken by God the Father. It reminded me of another scene I'd struggled with – the scene in the Garden of Gethsemane when He was so filled with dread and anguish that He sweated blood, praying for to the Father to remove the cup that had been set before Him – but only *if* that were the Father's will.

But the Father's answer to that prayer was no – it was not His will to remove the cup – and Jesus remained perfectly obedient all the way to the cross, laying down His life like the penultimate Passover lamb He was prophesied to be, quietly, without a word of protest, on the exact day God had ordained - Passover. I understood the drama of the scene but if Jesus knew everything that was coming, what was it that He feared so much?

Then, for the first time, the dots began to connect in my mind.

I'd always thought of Jesus' fear as being related to the horror and revulsion of knowing in advance that every sin that ever had been or ever would be committed was about to be piled on His sinless shoulders but that night, for the first time I considered the possibility that what Jesus would be facing was something unimaginably painful to Him: the total severing of the lifeline of love that had always connected Him to the Father and Holy Spirit. An eternity spent in a relationship of pure love and perfect holiness was about to end and *that* was infinitely worse than any physical suffering He would have to endure.

"My God, my God, why have you forsaken me?"

For the first time, I grasped that during His time on the cross, a period of finite time in our world yet timeless in the realm of the eternal God, a righteous God the Father had to mete out complete and total justice, punishing a willing Jesus for the sins of billions. That punishment included spiritual death – complete and total separation from God. The Father turned His back in every way, spiritually abandoning Jesus as He hung there on the cross, completely alone for the first time in all of eternity. Why would Jesus do this?!?! He was GOD! What made Him do it??

Nothing made Him do it.

The small, quiet words broke like a tidal wave, crashing through my consciousness to the depths of my heart. As I lay in the dark, I felt part of the terrible scene on Golgotha that day, as Jesus hung in helpless agony . . . beaten and bleeding . . . skin hanging off His body . . . nails driven through His hands and legs . . . in unimaginable agony as the weight of his body caused Him to slowly, painfully suffocate. He was willingly accepting the justice that we deserved so that we could receive the mercy God was offering.

I thought of His promise of salvation and forgiveness to the thief on the cross next to Him . . . I thought of Him praying for His tormentors *"Father, forgive them, for they know not what they do"* . . . of crying out in agony to God the Father . . . and of breathing His last breath.

Nothing made Him do it.

As I lay there, another Bible verse from John's gospel suddenly popped into my head.

No one takes it from me, but I lay it down of my own accord.

Jesus had *allowed* Himself to be arrested, stripped, mocked, beaten, scourged, ridiculed, humiliated, tortured and put to death in the most horrific manner ever devised – crucifixion. He was in full and total control of what was happening, able to call it off at any second. The thought that He *chose* to lay His life down in a seemingly incomprehensible atrocity prompted another Bible verse to pop into my head, perhaps the most famous in the entire Bible, John 3:16.

For God so loved the world that He gave His one and only Son, that whoever believes in Him shall not perish but shall have eternal life.

As the words hung in my mind, the still, small voice in my head completed the picture, personalizing what the Father had planned and the Son had accomplished.

For God so loved you, Scott, that He gave His one and only Son, that if you believe in Him you shall not perish but shall have eternal life.

The thought took my breath away.

Here was Jesus, the Lord of the universe through whom *all* things were made, freely choosing to accept the penalty for *my* sins in order to redeem *me*. God's plan for redemption had always been all about mercy, love and forgiveness, about giving us every opportunity to love and trust Him as our loving Creator, however imperfect or rebellious we were or are. He never turned away from us. We turned away from Him, just as He knew we would.

Jesus didn't die for the rich or the powerful or the Jews or the Gentiles or the good or the evil of mankind and He doesn't want rules or rituals taking the place of loving Him, learning about Him and drawing closer to Him. When we choose to love Him, we choose to obey Him as our Creator and that means two things. First, we should love Him with all our heart, our mind, our soul and our strength. That should come from gratitude, the natural product of understanding what He has done for us and how much He loves us. Second, we must love and serve one another – all mankind – just as Jesus loved and served us during His life. He loved us before we ever loved Him, *proving* the depth of His love in the most amazing way possible – dying for us so that we could live with Him. We were given free will and with that, God wants us to *choose* to love Him as He loves us.

As I lay there in bed, the tears flowed down my cheeks as I was overcome with a totally new and different emotion – *gratitude*. Salvation and forgiveness was a *free* gift from a Creator who loves me more than I can possibly imagine, who wants to bless me more than I would ever dare to ask and who gives us every chance to use the free will He gave us to choose . . . Him. The gift was right in front of me, where it had always been, waiting to be claimed. Now, finally, I grasped the size and scope and price of that gift, along with what it meant.

Gratitude!

My heart changed that night as I finally accepted Christ as my Lord and Savior. In less than a single year, my journey of discovery and inquiry had delivered me from wallowing in the wreckage of my own fleshly desires through the process of feeling I had to earn God's grace to finally understanding the full scope and sheer magnitude of what Jesus did. He had given His life for me and I could do no less than offer Him mine out of love and gratitude, knowing that I could trust Him, wherever He led me in life.

***

In 2007, the Cup fell by the wayside as many of us simply could not make it. Life, family and work have a way of getting in the way, after all, and despite everyone's best efforts, no one would ever fill Ian's immense shoes as England organizer. All, however, was not lost and in October, Smokin' Joe, Baz and Manson Hanson came across the pond for a week or so to play golf in northern NJ and we had a fantastic time culminating in a round at AJ's home course, the prestigious Montclair Country Club.

Invited to his home afterwards, we enjoyed a meal with his family along with several bottles of outstanding wine. As the evening waned, I found myself sitting and relaxing in the den with Jack Sr., talking about Ian. Eventually, talk turned to my newfound faith and all the remarkable things that had happened over the previous few years. It came as no surprise when Jack told me that others had also found a fledgling interest in Christ through the golf trip. They'd sought after Jack, engaging him because of simple curiosity concerning his depth of belief, wanting to better understand what it was that gave Jack the contentment and faith we all saw in his life. Jack, of course, neither sought nor claimed any credit.

"The words of any man can only effect so much change in the human heart. After that, it is up to God. We are called to lay our lives down for Christ, letting His light and love shine through us in our actions and to speak boldly of our hope in Him when the opportunity presents itself. I try to make my life an offering to Christ, just as He made His life an offering for us. But words will only go so far. If the sincere seeker stays with it – and the key word is <u>sincere</u> – the Holy Spirit will come to finish the work, convicting the seeker deep within his heart. The Spirit councils and guides us but we must learn to listen."

Without thinking, I offered up something I'd been wondering about for some time.

"I just can't believe how remarkable it was that Ian pulled us together into a group where so many could be touched by God, changing their lives forever. Here was a man who was given a lion's share of God's gifts yet never gave a thought to God until the very end when he was facing death."

An amused look came over Jack's face and he chuckled as I looked at him, puzzled.

"I have a slightly different take. The first few years of the Cup I didn't think much of it but in 2001, when the Brits first came over as a team, I found myself wondering what purpose God had for this trip. Of course, I didn't know - I rarely do . . . and even when I think I do, I'm usually wrong - but I did know that God always has a purpose and He would reveal it in His time. Today, I see His plan continuing to be revealed. Through any seemingly senseless loss, any tragedy, God can work miracles. Look at what He has done through Ian's death, how many people He has drawn back to His love, including the priceless hope that Ian now waits for us in heaven. I have come to learn that no matter what my circumstance, I trust in God to care for me."

Recognizing my own foolishness, it was suddenly clear just how God's hand had been on the trip from the beginning. I, and perhaps others, had been motivated to turn back towards a God who had been was there all along, ready and waiting to welcome us home. Jack was right; it was all to God's glory. My mind shifted, a smile coming over my face. When Jack noticed it, he chuckled.

"What? What are you smiling about?"

"Huh? Oh, nothing. I was just thinking about Ian."

While partly true, what I was really thinking was that I didn't think God's plan was quite done yet. Through an unwitting servant, God had documented virtually every aspect of the story and I was thinking about the book I had already begun, a book that would recount an incredible story of love, friendship, tragedy and salvation. God had blessed me with a friend like Ian, a friendship that resulted in this amazing Flem Cup story. What else could I do but bring glory to God by telling that story, praying only that it would lead others to find God in whatever way He had planned for them. After all, all things are possible with God - even my salvation - and I had come to realize that somehow, in some small way, this wonderful story was part of His plan.

"I was wondering if we could say a prayer for Ian before we rejoin the others."

"Sure."

I bowed my head as Jack began.

"Father in Heaven . . ."

Author's Note

I'd like to thank you for taking the time to read *The Flem Cup*. It was an incredible story to be a part of and to write about and if you enjoyed reading it *half* as much as I enjoyed writing it, I know you loved it! And if you did love it, please leave a review on Amazon.

As mentioned in the Preface, of the 110 or so articles originally posted to the website from its inception in 2001 through 2005, only about 15 or so made it into the book. If you would like to dig deeper into the rest of those stories, results, mental games and sub-plots, please visit the website at Flemcup.com, link through to the Story Vault.

Although The Flem Cup makes for a great golf story, what makes it truly remarkable, at least to me, is the underlying story of redemption. Only a tragedy like Ian's untimely passing could have served to lead the two of us - hopeless sinners, both - to seek out and find God. What we found was an incredible, loving God who can use any tragedy for His own purposes. My inspiration in completing the book was the hope of inspiring others to take the time and make the effort to find God for themselves.

My path was an intellectual one and while that is certainly not the only route, it is an undeniably powerful and, for many, necessary one. To paraphrase Jack,

God ultimately wants your heart but He'll gladly get there through your head. I believe there are many people like me, perhaps prejudiced by experiences in life against the general concept of religion but nevertheless curious as to life's great questions, in need of an intellectual nudge to take those first few steps of honest inquiry in search not of religion but of the existence and nature of God.

To help with those steps, the website also has an ever-growing selection of articles on a variety of subjects (including Christian Apologetics) as well as links to other sites and resources. I invite you to begin your own journey of discovery by visiting those sections (and revisiting periodically as new articles get posted). Whether you are an atheist or an agnostic, a seeker or a mature believer, I'm confident you will find something fascinating that you never knew before. My only request is that you come with an open mind and heart.

You will also be able to contact me directly with questions and comments but please bear in mind that while I love to engage in respectful conversation and debate, I do not consider myself a scholar or expert in any specific biblical area. While I have learned an incredible amount since my studies began, that is dwarfed by what I have yet to learn. If you raise a question I don't know the answer to, I will do my best to find an answer and provide the source. After all, one thing I am always interested in doing is learning something new.

One thing I am absolutely confident of is that if you embark on your own spiritual journey with a sincere desire to seek out God, you will not only find Him but you will discover that He has been there all along, waiting for you, and all of heaven will rejoice at the return of yet another prodigal son or daughter. In the Gospel of Matthew (7:7-8), Jesus makes that very promise in no uncertain terms:

Ask and it will be given to you; seek and you will find; knock and the door will be opened to you. For everyone who asks receives; the one who seeks finds; and to the one who knocks, the door will be opened

Thanks again, and may God bless!

Made in the USA
Lexington, KY
24 November 2019